Inquiry by Design

Julia Gooding
Bill Metz

RoseDog Books

PITTSBURGH, PENNSYLVANIA 15222

ISBN-10: 0-8059-8923-4
ISBN-13: 978-0-8059-8923-6

Printed in the United States of America

First Printing

For information or to order additional books, please write:
RoseDog Books
701 Smithfield St.
Third Floor
Pittsburgh, PA 15222
U.S.A.
1-800-834-1803
Or visit our web site and
on-line bookstore at www.rosedogbookstore.com

This book is dedicated to those of our students, teachers and colleagues who not only challenged us, but questioned us and encouraged us to question in return.

Table of Contents

Earth Science

Environmental Science

Forces and Motion

Forensic Science

Heat

The Patent Office

Scientific Reasoning

Teacher Support Materials

Preface

"Houston, we have a problem." Those were the words spoken by actor Tom Hanks, in his role as the Commander Jim Lovell in the 1995 movie, *Apollo 13.* What transpired was a unique, real life problem situation, the outcome of which would determine the fate of the Apollo 13 crew. Recall that the capsule had lost its service module cryogenic oxygen system, as well as the capability of generating electricity, oxygen and water. The engineers in Houston had to somehow jury rig the failed system. As they gathered around a table with a box of materials, they were issued the following challenge, "This is the stuff they have on board...we need to make it work!" Looking at the limited materials, and knowing that lives were on the line, the engineers began what some might have called and impossible task.

Based on actual events, this movie scenario is an example of a **design brief** – a plausible situation in which the participants must solve a problem given limited materials, a specific time frame, and the necessity of being successful while working under a number of constraints...the inquiry process in action.

This book is a collection of content applications that address the most common science areas found in the middle and junior high school settings. Each challenge is introduced with a *context statement* and a brief *scenario* that helps to set the stage for introducing the dilemma. *The challenge* invites the students to solve the problem while adhering to specific *limitations and rules*. Whether using a kit program, a textbook, or a self-developed curriculum, this publication is a valuable asset to any collection of science education resources.

While possible procedures are provided for all the design briefs they should never be considered the only procedures. The rationale for this position stems from our belief that the process of true inquiry is unique to each individual problem solver or team. While the final outcome may be specific, the means by which that outcome is reached can be as varied as the people searching for it.

Introduction

Science is something that students do, not something that is done to them. As such, children should encounter science through a variety of experiences that actively engage them in the construction and pursuit of ideas, the crafting and implementation of a course of action, and the evaluation and interpretation of their results. Support for this position is found in the *National Science Education Standards, NSES,* (1996) as the document states, "Inquiry into authentic questions generated from student experiences is the central strategy for teaching science" (p. 31). Equally important is their comment about extending student investigations, "In the middle-school years, students' work with scientific investigations can be complemented by activities that are meant to meet a human need, solve a human problem, or develop a product" (p. 161). This is the purpose of a design brief.

The design brief concept has been used in Technology Education for a number of years as a means of problem solving and product development. However, according to the National Academy of Engineering (2002), "Science and technology are tightly coupled. A scientific understanding of the natural world is the basis for much of technological development today" (p. 13). In fact, technology as design is even included in the *NSES* as a parallel to science as inquiry. Because of this overlapping of ideas and skills, the design brief has been adapted and integrated into the science activities herein. This creative adaptation of the design process sets the stage for the realistic application of science content knowledge and critical thinking by the students.

The design briefs also provide instructional strategies for teachers who want to raise the cognitive level of their existing lessons. It is our hope that, as teachers become conversant with the design brief format, they will also become more comfortable with crafting additional investigations like those included here. Additionally, we hope that they will challenge students to go beyond the scripted nature of many hands-on activities and take up the challenge of applying that which they have learned.

Just as in Technology Education, each design brief begins with **The Context**, a statement that provides the rationale for the activity. This is followed by **The Scenario**, a description of a plausible, real-life situation. The next segment is **The Challenge**, wherein the task is described. The remaining sections are **The Limitations** or constraints and **The Rules** for judging the quality or efficiency of the project. (See "How to Create Your Own Design Briefs" for a more detailed description of these sections).

NSES (1996) Content Standard A for Grades 5-8 states that "all students should develop (a) abilities necessary to do scientific inquiry and (b) understandings about scientific inquiry" (p. 143). In concordance with the means by which these standards indicate that students will demonstrate proficiency in these skills, each design brief in this text attempts to place students into their own *Apollo 13* setting. In order to accomplish the task at hand, student design teams must understand and pool their resources. They are challenged to collaborate on each phase of the project, apply knowledge, collect and process information, communicate findings and continuously self evaluate. The situation at Mission Control was an extreme example of the design process, one in which actual lives were on the line. Most problem solving situations may not have such severe consequences, but the method of resolving issues is nonetheless the same.

With the advent of *No Child Left Behind*, states are revamping and developing science curricula and assessment measures to encompass a broader range of student abilities. They are also expanding their criteria of how students can demonstrate that learning has occurred. The investigations in this book attempt to provide additional means for teachers to differentiate the delivery of their instruction through real life challenges while capitalizing on the positive interaction of the collaborative group format. Design briefs offer open ended teaching/learning opportunities for the acquisition and application of knowledge.

The National Research Council (2005), in their publication *How Students Learn: Science in the Classroom*, states that learning experiences need to develop from first-hand concrete experience and that "students need opportunities to learn and inquire in the discipline [of science]" (p. 512). Consequently, the challenges in this book are crafted to be content application activities. However, they can be relevant at any point in the science program depending on the need or structure of the curriculum. In addition, the layout of the investigations provides a student sheet for duplication purposes with teacher information on the reverse side.

We invite you to alter these challenges to best meet the needs of your students, the availability of materials, and the time restrictions of your curriculum. Be aware that while the problem solving techniques used by each team may be different, the diversity of thinking is beneficial for enhancing the problem solving repertoire of each student. Sharing is not only encouraged it is a strategy used throughout the program.

Design Brief Format and Explanation

Design briefs can help students engage in creative problem solving activities by providing a structure in which they can work. There are many different formats for design briefs, but each should include a clear statement of the design task and a description of the parameters. The following format will be used in this publication. The examples listed below reference the challenge posed in the preface.

The Context: This is a general statement describing the concept.

> Engineers are responsible for the design, improvement, and installation of integrated systems in industry. They make products that perform specific functions.

The Scenario: This is a story that "sets the stage" for the reader.

> You are a design engineer for a major company. Your supervisor approaches you with a problem that must be solved immediately. He tells you that you need to make an air purification system for a closed living environment using non-traditional materials.

The Challenge: This is a detailed description of the problem.

> Your design team must develop a makeshift air purification system that will be capable of reducing the amount of carbon dioxide in the Apollo 13 spacecraft and you must have it completed and functional in two days. You are given a bizarre compilation of materials such as canisters, cardboard, large hoses, duct tape, and storage bags to name a few, and told that this is what the Apollo crew has on board. These are the only materials you have to work with and you must fix the problem. The lives of the Apollo Crew are at stake and they are relying on your expertise. "Failure is not an option."

The Limitations: This is a list of constraints or specifications that must be met in order for the project or process to meet minimum requirements.

> - Your design must be completed and functional in two days.
> - Your team can only use the materials provided.
> - The team must craft a set of installation instructions that will ensure successful system assembly by the Apollo crew.

The Rules: These are the testing procedures for products and processes that meet established specifications.

> - Testing of all air purification prototype systems will be conducted on day two.
> - Once testing begins no system modifications will be allowed.
> - Each design team will take a turn serving as the "fabricators" for another design team to test the clarity of the installation instructions.

Rationale for Incorporating the Design Brief into Science

The design brief has been primarily used both here in the United States and in the United Kingdom as a standard curriculum format in Technology Education for many years. In its most simplified form a design brief can be thought of as a process for identifying, investigating and analyzing problems. During this process, students engage in researching existing ideas, crafting new thoughts, selecting and testing possible solutions, analyzing data and evaluating and presenting outcomes. In alignment with the *NSES*, design briefs allow students to develop their skills of acquiring science knowledge and using high-level reasoning. Students are then obliged to apply their existing understanding of scientific ideas and to communicate scientific information.

Recently, design technology has considered the integration of other subjects to enhance its overall effectiveness. According to Bernard Zubrowski (2002), "design projects at the elementary and middle school levels will be much enriched and put on a firmer pedagogical foundation if there is an infusion of science process and content". He also contends that science teaching will be enhanced if it occurs in a design context and that "students are highly motivated when working on a challenge or problem that is related to their personal lives or the world outside the classroom."

While Zubrowski (2002) encourages the infusion of science to support design technology, in his work the latter content area still remains the primary instructional agenda. Reversing this focus is the intent of *Inquiry by Design.* It is our contention that the design brief, a proven format in Technology Education, would serve as a unique approach for extending the content of hands on science instruction through direct application. We are not alone in this belief according to a report by the National Research Council. As reported in *Inquiry and the National Science Standards* (2000), "The emphasis of recent research has been on learning for understanding, which means gaining knowledge that can be used and applied to novel situations" (National Research Council, p. 116). According to the *NSES* (1996), one basis for understanding the similarities, differences, and relationships between science and technology should be experiences with design and problem solving in which students can further develop some of the abilities previously introduced. The *NSES* also reports that the tasks chosen should involve the use of science concepts already familiar to students or should motivate them to learn new concepts needed to use or understand the technology.

By organizing these activities in the design brief format, we are simply providing teachers and students with a structure in which to operate.

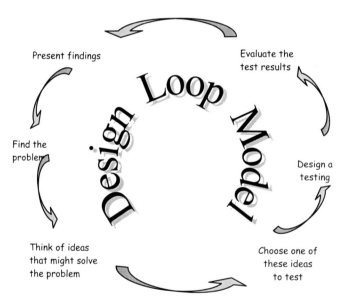

Present findings

Evaluate the
test results

Find the
problem

Design a
testing

Think of ideas
that might solve
the problem

Choose one of
these ideas
to test

However, "students need opportunities to see where ideas come from, and they need to be held responsible for knowing and communicating the origins of their knowledge" (Donovan and Bransford, 1999, p. 512). This format provides students with the opportunity to do just that. They now have a reason to solve the problem, to which they can apply their prior content knowledge. This format meshes well with the *NSES* (1996) position that "students need opportunities to present their abilities and understanding and to use the knowledge and language of science to communicate scientific explanations and ideas" (p. 144).

The Design Loop is the basic strategy used for solving problems written in the Design Brief Format. There are more elaborate versions of this schematic and some that are more simplified. Regardless, they all direct the learner to isolate a problem and pursue it in a systematic fashion. A traditional design loop is illustrated previously and is similar to the conventional "scientific method." Finding a problem is the usual starting point in this time honored scheme.

However, research from the NRC suggests that simply asking students to follow the steps of "the scientific method" is not sufficient to help them develop the knowledge, skills and attitudes that will enable them to understand what it means to "do science" and participate in a larger scientific community. Toward that end, the following diagram represents the opinion that ideas can originate from anywhere in the loop and that the loop can be entered from any point. There are also mini-loops within this model. Very often during the evaluation of a project, additional "tinkering" becomes necessary as a result of feedback. In point of fact, the mini-loop of testing, modification, and retesting is common in most design projects. This model is supported by *NSES* Content Standard A in that the conceptual and procedural abilities suggest a logical progression, but they do not imply a rigid approach to scientific inquiry. Specifically, they state that this standard should not be interpreted as advocating a "scientific method," and that it cannot be met by having students memorize the abilities and understandings. Rather, it can only be met when students frequently engage in active inquiries.

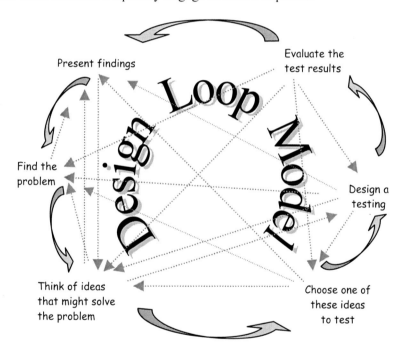

Frequently Asked Questions

Does *Inquiry by Design* align with the National Science Education Standards?

By its very nature, each design brief aligns with NSES Content Standard A (Science as Inquiry) and Content Standard E (Science and Technology). Additionally, each brief contains a reference to the content standard to which it coincides.

Furthermore, the most applicable standards from the National Council of Teachers of Mathematics and those from the National Council of Teachers of Language Arts are referenced with each challenge. Other problem-based learning programs contain opportunities for students to apply mathematical principals and functions or to write in either a reflective, persuasive, narrative, or informational manner. Research cited in the NSES supports the contention that deeper learning is achieved through the application and integration of information. It is for that reason that we have required the use of mathematics and language arts skills as an essential part of most design briefs.

Where does *Inquiry by Design* fit with the regular science curriculum?

A majority of the design briefs found in **Inquiry by Design** have been written as extensions, or application lessons. They are not intended to replace the regular middle school science curriculum, but rather to supplement it. The placement of these challenges in the standard curriculum has been left up to the discretion of the teacher. However, the design briefs are most appropriately placed after the students have and some experience with the science concepts and content extended by the challenge. Design brief challenges can also be considered performance assessments that require students to apply pertinent science content in their quest to solve credible problems.

What is the most appropriate use for a design challenge?

As stated previously, a majority of the design brief challenges require students to have prior knowledge of specific science content. This fact, therefore, necessitates introducing the challenge later in the learning sequence. However, while these challenges are often used as performance assessments or culminating investigations, their use should not be limited solely to this function. Some challenges can even be used as introductory activities to motivate students or to serve as a formative assessment tool. Additionally, many briefs contain opportunities for students to research, to adapt or repurpose materials, to create appropriate data displays, to develop process skills and content knowledge and to demonstrate what they have learned in a variety of ways. There is a "Suggested Use" subdivision in the "Teachers Notes" section of each design brief challenge to serve as a guide for the placement of the challenge within the regular science curriculum

What if I do not have all the materials suggested in design brief challenges?

In most of the design brief challenges, the materials listed are only suggestions. However, some activities do require specific materials. Therefore, design briefs should be reviewed in light of these material needs. Generally, standard middle school laboratory equipment will be needed in addition to everyday classroom supplies. To reduce additional costs, we suggest that the student teams be held responsible for obtaining any materials beyond those available in school. If imposed, all groups must follow this rule in order to meet the requirements of the assignment.

Are these challenges designed for a particular type of learner?

As schools are becoming more differentiated, a single approach to curriculum delivery does not address the variety of learning styles found in most classrooms. ***Inquiry by Design*** is a unique approach to lesson design and delivery. These lessons are, by intent, more open-ended and inquiry-oriented than typical lessons. As such, the responsibility for much of the lesson procedure is placed in the hands of the students, guided only by the challenge rules and limitations. Procedural differences are therefore expected.

According to brain research, since no two of us have the same data in our cognitive belief systems, no two people see the world in exactly the same way. "There are many ways that people can put the same data together" (Sousa, 1995). The acceptance of diverse ideas is not only encouraged in each design brief it is an expectation—one that allows students to interpret, process, and analyze a problem on their own terms.

How accurate are the time allotments suggested for each lesson?

The suggested time allotments are estimates based on actual classroom experience. However, there are a number of variables that influence the length of any lesson. These include the number of students, the amount of material available, the background of the students, and so on. With few exceptions, the time allotment for the challenges can be altered to better suit the needs of individual teachers and their students.

Are there design brief challenges for all content areas of science?

Inquiry by Design provides application challenges for many of the common content areas found in middle school science curricula. However, not all areas could be included in this publication. Should teachers not find a design brief to meet a specific need, they have the option of crafting one. Our process for creating design briefs is included herein. It is our hope that this book will be used by teachers as a resource for developing and expanding their own repertoire of design brief challenges.

What considerations should be made when forming teams for the challenges?

Traditionally, teams of four students are assigned to a collaborative group. In addition, it is suggested that team members reflect the diversity of the class and that groups be multi-leveled, as a majority of the design challenges require a variety of skills to complete. However, the number of students assigned to each design team may also depend on the specifics of the challenge, the amount of necessary materials, the allotted time and/or the subsequent challenge rules and limitations. Teachers must ultimately make this decision.

How are the lessons formatted?

Most of the lessons found in Inquiry by Design are formatted as a two-sided page, one side for each component of the brief. The first component is the student section or design brief challenge, which can be duplicated for student use. On the reverse side of the student page is the teacher component containing pertinent information about materials, suggested use, background material, safety issues, and a possible procedure. It is most important to remember that authentic inquiry assumes a variety of potential solutions to a problem. As stated at the bottom of each Teacher Notes page, "While the problem solving techniques used by each team may be different, the diversity of thinking is beneficial for enhancing the problem solving repertoire of each student. Sharing is not only encouraged it is a strategy used throughout the program."

Can the design briefs be changed?

The design challenges in ***Inquiry by Design*** were written for teachers and students who want to go beyond the scripted nature of the regular science curriculum. Therefore, we hope that teachers will feel comfortable altering these challenges to better meet the needs and abilities of their students, the availability of materials and the issues of time constraints.

Altering the instructional delivery is also an option that may be considered. The format of the design brief often establishes an unstated competition between collaborative groups. While some students thrive in this environment, others may be stifled or thwarted by this pressure. Should this be a concern, keep in mind that these challenges allow for the acceptance of multiple procedures. Remind students that their results are acceptable if the outcomes adhere to the limitations and rules of the challenge, if they make data based decisions and construct justifiable conclusions and/or appropriate models. Having students share their unique ideas, procedures and results is extremely beneficial because this process not only reduces the competitiveness of the challenge but tends to enhance the problem solving abilities of every student.

Above all, we encourage teachers to make changes in these investigations and to use this information as a guide for creating their own lessons. However, we caution against making alterations that would compromise the spirit of the challenge. Eliminating a collaborative activity in which the students are required to produce an advertising campaign might save time, but it may weaken the challenge.

How may design briefs assessed?

The assessment of a design brief is an integral part of each challenge. Prior to using an appropriate rubric, students in a collaborative group must adhere to all the stated limitations, rules, and guidelines. Each group which adheres to these criteria should have its work considered complete and acceptable. In this case, it is the students' responsibility for assessing the quality of the assignment before submitting it to the teacher. For example, a challenge may require students to craft a device that floats and holds a given amount of weight. If the craft sinks, it is not the teacher who has judged the project as unacceptable, but the laws of physics. We have included the *Project Assessment Rubric* to help with the assessment of projects. In addition, if a student group is required to present its project, teachers may choose to use the Team Presentation Rubric as an additional assessment tool, or create their own assessment tools for the activities.

Throughout ***Inquiry by Design***, care has been taken to account for the assessment of individual students. It is our belief that while collaborative group work is a necessity for the collection of data and the completion of many of the challenges, it is the responsibility of each student to individually process that data. Students could theoretically receive a laboratory grade for what they physically do during a class session, a group grade for the collaborative nature of the work done, and an individual grade for processing and interpreting the collected data.

Additionally, we support writing across the curriculum. It is an important practice, and one that is supported by many brain researchers because of its positive affects on memory (Klein, & Boals, 2001). That considered, ***Inquiry by Design*** is an example of putting theory into practice for there many occasions in which students are asked to write as part of a design challenge. These writing assignments are generally of a descriptive or persuasive nature and are the responsibility of each student. Assessing the student writing assignments could be done via a teacher-made, school-adopted or standardized writing rubric.

These design challenges inherently rely on the appropriate use of the process skills. We have included a listing of these skills, their definitions and a sequentially developed matrix showing appropriate process expectations for each grade. Should students not be conversant with these skills, or need additional background, the matrix can be used as a guide for teachers in crafting a remediation program to reinforce these necessary skills.

CHEMISTRY

WEATHER WATCH

- Design a solution to a problem. *NSES*
- Implement a proposed design. *NSES*
- Apply and adapt a variety of appropriate strategies to solve problems. *NCTM*
- Students adjust their use of spoken, written, and visual language (e.g., conventions, style, vocabulary) to communicate effectively with a variety of audiences and for different purposes. *NCTE*

The Context: The Department of Transportation is responsible for keeping the roads clear and passable throughout the year. This is especially true during the winter months when the weather can offer an additional challenge.

The Scenario: To keep the roads clear of ice and snow, road crews sometimes spray the road surface with a concentrated salt solution. The concentration of this solution can be changed according to the outside temperature. The colder the temperature the more concentrated the solution needs to be. The Department of Transportation has requested the help of your engineering team. It seems that a severe winter storm, with very low temperatures, is quickly approaching and they are not sure which of two salt solutions to use. It seems that labels have fallen off the two brine tanks and no one knows how to tell the concentrated solution from the super-concentrated solution.

The Challenge: Your challenge is to develop and implement a procedure by which the Department can distinguish the concentrated salt solution from the super concentrated salt solution.

The Limitations:
- Because a sever storm is quickly approaching, time is of the essence. Each team will be given one class period complete this challenge.
- Action plans must be approved prior to gathering materials.
- Each team will have access to general laboratory equipment.
- Each team must design both data display and data communication formats.
- Results must be <u>quantifiable</u>.

The Rules:
- Each team member must write a set of directions to the Department of Transportation for finding the most concentrated solution. The directions must be supported by data.
- Each team must follow approved safety procedures when conducting their laboratory investigations.
- Safety glasses are required at all times.
- Standard laboratory equipment will be available for each team.

Extended Challenge: Suppose the Department of Transportation had to make up its own salt solution to match the concentration of either tank. Have the students demonstrate, and explain how they would do this if the tank contained 500 ml. For presentation purposes refer to the *Team Presentation Rubric* in the Teacher Support Section. Students might also be asked to determine the concentration of each solution using percent by mass, in order to make their own solutions.

TEACHER NOTES

Suggested Materials: Standard laboratory equipment and general school supplies may be needed for this challenge. Students will also need a supply of two different salt solutions one concentrated the other not. It is recommended that Kosher salt be used for this challenge since it dissolves readily and the water will remain clear.

Suggested Use: This design brief was written to extend and apply the content associated with the study of mixtures and solutions. A solution is made more concentrated by dissolving more and more solute in the same volume of solvent. Students should be familiar with this process. Because density increases if more solute is dissolved in an equal volume of solution, this activity could also be used after a study of density, or as a discrepant event at its introduction.

Ties to Content: Solutions can be solids, liquids, gasses as long as the mixture is homogeneous and the particles of the subsequent materials are evenly distributed.

Solutions can be solids, liquids, gases, or combinations thereof. They are homogeneous mixtures in which the solute particles are evenly distributed throughout the solvent particles. In this case, the salt water solution is composed of salt (solute) and water (solvent). The salt is an ionic compound which dissociates in water, meaning that it breaks down into positive and negative ions. This occurs partly because of the polar nature of water, meaning that it has a slightly positive end and a slightly negative end. The positive end of the water attracts the negative ions of the salt, and the negative end of the water attracts the positive ions of the salt, causing it to dissociate.

Increasing the rate of solubility of a solid, like salt, in a liquid, like water, can be achieved by heating the solution, stirring the solution, or increasing the surface area of the solute particles (by crushing them into smaller pieces). Lastly, the concentration of a solution can be indicated in a variety of ways, including percent by mass, which is a ratio of the mass of the solute to the mass of the solution (mass of solute/mass of solution X 100). As the concentration of a solution increases so does its density.

Possible Procedures(s): There are several ways that students could determine the most concentrated salt solution but weighing may be the most straight forward. Using pure water as the standard (1 ml = 1 cc = 1 g) students could weigh out equal volumes of the two salt solutions, the heavier of the two would be the most concentrated.

Precautions: Students will be expected to wear appropriate eye protection during this investigation. Care should be taken when using any chemical. Check the MSDS sheet for each chemical prior to use. Should these sheets not be available check the Flinn Scientific Catalog or the Flinn Scientific website, www.flinnsci.com. Click on the chemistry link and then the MSDS link.

While the problem solving techniques used by each team may be different, the diversity of thinking is beneficial for enhancing the problem solving repertoire of each student. Sharing is not only encouraged it is a strategy used throughout the program.

THE HIDDEN RAINBOW

> - Design a solution to a problem. *NSES*
> - Implement a proposed design. *NSES*
> - Apply and adapt a variety of appropriate strategies to solve problems. *NCTM*
> - Students adjust their use of spoken, written, and visual language (e.g., conventions, style, vocabulary) to communicate effectively with a variety of audiences and for different purposes. *NCTE*

The Context: Clues to the solution of a mystery can often be hidden from plain sight.

The Scenario: One morning as you quickly go through your locker you find the following note:

So, you think you got away with stealing pencil #6 from the sign out section of the front desk? You had better return my property or else!
> *I'll be waiting,*
> *Ann L. Retentive, Librarian*

You decide to get to the bottom of this because you did not take her precious pencils and already owe $2000 dollars in library fines for overdue books. You certainly can't afford to make Miss Retentive any more upset than she already is, so you gather your investigative team together to discuss what to do. Consensus is reached, and the team suspects that the entire incident and believe that a joke is being played and that Ann never wrote the note in the first place.

The Challenge: You know that if you could find the pen used to write the message you'd have a critical piece of evidence in solving this problem.

The Limitations:
- Each team must prepare a detailed procedure and rationale before gathering any equipment or related materials.
- Each team must design a way to display its collected data.
- Each team will have one class period to complete this challenge.
- Each team will be given a sample of the ransom note for testing and comparative analysis.

The Rules:
- No team will get more than one piece of the ransom note.
- Each team member much individually interpret the results and provide a written justification for the decision about the librarian's role in this mystery.
- Each team must follow approved safety procedures when conducting their laboratory investigations.
- Safety glasses are required at all times.
- Standard laboratory equipment will be available for all each team.

TEACHER NOTES

Suggested Materials: Students should have access to general laboratory equipment. In addition, a supply of black, water-based fine-line, markers need to be available as well as a piece of the "ransom note" to serve as a comparison when testing the markers. Standard filter paper, or even regular white paper towels, will suffice. The students will also need containers of water and some way of suspending the paper strips.

Suggested Use: This design brief was written as a real-life application of the concept of chromatography. It should be noted that each research team should receive a simulated sample of the ransom note for testing purposes. This note should contain a line or heavy dot of ink from the pen used to write the ransom note. These samples should be prepared by the teacher prior to the lesson by using one of the pens available.

Ties to Content: Paper chromatography is a separation technique that depends upon differences in how strongly the dyes are adsorbed onto the paper and how soluble the dyes are in the solvent in which they are immersed. In paper chromatography, a sample of the material to be separated, such as ink, is placed close to the edge of a piece of paper. The edge of the paper is then immersed in a developing solution and as the developing solution is absorbed by the paper through capillary action, the composite materials of the sample are carried along at different rates.

In the case of our pen mystery, the chemical composition of the water-based inks will probably vary between manufacturers and thus will produce a unique chromatograph.

Possible Procedures(s): Students should be instructed to make a dark horizontal line across the paper strip about 3 centimeters from the bottom. The prepared strips should be suspended above a container of water so that the "inked" ends are just touching the surface, making sure the ink does not touch the water. As the paper absorbs the water, through capillary action, the different ink components will separate at different rates, and will thus be deposited at different locations over the length of the paper.

Precautions: Students will be expected to wear appropriate eye protection during this investigation.

While the problem solving techniques used by each team may be different, the diversity of thinking is beneficial for enhancing the problem solving repertoire of each student. Sharing is not only encouraged it is a strategy used throughout the program.

CHROMATOGRAPHY EXTENSIONS

1. Can the colors displayed on a chromatograph be rejoined to produce the original color?

2. Will all marker colors produce a rainbow?

3. Will a darker mark produce a darker rainbow?

4. Will all kinds of paper work for this investigation?

5. Does the temperature of the water make a difference in the speed or the pattern produced?

6. Will other liquids like salt water or alcohol work in making chromatographs?

7. Can the rate of chromatography be increased or decreased?

8. If the rate of the chromatography process can be increased or decreased does this affect the pattern produced or the quality of that pattern?

9. Would the chromatography pattern change if the color spreading was circular (outward) rather than straight up?

10. Will water color paints work as well as water based markers?

11. How do you think you could use the process of chromatography to produce a piece of artwork?

12. What if water was allowed to run downward through a chromatography mark? Do you think a chromatograph would be produced *below* the mark?

13. Could chromatographs be made with M & M's or Skittles?

14. Could green leaves be made to produce a chromatograph?

NATURAL INDICATORS

- Design a solution to a problem. *NSES*
- Implement a proposed design. *NSES*
- Apply and adapt a variety of appropriate strategies to solve problems. *NCTM*
- Students adjust their use of spoken, written, and visual language (e.g., conventions, style, vocabulary) to communicate effectively with a variety of audiences and for different purposes. *NCTE*

The Context: Color change is a way of indicating the presence of acids and/or bases.

The Scenario: The Chameleon Litmus Company is searching for a new product that can replace the standard pink and blue litmus paper it has sold for many years. Lichens are used to manufacture litmus paper and are becoming scarce. If the company cannot find a natural alternative, it may have to close its doors.

The Challenge: Your chemical research team has been contacted to help with this challenge. You know that red cabbage, when boiled produces a blue-purple solution that can be used to treat absorbent paper. This paper can then be used like litmus to identify acids and bases. The purple paper will turn red in the presence of acids and green when exposed to bases. The company is aware of this but needs other natural options as well.

The Limitations:
- Each team will have two lab periods to complete this challenge. It is expected that student teams will conduct appropriate research outside of class.
- Each team must design a testing procedure with appropriate safety notations that must be approved before testing begins.
- Each team must test three different natural materials (supplied by the teacher) to determine if they could be used as a natural acid-base indicator.
- Students are also responsible for gathering three additional products to test.

The Rules:
- Each team will be using dilute acid and base solutions for this challenge. Solutions will be prepared by the teacher.
- All testing must be conducted in school.
- Each team must follow approved safety procedures when conducting their laboratory investigations.
- Safety glasses are required at all times.
- Standard laboratory equipment will be available for each team.
- All research gathered by each team must be noted in bibliographical form.
- Each team must design data displays for all collected information.
- Each team member will be responsible for interpreting and presenting the results of its investigation in the form of a written letter to the Chameleon Litmus Company. Supportive data must be noted in this document.

TEACHER NOTES

Suggested Materials: Standard laboratory equipment will be needed for this challenge. In addition three different fruits, flowers or vegetables containing anthocyannin need to be made available for testing. Be aware that living material that is purple in color usually contains anthocyannin. This design brief also requires students to test three other natural products of their own choice for appropriateness as an acid-base indicator. A selection of weak acids, strong acids, weak bases and strong bases should be available for testing with the indicators. These solutions can be prepared with common materials or with those commonly available in a science lab. Examples include ammonia (weak base), vinegar (weak acid), crystal Draino (strong base), and muriatic acid (strong acid-available at most hardware or home improvement stores). To prepare these solutions, add some of each of these to distilled water. The concentration of each solution will not matter, but using similar amounts of solutes per similar amounts of water may be helpful. Remember, **always add the acid (or base) to the water, never the reverse.** This is especially true in the cases of the strong acids and bases mentioned here. Crystal Draino is actually made of sodium hydroxide pellets, and can burn the skin if contacted directly, so protective gloves may also be helpful. Muriatic acid should be treated in a similar fashion, as it is simply hydrochloric acid. Buffer solutions ordered from a chemical supply company could also be used to represent specific pHs.

Suggested Use: This design brief was written to extend the study of acids and bases through exploring natural materials that can be used as acid-base indicators. Additionally, students could be asked to decide which indicators might be appropriate for different situations involving specific pH ranges.

Ties to Content: There are many natural acid/base indicators, purple cabbage juice being the most common. The extract (or juice) of any plant part that contains anthocycanin (Hoffman's Violet) will produce a color change when in the presence of an acid or base but some are better than others. Some extracts will react better with acids, some with bases and some, like purple cabbage, will react with both. Examples of common plant extracts include, grapes, cherries, corn flowers, red poppies, blue berries, iris, clematis and red impatients to name a few.

Possible Procedures(s): There are two basic ways of extracting the anthocyannin from vegetable material, boil it or blend it boiling tends go be the better of the two methods In either case the cell walls of the vegetable material are broken thus permitting the distinctive indicator to be released. For the record, boiling the material is the preferred method. Once the anthocyannin is extracted it can be transferred to pH neutral paper to create litmus paper or used in liquid form.

Precautions: Students will be expected to wear appropriate eye protection during this investigation. Care should be taken when using any chemical. Check the MSDS sheet for each chemical prior to use. Should these sheets not be available check the Flinn Scientific Catalog or the Flinn Scientific website, www.flinnsci.com. Click on the chemistry link and then the MSDS link.

While the problem solving techniques used by each team may be different, the diversity of thinking is beneficial for enhancing the problem solving repertoire of each student. Sharing is not only encouraged it is a strategy used throughout the program.

STOMACH PAINS

> - Design a solution to a problem. *NSES*
> - Think critically and logically to make the relationships between evidence and explanations. *NSES*
> - Apply and adapt a variety of appropriate strategies to solve problems. *NCTM*
> - Students employ a wide range of strategies as they write and use different writing process elements appropriately to communicate with different audiences for a variety of purposes. *NCTE*

The Context: The results of product testing are somewhat suspect if the evaluation of the product is done by the manufacturer. This is known as experimenter bias.

The Scenario: The responsibility of a marketing department is to positively advertise products in hopes that consumers will be encouraged to buy them. While some products perform as advertised, others do not. A "fair test" can only be done by an agency that has nothing to gain other than finding the truth.

The Challenge: Your laboratory team has been asked to evaluate over-the-counter antacids. The most common claims for these products are that they work fast and that they neutralize more stomach acid than other brands. As independent testers, your challenge is to answer the following questions: "Which antacid works the fastest?" and "Which neutralizes the most acid?"

The Limitations:
- Each research team will have three class periods to complete this investigation.
- Each team will have access to all laboratory equipment but, due to costs, will have a limited amount of product to test.
- Each team must detail a "fair test plan" describing how it will answer the research question.
- No team may begin testing until its "fair test plan" has been approved.
- Test results must be <u>quantifiable</u>.
- Each team will be responsible for testing all the brands of antacid supplied.
- The recommended dosage of each antacid will be compared.

The Rules:
- Data collection and display formats must be created by each research team.
- Each team member must prepare a report including the procedure followed, appropriate data charts/graphs, a review of the results, a summary statement supported by data and recommendations to consumers about the products tested. A comparison of product performance and price will also be required.
- Each team must also prepare a two minute presentation of its fair test procedure and the results of its investigation.
- Each team must follow approved safety procedures when conducting their laboratory investigations.
- Safety glasses are required at all times.
- Standard laboratory equipment will be available for each team.
- For presentation purposes refer to the *Team Presentation Rubric* in the Teacher Support Section.

TEACHER NOTES

Suggested Materials: This investigation will require basic laboratory equipment such as, graduated cylinders, pipettes, glassware, an indicator such as phenolphthalein or wide range pH paper, vinegar (or HCl to simulate stomach acid-this is sometimes found in home improvement stores labeled as muriatic acid), stirring sticks, funnels, stop watches, balance sensitive to .001 grams, filter paper, a variety of over-the-counter antacids and some way to crush or powder the antacids such as a mortar and pestle. It is suggested that the students have a copy of the *Team Presentation Rubric* to use as a guide as they craft their presentations.

Suggested Use: This design brief was written to extend the study of acids and bases through exploring indicators and titrations or as part of a unit on consumer science or customer awareness. This challenge can also be used as a performance assessment in a number of areas including quantitative analysis, laboratory procedures, and proficiency in recording and reporting.

Ties to Content: Taking an antacid is usually done to help with an upset stomach. If we are to believe the antacid commercials, neutralizing excess stomach acid is the key to relief. This challenge addresses simple acid-base chemistry including the concepts of pH, replacement reactions and neutralization reactions. In this case, an aqueous solution of the base (antacid tablet) is being titrated with a "mock" stomach acid (vinegar will suffice, but dilute hydrochloric acid, HCl, could also be used). An indicator such as phenolphthalein is added to the basic solution prior to titration (drop by drop addition of the acid) until a color change is observed. Phenolphthalein is magenta in a basic solution but becomes clear in neutral and acidic solutions. The more effective the antacid the more vinegar will be required to reach the equivalence point (the point at which the color of the solution changes).

Possible Procedure(s): Students could approach this challenge by first massing out equal amounts of each antacid supplied, powdering each sample and mixing it with 20 ml of water. To ensure that the equivalence point will be visible, a few milliliters of phenolphthalein should be added to this basic mixture. Acid should then be added, drop by drop, until the basic solution of water and antacid loses its distinctive magenta color. This indicates that the endpoint has been reached, and that the base has been neutralized.

Initially, the teacher must determine the number of antacid brands for testing and the amount of time that will be devoted to this investigation. The investigation could also be restructured to be a comparison between two brands of antacid, or as a comparison between antacid brands and sodium bicarbonate (baking soda)

Precautions: Students will be expected to wear appropriate eye protection during this investigation. Care should be taken when using any chemical. Check the MSDS sheet for each chemical prior to use. Should these sheets not be available check the Flinn Scientific Catalog or the Flinn Scientific website, www.flinnsci.com. Click on the chemistry link and then the MSDS link.

While the problem solving techniques used by each team may be different, the diversity of thinking is beneficial for enhancing the problem solving repertoire of each student. Sharing is not only encouraged it is a strategy used throughout the program.

CONCENTRATION

- Design a solution to a problem. *NSES*
- Implement a proposed design. *NSES*
- Apply and adapt a variety of appropriate strategies to solve problems. *NCTM*
- Students adjust their use of spoken, written, and visual language (e.g., conventions, style, vocabulary) to communicate effectively with a variety of audiences and for different purposes. *NCTE*

The Context: The results of an investigation can be duplicated if accurate laboratory notes are available.

The Scenario: The Colorado Concentrate Company (CCC) is in the business of preparing and bottling saturated solutions. While the company has a standard line of products and also makes up special orders when needed. For example, during the winter season, saturated brine solution is the biggest seller as this product is sprayed on road surfaces to prevent ice build-up. The brine, like all solutions, is prepared following a specific procedure: one of many that were recently destroyed in a small, but costly office fire.

The Challenge: CCC has contacted your research team for help. The company has a large supply of 0.5 liter bottles in stock but, because of space considerations, the solutes need to be ordered from the supply house each day. This is the major problem. No one knows how much of each solute to order because no one knows how much solute is needed to make each saturated solution. CCC needs specific procedures for preparing each of their saturated stock solutions. Solutes include salt, sugar, citric acid, alum, sodium hyposulfite (photographic hypo) and Epsom salts.

The Limitations:
- Each team must prepare an action plan describing how they will create the saturated solutions that CCC requires.
- Each team must *jointly decide* at which point saturation has been reached.
- Each team may request any equipment normally found in the room.
- Each team may also supply some of its own equipment.
- Each team must design a way to collect and display its experimental data.

The Rules:
- Each team must use 100 ml of room temperature water in each of their saturated solutions.
- Each member of the team will be responsible for individually interpreting the data and crafting a summary statement supported by the collected data.
- Each team member must write a letter to CCC outlining the investigative procedure and presenting the "recipe" for making each saturated solution.
- All "recipes" must be reported in grams of solute/ml of water.

TEACHER NOTES

Suggested Materials: Standard laboratory equipment and general school supplies may be needed for this challenge. The solutes that need to be supplied could include: salt, sugar, citric acid, alum, sodium hyposulfite (photographic hypo) and/or Epsom salts. Other soluble solids could also be used providing appropriate safety precautions are followed. In addition, a supply of .5 liter water bottles should be on hand for student use.

Suggested Use: This design brief was written to extend and apply the content associated with the study of mixtures and solutions. While students may understand the concept of creating a saturated solution they may not realize that different solutes will dissolve in different amounts given the same amount of water. It is suggested that kosher salt be used because solution made with this compound remains clear.

Ties to Content: Solutions can be solids, liquids, gasses as long as the mixture is homogeneous and the particles of the subsequent materials are evenly distributed. When a solid, like sugar, is dissolved in a solute, like water the process occurs on the surface of the sugar. Water molecules are said to be polar which means they have a positive and a negative area. As the water molecules move about they come in contact with the molecules of sugar and the negative areas of the water molecules are attracted to the positive areas o the sugar molecules. The water molecules continue to move about and strip the attracted sugar molecules with them eventually dispersing them evenly throughout the solution. The rate of dissolving for a solute, like sugar, can be increased by enlarging the surface area of the solute by grinding it into smaller pieces, increasing the temperature of the solute, or stirring or shaking the mixture of solute and solvent.

Possible Procedures(s): Prior to beginning this challenge, each team must operationally define what it is that they mean by dissolving and saturation. Generally, **dissolving** means that after 100 vigorous shakes no more solute remains visible in the bottle. **Saturation** means that some solute is visible after 100 vigorous shakes. Additionally, each team must reach consensus regarding the mixing procedure for the solutions. Shaking the solution vigorously 100 times in a closed container is generally accepted as the standard. Once everyone agrees, each team is free to decide how it will proceed. Each team might begin with 100 ml of room temperature, add a small amount of solute and vigorously shake the closed container 100 times. As long as the solute dissolves in the water then the procedure should continue until saturation is reached...that point at which the solute no longer dissolves. The students have to keep track of the amount of solute they add to the 100 ml of water. They could, of course, weigh the solute out prior to mixing or they could weigh the saturated solution and subtract 100 grams (the weight of the solvent alone). Students could be asked to extend this challenge by predicting the amount of solute would be needed to create different quantities of saturated solutions. They could also be asked to investigate the affect of water temperature or powdering the solute (increasing the surface area) on the rate of dissolving.

Precautions: Students will be expected to wear appropriate eye protection during this investigation. Care should be taken when using any chemical. Check the MSDS sheet for each chemical prior to use. Should these sheets not be available check the Flinn Scientific Catalog or the Flinn Scientific website, www.flinnsci.com. Click on the chemistry link and then the MSDS link.

While the problem solving techniques used by each team may be different, the diversity of thinking is beneficial for enhancing the problem solving repertoire of each student. Sharing is not only encouraged it is a strategy used throughout the program.

EXO-EXCITING

> - Design a solution to a problem. *NSES*
> - Implement a proposed design and evaluate completed technological designs or products. *NSES*
> - Apply and adapt a variety of appropriate strategies to solve problems. *NCTM*
> - Students adjust their use of spoken, written, and visual language (e.g., conventions, style, vocabulary) to communicate effectively with a variety of audiences and for different purposes. *NCTE*

The Context: Changing a product does not guarantee improved performance.

The Scenario: The "Inferno" Heat Pack Company has been manufacturing the same size, rechargeable hand warmers for a number of years. The "Inferno" marketing department is interested in expanding the product line but needs research data to guide its decision making.

The Challenge: Your research team has decided to take on the challenge of determining if there is a relationship between the size of a hand warmer and the amount of heat it generates. A second question that also needs to be answered refers to the length of time that a specific hand warmer will continue to generate heat.

The Limitations:
- Each team will have three class periods to complete this challenge.
- As a class, teams must work together to operationally define what size means in reference to hand warmers (mass, volume, surface area or something else). Each team will be responsible for investigation and manufacturing a different size warmer.
- As a class, teams must also decide how long their tests should last and what kind of data needs to be compiled.
- As a class, teams must decide how they intend to accurately measure the heat generated from the hand warmer. Once the temperature begins to drop the heat generating properties of the hand warmer should be considered ended.
- As a class, teams must create an action plan prior to gathering materials.
- Each team will use the same super saturated solution to manufacturer its hand warmer.
- General science equipment will be available for each team.
- Each team must design both data display and data communication formats.

The Rules:
- Each team must collect investigative data from the other teams.
- Each team must design both data display and data communication formats for <u>class data</u>.
- Each team member must prepare a brief report to the "Inferno" company that will include a synopsis of the investigation, an analysis the data, and predictions of what would result from manufacturing hand warmers for three sizes that were not tested.

TEACHER NOTES

Suggested Materials: Suggested time allocations for this challenge include: one period for planning and class decision making, one period for laboratory and data collecting and one period for collating data and writing final reports. Materials needed for this investigation include general science equipment, approximately 1 L of super saturated sodium thiosulfate solution, a supply of sodium thiosulfate seed crystals, and a supply of different size plastic zip lock bags. Real hand warmers are common products and can be found in many stores during the winter months.

Suggested Use: This design brief is most appropriately used as an extension activity associated with the study of endothermic and exothermic chemical reactions.

Ties to Content: All chemical reactions need energy to get started. This is called activation energy. Reactions which have low activation energies occur spontaneously. Others require the addition of energy to get started. Once the reaction begins, however, other energy changes occur which determine whether the reaction is endothermic (one which absorbs heat from the environment) or exothermic (one that gives off energy to the environment). Generally, chemical reactions involve the breaking and formation of chemical bonds, which requires energy. This net energy change determines whether a reaction is endothermic or exothermic. The crystallization of a supersaturated sodium acetate solution is a common exothermic process and is commercially available in the form of hand warmers.

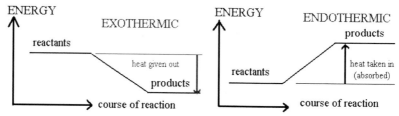

Possible Procedures(s): Heat packs can be made by using two different size zip lock bags, some water, and a supply of sodium thiosulfate. Place 440 g of sodium thiosulfate and 30 ml of water into a beaker or Pyrex glass. Using a double boiler type set up, place the beaker and its contents in a pan of water and heat the water until it boils. Stir the sodium thiosulfate with a metal spoon until it melts. Continue stirring for a few minutes. Remove the solution from the heat and allow it to cool. Be sure to spoon some of the liquid on the insides of the container to dissolve any crystals that might have formed. When cool, pour the liquid into a plastic sandwich bag. Place a few seed crystals of sodium thiosulfate in a larger zip lock bag, along with the smaller sealed zip lock bag containing the super saturated solution of sodium thiosulfate. The heat pack is now ready for use or storage. To activate the homemade heat pack, place a few seed crystals from the outer bag into the solution in the inner bag and reseal both bags. The solution will begin to solidify and heat will be given off for about an hour (about a maximum of 48°C). Recharging the heat pack can be done by removing the solid sodium thiosulfate from the inner bag, liquefying it as before, and placing it inside a new bag. Additional ideas for home made hand warmers can be found online.

Precautions: Students will be expected to wear appropriate eye protection during this investigation. Care should be taken when using any chemical. Check the MSDS sheet for each chemical prior to use. Should these sheets not be available check the Flinn Scientific Catalog or the Flinn Scientific website, www.flinnsci.com.

While the problem solving techniques used by each team may be different, the diversity of thinking is beneficial for enhancing the problem solving repertoire of each student. Sharing is not only encouraged it is a strategy used throughout the program.

WARM HANDS, COLD HEART

- Design a solution to a problem. *NSES*
- Implement a proposed design and evaluate completed technological designs or products. *NSES*
- Apply and adapt a variety of appropriate strategies to solve problems. *NCTM*
- Students adjust their use of spoken, written, and visual language (e.g., conventions, style, vocabulary) to communicate effectively with a variety of audiences and for different purposes. *NCTE*

The Context: Product comparison is a very common marketing tool.

The Scenario: The "Sportsters" Company sells equipment and apparel for every sport. One of their "hottest" selling items during football season, is the personal hand warmer. Some of these devices use a chemical reaction to generate heat while others use the principle of a phase change. Sportsters needs to place an order for next year, and since all the hand warmers are about the same price, they would like the most affective product for their customers.

The Challenge: Sportsters has contacted your research firm to help them with this dilemma. Which type of hand warmer produces the most heat?

The Limitations:
- Each team will have three class periods to complete this challenge.
- Because this is a comparative study, all groups must reach consensus on the operational definition of product size. Suggestions might include mass, volume, surface area, etc.
- Each team must create an action plan prior to gathering materials.
- Each team must decide how it intends to accurately measure the heat generated from the hand warmers, the duration of the test and the data to be gathered.
- General science equipment will be available for each team.
- Each team will receive the same number and types of hand warmers.

The Rules:
- Each team must identify the heat generated from their hand warmers as a chemical change or a phase change and explain its decision.
- Each team must design both data display and data communication formats.
- Each team member must present a synopsis of the investigation.
- Each team must display, interpret and present the results of the investigations.
- Each team must provide analyses of which type of hand warmer is the best buy and explain the decision with supportive data.
- Each team should refer to the *Team Presentation Rubric* for guidance in crafting the presentation.

TEACHER NOTES

Suggested Materials: A supply of chemical change and phase change hand warmers will be needed for this investigation and the price for each type of hand warmer may vary. These can be purchased at sporting goods stores. Be sure to check each team's action plan prior to allowing the investigation to proceed as this will help avoid wasting materials. Phase change hand warmers are not consumable as they can be recharged by placing them in boiling water. General laboratory equipment, including thermometers, will be needed for this challenge.

Suggested Use: Hand warmers are a common product and can be found in many stores during the winter months. This design brief is most appropriately used as an extension activity associated with the study of endothermic and exothermic chemical reactions. Suggested time allocations include one period for planning and class decision making, one period for conducting laboratory tests and collecting data and one period for processing data and writing final reports. Teachers should also be aware that once the hand warmers are activated they may generate heat longer than the given class period. Consider this possibility and make allowances for this possibility.

Ties to Content: All chemical reactions need energy to get started. This is called activation energy. Reactions which have low activation energies occur spontaneously. Others require the addition of energy to get started. Once the reaction begins, however, other energy changes occur which determine whether the reaction is endothermic (one which absorbs heat from the environment) or exothermic (one that gives off energy to the environment). Generally, chemical reactions involve the breaking and formation of chemical bonds, which requires energy. This net energy change determines whether a reaction is endothermic or exothermic. The crystallization of a supersaturated sodium acetate solution is a common exothermic process and is commercially available in the form of hand warmers.

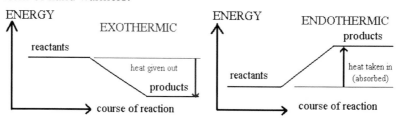

Possible Procedures(s): In order to compare hand warmers it will be necessary to equate them. Because these devices are sealed their size or contents cannot be altered, however it may be possible to account for this discrepancy through the testing process. For example, if the effectiveness of the different hand warmers is determined by how much they increase the temperature of a given amount of water, then adjusting the amount of water could possibly negate any size differences in the hand warmers.

Students might also collect temperature data by placing the devices directly on thermometers or by placing the hand warmers in large, insulated drinking cups with lids (like coffee cups) and recording changes in the air temperature inside the cup over time.

Precautions: Students should wear safety glasses during the course of this challenge. In addition, safety practices associated with the handling of hot materials should be followed.

While the problem solving techniques used by each team may be different, the diversity of thinking is beneficial for enhancing the problem solving repertoire of each student. Sharing is not only encouraged it is a strategy used throughout the program.

CONSUMER PROTECTION

CAVEAT EMPTOR

- Design and conduct a scientific investigation. *NSES*
- Design a solution to a problem. *NSES*
- Apply and adapt a variety of appropriate strategies to solve problems. *NCTM*
- Use mathematical models to represent and understand quantitative relationships. *NCTM*
- Students adjust their use of spoken, written, and visual language (e.g., conventions, style, vocabulary) to communicate effectively with a variety of audiences and for different purposes. *NCTE*

The Context: Consumers purchase many products every year. Some products perform as advertised others do not and consumers often compare products before making a selection.

The Scenario: Advertisers use many strategies in an attempt to convince consumers to buy their products. These techniques include: bright colors (*eye catching*), performance data (*faster, less work, more powerful*), convenience features (*easier to use, disposable*), endurance qualities (*lasts longer, stronger, best material*), economic considerations (*less expensive, more for the money*), societal issues (*biodegradable, less polluting*) and personal appeals (*fat free, makes you look and feel better).* Remember, the advertisers are competing for your money, so stretching the truth is not out of the question!

The Challenge: Your task is to select a consumer product to test. Are the advertising claims true or are they false? You team will be responsible for designing, scientifically testing, and presenting the results of a product investigation.

The Limitations:
- Each team must first create an action plan including a problem question that will be investigated about a selected product.
- The product, the problem question and the testing procedure must be completed and approved before product testing may start.
- Each team is solely responsible for its materials.
- Each team will have three weeks to complete this challenge. Working at home is strongly encouraged since teams may need more time than can be afforded at school.
- Each team will present its findings on the same day. Presentations will be limited to five minutes.

The Rules:
- Products must be tested at least three times and the data averaged.
- Each team needs to create a way to store and display collected data.
- All references must be noted in a bibliography
- All data must be displayed with accompanying graphs.
- Team members must individually process investigative data and craft data supported concluding statements.

TEACHER NOTES

Suggested Materials: While teams are responsible for their own materials, make standard laboratory and classroom equipment available for their use. Students should also have copies the *Team Presentation Rubric* and the *Advertising Guidelines* for reference purposes.

Suggested Use: This design brief is a consumer protection challenge and can provide an opportunity for teachers to observe the problem solving and data processing abilities of students. This type of activity requires students to question the product claims of manufacturers and to devise ways to "test" the authenticity of these assertions. Throughout this investigation students will also be expected to apply the process skills in meaningful ways. Therefore, this design brief can be used during a study of scientific thinking and problem solving. Additionally, this brief could be used in any content area if the products are selected ahead of time by the teacher. For example, it could be used in chemistry to study the amount of iron in breakfast cereals; in physics to study the tensile strength of fishing line, etc.

Ties to Content: This brief has no direct ties to any specific science content but addresses the process skills of identifying and controlling variables, data collection, hypothesizing, communication and interpretation. Students will be expected to craft a fair test procedure, collect appropriate data, process and display this data in an acceptable manner and draw reasonable, defendable conclusions.

Possible Procedures(s): The procedures devised by students will, in all likelihood, vary greatly because of the open ended nature of this challenge. Regardless, it is a requirement that each testing procedure be a "fair test" of the product being assessed. Students will also be required to collect quantifiable data and create appropriate data displays. It should also be noted that while the procedure, testing and data collection/displays are the responsibility of the "team", the processing and interpretation should be the responsibility of each individual student.

Precautions: The overarching purpose of these consumer investigations is to develop a healthy sense of skepticism in students. Since students are not permitted to advance past the planning stage without your permission, make every effort to check for safety issues in testing procedures and product selection.

While the problem solving techniques used by each team may be different, the diversity of thinking is beneficial for enhancing the problem solving repertoire of each student. Sharing is not only encouraged it is a strategy used throughout the program.

ADDITIONAL CONSUMER PROTECTION IDEAS

The over-arching purpose of any consumer investigation is to develop a healthy sense of skepticism. Collecting and processing quantifiable data is considered a primary skill for evaluating test results. Some of these investigations are straight forward, while others require the students to be creative in designing ways to collect quantifiable data.

⇒ Which is the longest lasting flashlight battery?
⇒ Which toothpaste is the most abrasive?
⇒ Does temperature affect the life of a flashlight battery?
⇒ Does all popcorn pop equally well?
⇒ Are water proofing sprays all the same?
⇒ What is the best insulating material?
⇒ Is chip proof nail polish really chip proof?
⇒ Just how effective is plastic food wrap? Are they all the same?
⇒ Which disposable diaper is the most absorbent?
⇒ Which paper towel absorbs the most? Is the quickest? Strongest?
⇒ Which breakfast cereal stays crunchy the longest?
⇒ Which breakfast sausage shrinks the least when cooked?
⇒ Which cereal floats the longest?
⇒ Which bar soap is the longest lasting?
⇒ Are all band aids equal?
⇒ Do dogs or cats prefer one brand of food over another?
⇒ Which is the thickest ketchup?
⇒ Do double stuff cookies really contain twice the stuffing?
⇒ Do all fingernail polishes dry quickly?
⇒ Which paper plate is the strongest?
⇒ Which brand of dish detergent provides the longest lasting suds?
⇒ Which hot dog "plumps" the most?
⇒ Which brand of facial tissue has the greatest strength?
⇒ Which is the best zip lock bag?
⇒ Are lite foods really lite?
⇒ What is the trade off for the reduced fat brand of a particular food?
⇒ Sand paper prices vary. Do you really get what you pay for?
⇒ Is waterproof mascara really waterproof?
⇒ Which kitty litter is the most absorbent?
⇒ Are all golf balls equal? Tennis Balls? Basketballs? Etc.
⇒ Masking tape…do they all hold equally well?

SUPER SNACK

- Design a solution to a problem. *NSES*
- Understand meanings of operations and how they relate to each other. *NTCM*
- Students adjust their use of spoken, written, and visual language (e.g., conventions, style, vocabulary) to communicate effectively with a variety of audiences and for different purposes. *NCTE*
- Students conduct research on issues and interests by generating ideas and questions, and by posing problems. They gather, evaluate, and synthesize data from a variety of sources (e.g., print and non-print texts, artifacts, people) to communicate their discoveries in ways that suit their purpose and audience *NCTE*.

The Context: Food companies are always developing new products in an effort to increase profits.

The Scenario: Double Stuff Snack Company is in a tailspin and the marketing department has decided that a new snack product might save the company from going bankrupt.

The Challenge: Your design team has been given the task of creating a new snack targeted at children between the ages of 6 and 16. Since your small company is unable to manufacture the various snack ingredients, it will be necessary to create the new snack from combining products that already exist.

The Limitations:
- Each team has two class periods to complete this challenge at the discretion of the teacher.
- The serving size listed on each ingredient package will be considered the unit of measurement for that product. *The serving size and the unit of measurement should be considered the same.*
- Each team may use ½ unit (serving size) of any product as long as the finished Super Snack does not exceed five total units. It does not matter that the serving size for each product may be different since it is relative to the product.
- Super Snacks must be limited to a total of five units.
- The five units selected must be from two or more of the ingredients provided.

The Rules:
- Each team must create a Super Snack container with appropriate advertising and nutritional information.
- Each team must present its Super Snack and container to the Double Stuff Snack Company
  Board of Directors.
- Each team must also write a newspaper or magazine article announcing the new product (remember the target audience) or create a television or radio commercial introducing the product.
- Each team should refer to the *Team Presentation Rubric* and the *Advertising Guidelines* as it prepares its package and presentation.

TEACHER NOTES

Suggested Materials: To defray the costs associated with this challenge it is suggested that parents be contacted for donations of specific food products. Examples of snack foods that can be used in this investigation include, but are not limited to: peanuts, breakfast cereal, small pretzels, small candies like M&Ms, corn twists, cheese crackers, dried fruit, and so on. Small zip lock bags are recommended as container liners for the finished product. For presentation purposes students should have copies of the *Team Presentation Rubric* and *Advertising Guidelines*.

Suggested Use: This design brief was crafted as a real life application of nutrition awareness and would be appropriately used with such a unit in the science or health class. It could also be used in a life science class during or as an introduction to the study of the classes of organic macromolecules: carbohydrates, lipids, proteins and nucleic acids. Lastly, it could be classified as a general consumer protection challenge and can provide an opportunity for teachers to observe the problem solving and data processing abilities of students.

Ties to Content: Food is a complex combination of nutrients used by humans to build tissue or to provide energy. Good nutrition generally assures a healthy body while poor nutrition can set the stage for health problems. Nutrients fall into six categories: proteins, fats, carbohydrates, minerals, vitamins and water. Everything we do requires energy, from playing tennis to sitting in a chair reading a book. The only way we can acquire this energy is by eating food. Additionally, what we eat is very important to how we look and how we feel. The energy obtained from food is measured in Calories, or the amount of energy required to raise one liter of water one degree Celsius. The number of calories we need varies with our age and our activity. If we ingest more Calories than we burn, we tend to gain weight. Conversely, if we burn more Calories than we ingest, we tend to lose weight. In order to use more Calories, we exercise. Keeping track of our activities and the types and amounts of food we consume is essential to good health.

Possible Procedures(s): In addition to developing a new snack, the students are responsible for creating their own container for their snack food. An easy way for them to accomplish this is to "re-purpose" an existing paper container by carefully separate the seams of the box, turn it inside out and glue or tape it back together. This procedure will create an instant box ready for advertising. The nutritional information of the products used can be found on its container. This information reflects the nutritional value found in one serving size. The total nutritional value for the entire package will require a little math. When students create the nutritional information of their Super Snack they may add the nutritional information of each of the components. In the event that students decide to use half a unit of any existing snack then the nutritional information must also be halved for that ingredient. Assume a homogeneous mixture of ingredients to determine the product information. If the product contains three parts, one of which is peanuts, then one third of the snack's nutritional value will come from the peanuts. A sample nutritional facts label follows this activity and may be copied and pasted onto student containers.

Precautions: It is suggested that teams wear protective gloves when handling any food product. Although tasting is not recommended in any science lesson the students, will probably want to sample the completed products. An option would be to have them conduct the taste test in the lunchroom or outside if it's a nice day. Allergic reactions to latex or food products may also be an issue. Be sure to obtain parental permission to check student medical records.

While the problem solving techniques used by each team may be different, the diversity of thinking is beneficial for enhancing the problem solving repertoire of each student. Sharing is not only encouraged it is a strategy used throughout the program.

Nutritional Facts

Serving Size
Servings per Container

Amount Per Serving

Calories   Calories from Fat

% Daily value

Total Fat

Saturated Fat

Trans Fat

Polyunsaturated Fat

Monounsaturated Fat

Cholesterol

Sodium

Total Carbohydrate

Dietary Fiber

Sugars

Protein

Vitamin A   Vitamin C

Calcium   Iron

Percent Daily values are based on a 2,000 calorie diet.
Your daily values may be higher or lower depending on your
calorie needs.

Calories 2,000   2,500

Ingredients:

COOKIE CAPERS

- Design a solution to a problem. *NSES*
- Implement a proposed design and evaluate completed technological designs or products. *NSES*
- Apply and adapt a variety of appropriate strategies to solve problems. *NCTM*
- Students adjust their use of spoken, written, and visual language (e.g., conventions, style, vocabulary) to communicate effectively with a variety of audiences and for different purposes. *NCTE*

The Context: Manufacturers encourage consumers to purchase products by using a variety of colorful images and written advertising ploys. But, how truthful are these enticements?

The Scenario: Your group is serving on a consumer awareness panel. The purpose of the panel is to develop easy-to-use product evaluation techniques for consumers.

The Challenge: Your team has been assigned the specific task of designing a four-point rubric for consumers to use when evaluating the quality of chocolate chip cookies (YUMMY). The ultimate goal is to combine all rubrics to create a master scoring device for evaluating chocolate chip cookies.

The Limitations:
- Each team will have one class period to develop its evaluation rubric.
- The testing of cookies and rubrics will occur during a second class period.
- No team may share the contents or the criteria of its rubric with other teams.
- Each team must design a graphic organizer to display the selection criteria (like chip size) that they consider to be important in evaluating the quality of a chocolate chip cookie.
- The criteria must appear in the chart along with a written expectation for each scoring level, 4 through 1, with 4 being the top rating.

The Rules:
- The rubric must be based on a four-point scale with clearly stated selection criteria such as Number of Chocolate Chips, Size, Mass, and so on.
- Each team will evaluate the sample cookies independently. Results will be shared at the conclusion of testing and evaluated to develop a master scoring device.

TEACHER NOTES

Suggested Materials: The materials for this challenge are limited, but can be expensive. It is suggested that parents be made aware of this challenge and be asked to donate a specific brand of cookies. In this way you can help assure a variety of cookies for testing purposes. In addition to the cookies, paper plates and napkins should be on hand.

Suggested Use: This design brief can be classified as a general consumer protection challenge and can provide an opportunity for teachers to observe the problem solving and data processing abilities of students. Students should have some experience with rubrics prior to this activity.

Ties to Content: This design brief does not focus on any specific science content but rather provides an opportunity for students to apply the process skills for gathering, organizing, analyzing and presenting data. It also provides students with an opportunity to experience a real life experience of working in teams, competing, collaborating with other work groups and reaching consensus to develop a research tool.

Possible Procedures(s): Students may be accustomed to using rubrics but creating them is another story. It is suggested that students be given a number of rubrics to observe, compare, contrast and generally process prior to being expected to develop their own. Before attempting to construct a rubric, students really have to understand the features common to all rubrics.

Precautions: Students may need to break apart the cookies in an attempt to count the number of chips. They may also want to eat the cookies. Since tasting is not recommended in any science lesson, and for sanitary purposes, it is suggested that the cookies be placed in a large plastic bag prior to any manipulation. In this way students can perform any number of investigations without directly touching the cookies. When the lesson is over the bags of cookies can be taken to lunch and everybody can enjoy. If you choose to allow students to manipulate the cookies directly, please dispose of them properly, making sure they are not eaten after extended handling.

Allergic reactions to latex or food products may also be an issue. Be sure to obtain parental permission to check student medical records for such adverse reactions.

While the problem solving techniques used by each team may be different, the diversity of thinking is beneficial for enhancing the problem solving repertoire of each student. Sharing is not only encouraged it is a strategy used throughout the program.

RAISIN PACKS*

- Design a solution to a problem. *NSES*
- Implement a proposed design and evaluate completed technological designs or products. *NSES*
- Use visualization, spatial reasoning, and geometric modeling to solve problems. *NCTM*
- Students adjust their use of spoken, written, and visual language (e.g., conventions, style, vocabulary) to communicate effectively with a variety of audiences and for different purposes. *NCTE*
- Students conduct research on issues and interests by generating ideas and questions, and by posing problems. They gather, evaluate, and synthesize data from a variety of sources (e.g., print and non-print texts, artifacts, people) to communicate their discoveries in ways that suit their purpose and audience *NCTE*.

The Context: There are many items in our daily lives that we take for granted and closer inspection can sometimes change an opinion.

The Scenario: The Casablanca Container Corporation of Carlsbad, California is interested in expanding its line of unique product containers. Need a job?

The Challenge: Your design/engineering team decides to accept the task. The company wants you to design, and construct a package for one of the state's major industries...raisins. In addition to manufacturing the package, the company also expects you to create the advertising campaign and craft a dynamic sales presentation.

The Limitations:
- Each team will have three class periods to complete this challenge.
- Each team will be required to use the container evaluation criteria prepared by the Casablanca Container Corporation (see Package Scoring Rubric).
- Each team is expected to assign each of its members to one or more of these roles.
- *Graphic Designer*: Responsible for images, lettering, and color selection for the package.
- *Construction Engineer*: Responsible for selecting packaging materials and design.
- *Contractor:* Responsible for constructing the package as per design specifications as set forth by the Construction Engineer.
- *The Advertising Coordinator*: Responsible for crafting the advertising campaign including product name, slogans, poems, and the general "flavor" of the sales pitch.
- *Director of Marketing*: Responsible for making sure the package meets, or exceeds, as many package selection criteria as possible.
- *Consumer Advocate*: Responsible for assuring product labels are accurate and complete.

The Rules:
- The managers are the bosses for their segment of the project and not solely responsible for completing their portion. This way, everybody gets a chance to be the boss.
- Each team must present its package to the other design teams and should refer to the *Team Presentation Rubric* and *Advertising Guidelines* to do so.
- Each package presentation must be accompanied by an analysis of how well the package fits the criteria of the scoring rubric.
- Presentations could also include an advertising poster, a slogan, song, poem, or a media commercial of some type.

TEACHER NOTES

Suggested Materials: The students should be able to gather everything they need for this challenge from within the regular classroom, except for the raisins. Students should also have access to general classroom supplies, including construction paper, masking tape, glue, transparent tape, crayons, colored pencils, markers, and other art supplies . Each design team should also receive approximately two ounces of raisins in a small zip lock bag. Students should have copies of the *Team Presentation Rubric* and *Advertising Guidelines* as they craft their projects and prepare their presentations.

Suggested Use: This design brief can be classified as a general consumer protection challenge and can provide an opportunity for teachers to observe the problem solving and data processing abilities of students.

Ties to Content: This design brief does not focus on any specific science content but rather provides an opportunity for students to apply the process skills for gathering and processing data and accomplishing a task in a collaborative group manner. However, this challenge is most closely aligned with the areas of Scientific Reasoning and Technology. Having students use the Design Loop, rather than the traditional, linear scientific method, allows them greater freedom in crafting and redesigning a solution to this challenge. The students will be expected to rely on a number of process skills in completing this challenge including: organizing, comparing, defining operationally and communicating. In addition, the students will also be required to produce a product that meets specifications and reflects a logical rationale.

Possible Procedure(s): This challenge is an open-ended project and should be approached in that manner. Nonetheless, as with many design problems, it will be necessary for student teams to be acutely aware of the time constraints. It is suggested that a completion schedule be provided to keep students on task. Three class periods have been allotted for this challenge. These periods are at the discretion of the teacher and could be spread over a longer period of time if necessary. Students are encouraged to work on this project outside of class. Students are provided with the guidelines for the challenge as well as an extensive rubric intended to serve as a course of action.

Precautions: For sanitary purposes it is suggested that teams wear protective gloves when handling any food product. Although tasting is not recommended in any science lesson the students will probably want to sample the completed products. A viable option would be to have them conduct the taste test in the lunchroom or outside if it's a nice day.

Allergic reactions to latex or food products may be an issue. Be sure to obtain parental permission to check student medical records for such adverse reactions.

* Adapted from Project 2061 Dissemination Workshop, School District Philadelphia, 1990

While the problem solving techniques used by each team may be different, the diversity of thinking is beneficial for enhancing the problem solving repertoire of each student. Sharing is not only encouraged it is a strategy used throughout the program.

PACKAGE SCORING RUBRIC

Package Criteria	4	3	2	1	Student Score	Teacher Score
Design	Package has unique shape or feature. When packaged in bulk, the space between individual packages is minimal.	Package serves purpose but is generally basic. When packaged in bulk, the space between individual packages is minimal.	Package serves purpose but is generally basic. When packaged in bulk, there is much wasted space between individual packages.	Package does not serve purpose well. When packaged in bulk, there is much wasted space between individual packages.		
Protective Qualities	Package protects contents from spoilage, breakage, spillage and tampering.	Package protects contents from spoilage and tampering.	Package protects contents from spoilage.	Package does not protect contents in any way.		
User Friendliness	Outside package is easy to open and to reseal. The same is true of the inner liner, if present. Package is sturdy and stores easily.	Outside package is easy to open and reseal. Inner liner if present does not re-seal easily. Package is generally sturdy and stores easily.	Outside package is easy to open but inner liner, if present, is difficult to open and does not re-seal easily. Package needs reinforcement and stores awkwardly.	Outside package opens with difficulty and can not be resealed. Inner liner necessary but not included. Package does not store easily.		
Environmental Friendliness	Package is recyclable, reusable, and/or biodegradable.	Package is recyclable, reusable, or can be re-purposed.	Most of the package is recyclable. Some of the package can be reused or re-purposed.	Most of the package is not recyclable or biodegradable. Nothing of can be reused or re-purposed.		
Cost Effectiveness	Package materials are easily obtained. Package design wastes very little material. Package allows for few manufacturing steps.	Package materials are easily obtained. Package design wastes some material. Manufacturing steps can be sequenced like an assembly line.	Most package materials are easily obtained. Package design is wasteful of raw materials. Manufacturing package is somewhat awkward.	Package materials are not easily obtained. Package design is very wasteful of raw materials. Manufacturing package is awkward and time consuming.		
Attractiveness	Design is eye catching and has attractive use of color. Graphics and lettering are clear, uncluttered, easily understood, and add to the overall effectiveness. Creative and interesting.	Design is eye catching and uses color. Graphics and lettering are neat and carefully done. Contents message is easily understood.	Design uses some color. Graphics are limited and lettering could be neater. Contents message is evident but lacks clarity.	Design uses no color. No graphics used and lettering is not neat and complete. Contents message is not evident.		
Information Quotient	Product name, description of contents, and amount appear. Manufacturer's address, phone #, website are evident. Price is supplied. Slogan or supportive product claim appears. For food products: Nutrition facts, serving size, and all ingredients are noted.	Product name, description of contents, and amount appear. Manufacturer's address and price of package are given. For food products: Nutrition facts, serving size, and major ingredients are noted.	Product name appears. Minimal manufacturing information present. Price of package appears. For food products: Limited information noted.	Product name appears. Manufacturer's information and package price do not appear. For food products: No information noted.		

TALE OF THE TAPE

> - Design a solution to a problem. *NSES*
> - Implement a proposed design and evaluate completed technological designs or products. *NSES*
> - Apply and adapt a variety of appropriate strategies to solve problems. *NCTM*
> - Students adjust their use of spoken, written, and visual language (e.g., conventions, style, vocabulary) to communicate effectively with a variety of audiences and for different purposes. *NCTE*

The Context: The results of product testing are somewhat suspect if the evaluation was done by the company that made the product. This is known as experimenter bias.

The Scenario: As Mrs. Baker entered her third grade classroom her mood immediately changed. She had spent two hours the day before decorating the room for Parent's Day and everything she had taped to the wall was now on the floor. Everything would have to be re-taped and put up again…but which kind of tape should she use?

The Challenge: Your independent research lab received a phone call from Mrs. Baker. She explained the problem and asked, "What kind of tape would be best to hold my heavy posters?" You assure Mrs. Baker that your crack research team will be able to find out which kind of tape will hold the most weight.

The Limitations:
- Your research team will have three class periods to complete this investigation.
- Each team will have access to all laboratory equipment and a variety of tapes.
- The wall surface selected for conducting the tape tests should be the same for all teams.
- Each team must detail a "fair test" plan of how it will answer the research question.
- Each team must identify and list the variables it intends to keep the same during the tests.
- No team may begin testing until its "fair test" plan has been approved.

The Rules:
- Each team will be responsible for testing all the tapes supplied.
- Each team may supply any additional materials it considers necessary.
- Quantitative data collection and display formats must be created by each team.
- Each team member must prepare a lab report. The report should include the procedure followed, a description of the variables, data charts/graphs, a written review of the results, conclusions supported by data and recommendations to Mrs. Baker about the products tested.
- Each team must present its findings to the rest of the class.
- Team members should refer to the *Team Presentation Rubric* in crafting their presentations.

TEACHER NOTES

Suggested Materials: This challenge requires variety tapes. In addition, general equipment and pieces of cardboard (18" X 24 ") could also be on hand to simulate the heavy posters.

Suggested Use: This design brief can be classified as a general consumer protection challenge and can provide an opportunity for teachers to observe the problem solving and data processing abilities of students.

Ties to Content: The focus of this design brief relies heavily on the appropriate use the design loop as students craft a fair test to determine the most effective tape. Students also need to describe how they intend to identify and control of variables in the investigation. Teachers should take notice of this and if students use appropriate process skills. The biggest challenge for the students will be to identify and control the variables associated with this investigation.

As with many design problems, it will be necessary for student teams to be acutely aware of the time constraints. In addition, students should refer to the *Team Presentation Rubric* in planning, construction, testing and presenting.

Possible Procedures(s): While there are a variety of ways students could approach this design challenge. In sum, students must design and conduct a controlled or "fair test" investigation to test the relative strength of a variety of different tapes. Students could design a comparative test between tape samples or test all the tape samples against a standard, like a spring scale or hanging uniform masses, both yielding quantifiable data.

Precautions: Whenever students are involved in a construction project there is the possibility of a mishap, especially if tools, hot glue guns and other sharp objects are available. Students should be shown proper tool use and be expected to sign a safety contract. They should wear safety goggles whenever working with sharp objects in close quarters. Appropriate safety contracts can be obtained from Flinn Scientific at www.flinnsci.com .

While the problem solving techniques used by each team may be different, the diversity of thinking is beneficial for enhancing the problem solving repertoire of each student. Sharing is not only encouraged it is a strategy used throughout the program.

LOOKS CAN DECEIVE

- Design and conduct a scientific investigation. *NSES*
- Design a solution to a problem. *NSES*
- Apply and adapt a variety of appropriate strategies to solve problems. *NCTM*
- Use mathematical models to represent and understand quantitative relationships. *NCTM*
- Students adjust their use of spoken, written, and visual language (e.g., conventions, style, vocabulary) to communicate effectively with a variety of audiences and for different purposes. *NCTE*

The Context: The results of product testing are somewhat suspect if the evaluation was done by the company that made the product. This is known as experimenter bias.

The Scenario: The role of marketing departments is to put a positive spin on the products they represent so consumers will buy them. Unwary consumers can easily be drawn in to the trap of believing what others tell them is true or what they think is true. One example of this perception problem is the size and shape of product containers.

The Challenge: Your research team decides to take on this challenge. For years consumers have been told that the giant, economy size boxes were the best value. Is this really true and is it true for all products?

The Limitations:
- Your research team will have three class periods to complete this investigation. One period to craft a plan of attack, one period to process and interpret collected data, and one period to present findings. These class periods will be at the discretion of the teacher.
- Additional time will be needed to collect data outside of class and that will be the responsibility of each team.
- Each team must detail a "fair test plan" of how it will answer the research question.
- Each team must establish a way to compare the amount of product in each container with the price of that container.
- No team may begin collecting data until its "fair test plan" has been approved.
- Six different products must be evaluated.
- Data collection and display formats must be created by each team.

The Rules:
- Testing results must be quantifiable.
- Each team member must prepare a written report and include the procedure followed, data charts/graphs, a written review of the results, conclusions supported by data and recommendations to consumers.
- Each team must present its findings.
- Team members should refer to the *Team Presentation Rubric* in crafting their presentations.

TEACHER NOTES

Suggested Materials: There are no specific materials associated with this deign brief. General school supplies may be provided if available. This challenge requires that students visit local stores to conduct product price/quantity comparisons. The food store is usually the most productive for this type of investigation. Teachers might consider having the students prepare a letter of introduction to the store management describing the project and asking permission. Remind the students that their challenge is to compare relative value of different size containers of the same product and manufacturer. They will also be responsible for investigating a minimum of six different products.

Suggested Use: This design brief can be classified as a consumer protection challenge and can provide an opportunity for teachers to observe the problem solving and data processing abilities of students. It also provides the opportunity to analyze and compare data. This may be an appropriate math lesson, as well.

Ties to Content: This brief has no direct ties to any specific science content but addresses the process skills of data collection, communication and interpretation. Students will be expected to craft a fair test procedure, collect appropriate data, process and display this data in an acceptable manner, draw reasonable, defendable conclusions and communicate their findings.

Possible Procedures(s): It is suggested that a work schedule be established to keep student teams on task. Three class periods are allotted to complete this challenge at the discretion of the teacher. The first period could be devoted to crafting a fair test plan and assigning responsibilities within each student group. The second class period could be devoted to processing and displaying the collected data. Student team presentations would take up the third class period. Students should be made aware that they will have to spend time outside of school collecting the required data. These three days need not be consecutive. In other words, they could be spread out over a period of weeks.

Precautions: No safety precautions are associated with this design brief.

While the problem solving techniques used by each team may be different, the diversity of thinking is beneficial for enhancing the problem solving repertoire of each student. Sharing is not only encouraged it is a strategy used throughout the program.

STUCK UP

- Design a solution to a problem. *NSES*
- Implement a proposed design and evaluate completed technological designs or products. *NSES*
- Apply and adapt a variety of appropriate strategies to solve problems. *NCTM*
- Students adjust their use of spoken, written, and visual language (e.g., conventions, style, vocabulary) to communicate effectively with a variety of audiences and for different purposes. *NCTE*

The Context: The results of product testing are somewhat suspect if the evaluation was done by the company that made the product. This is known as experimenter bias.

The Scenario: The Chippendale Furniture Company (CFC) has decided to expand its product line and include furniture with a more contemporary design. This modern style however, will put more stress on the wood joints. Therefore, the company believes that a stronger glue will be required in the manufacturing process.

The Challenge: Your independent testing facility has been contacted by CFC and asked to test the holding strength of common glue products. CFC wants you to find out, "What is the strongest wood glue?"

The Limitations:
- Each team will have three class periods to complete this investigation.
- Each team will have access to all laboratory equipment and a variety of wood glues.
- Each team will detail a "fair test" plan of how it will solve the problem.
- No team may begin testing until its "fair test" plan has been approved.
- Each team may supply any additional materials it considers necessary.
- Data collection and display formats must be created by each team.

The Rules:
- Each team will be responsible for testing all the glues supplied.
- Each team must list what variables will be held constant and how this will be accomplished.
- Each team member must prepare a lab report. The report should include the procedure followed, a description of the variables, data charts/graphs, a written review of the results, conclusions supported by data and recommendations to consumers about the products tested.
- A comparison of product performance and product price per gram or milliliter will also be required.
- Each team must present its finding to the rest of the class.
- Each team should refer to the *Team Presentation Rubric* when crafting its presentation.

TEACHER NOTES

Suggested Materials: This challenge requires variety wood glues. Tongue depressors or craft sticks could be used for testing but that is up to each research team. The biggest challenges to the students will be the control of variables and the collection of quantifiable data. Students should have copies of the *Team Presentation Rubric* when preparing for the presentation segment of this challenge. Small containers of a variety of wood glues need to be provided for this challenge.

Suggested Use: This design brief can be classified as a general consumer protection challenge and can provide an opportunity for teachers to observe the problem solving and data processing abilities of students.

Ties to Content: This design brief can be used to evaluate the process skills of science. It also can be used in a physical science lesson dealing with force, weight, mass, etc. This design brief is project-oriented and relies heavily on the appropriate use the design loop, the use of appropriate process skills, and the collaborative abilities of each team member. As with many design problems, it will be necessary for student teams to be acutely aware of the time constraints and the use the Design Loop. Students also need to be aware of the *Team Presentation Rubric* in planning, construction, testing and presenting.

Possible Procedures(s): While there are a variety of ways students could approach this design challenge. In sum, students must design and conduct a controlled or "fair test" investigation to test the relative strength of commercial wood glues. Students could design a comparative test between the glue samples or test all the glue samples against a standard, like a spring scale or hanging uniform masses, both yielding quantifiable data.

Precautions: Whenever students are involved in a construction project there is the possibility of a mishap, especially if tools, hot glue guns and other sharp objects are available. Students should be shown proper tool use and be expected to sign a safety contract. Students should wear safety goggles whenever working with sharp objects in close quarters. Appropriate safety contracts can be obtained from Flinn Scientific at www.flinnsci.com

While the problem solving techniques used by each team may be different, the diversity of thinking is beneficial for enhancing the problem solving repertoire of each student. Sharing is not only encouraged it is a strategy used throughout the program.

BAG IT

- Design a solution to a problem. *NSES*
- Implement a proposed design and evaluate completed technological designs or products. *NSES*
- Apply and adapt a variety of appropriate strategies to solve problems. *NCTM*
- Students adjust their use of spoken, written, and visual language (e.g., conventions, style, vocabulary) to communicate effectively with a variety of audiences and for different purposes. *NCTE*

The Context: The results of product testing are somewhat suspect if the evaluation was done by the company that made the product. This is known as experimenter bias.

The Scenario: The manner in which we dispose of our wastes is much different than it was 50 years ago. The increased use of plastic bags has had a great deal to do with this evolution. Yet, selecting the right plastic bag for a particular job is not always an easy task. All the bag manufacturers use words like tough, strong, flexible, puncture resistant, stretchable… but who do you trust? Which plastic trash bag is the strongest?

The Challenge: Your independent research team has decided to take on this challenge and conduct a fair test evaluation of plastic trash bags. Your goal is to determine, once and for all, which bag is the strongest…until some company develops a newer brand.

The Limitations:
- Each team will have three class periods to complete this investigation.
- Each team will have access to all laboratory equipment.
- Each team must clearly define what it means by strongest.
- Each team must detail a "fair test plan" of how it will answer the research question.
- No team may begin testing until its "fair test plan" has been approved.
- Special attention will be given to what, and how, teams will keep things the same between tests.
- Each team may supply any additional materials it considers necessary.
- Test results must be quantifiable.

The Rules:
- Data collection and display formats must be created by each team.
- Each team will be responsible for testing all the plastic bags as supplied by teacher.
- Each team member must prepare a lab report and presentation. The report should include the procedure followed, a description of the variables, data charts/graphs, a written review of the results, conclusions supported by data and recommendations to consumers about the products tested.
- A comparison of product performance and price will also be required.
- Each team should refer to the *Team Presentation Rubric* as it prepares the presentation.

TEACHER NOTES

Suggested Materials: This challenge requires variety plastic bags. To reduce costs it is suggested that parents be contacted and donations be requested. Be sure to get product labeling information with all donations as this may be helpful in product analysis. Students should have access to general laboratory equipment and standard classroom supplies.

Suggested Use: This design brief can be used to evaluate the process skills of science. It also can be used in a physical science lesson dealing with force, weight, mass, tensile strength, polymers, etc. This design brief can be classified as a general consumer protection challenge and can provide an opportunity for teachers to observe the problem solving and data processing abilities of students. In addition, students could be formatively assessed on their ability to design and implement a "fair test" procedure.

Ties to Content: The focus of this design brief relies heavily on the appropriate use of the Design Loop as students craft a fair test to determine the strongest plastic bag. Students also need to describe how they intend to identify and control of variables in the investigation. Teachers should take notice of the foregoing and if students use appropriate process skills.

As with many design problems, it will be necessary for student teams to be acutely aware of the time constraints. Students should refer to the *Team Presentation Rubric* in planning, construction, testing and presenting.

Possible Procedures(s): While there are a variety of ways students could approach this design challenge, students must design and conduct a controlled or "fair test" investigation to test the relative strengths of different plastic bags. Students could design a comparative test between plastic bags or test all the bags against a standard such as a heavy object (a bowling ball).

Precautions: Students will be conducting tests of their own design and should be closely monitored. They should not proceed with any tests unless approved by the teacher. Students should wear safety goggles whenever working with sharp objects in close quarters.

While the problem solving techniques used by each team may be different, the diversity of thinking is beneficial for enhancing the problem solving repertoire of each student. Sharing is not only encouraged it is a strategy used throughout the program.

EARTH SCIENCE

LANDSCAPE DILEMMA

- Design a solution to a problem. *NSES*
- Implement a proposed design and evaluate completed technological designs or products. *NSES*
- Apply and adapt a variety of appropriate strategies to solve problems. *NCTM*
- Students adjust their use of spoken, written, and visual language (e.g., conventions, style, vocabulary) to communicate effectively with a variety of audiences and for different purposes. *NCTE*

The Context: When it rains, water runs into gutters, down the street, into streams, or soaks directly into the ground. However, not all earth materials absorb water equally.

The Scenario: Your local township has decided to build a new community park on one of its plots of land. They are aware that water flow through the park is necessary, but must be managed in order to maintain the park's beauty and environmental friendliness. Because of this, they are willing to landscape and rebuild the area.

The Challenge: Your landscaping team has been hired by the township to address the issue of surface runoff in the proposed park. Each area may require a different combination of surface materials to manage the water. Therefore, your team must devise a method for creating and testing various mixtures of earth materials (using sand, gravel, humus, and clay) for their water holding characteristics. Some mixtures will be needed to shed the water while others will be needed to hold large quantities of water.

The Limitations:
- A detailed procedure must be completed and approved by the Commissioners (teacher) before testing begins.
- Each team must devise some way of determining how much water is absorbed by each material tested and each mixture of materials tested.
- Each landscaping team must document the formulas used to make each soil mixture.
- Each team must collect and display testing results and formulas in some colorful manner.
- No team may use any materials except those provided.

The Rules:
- All results must appear in chart form.
- Each team member must compose and a letter to the Board of Commissioners noting the recommendations for the use each of the materials created. Uses include the walking trails, the flower and shrubbery areas, the lake bottom, the playground and the sports fields.
- Recommendations must be supported by test data.

TEACHER NOTES

Suggested Materials: The materials needed for this challenge include a supply of water, humus, gravel, clay and sand. Additional materials might include hand lenses, balances, plastic spoons, coffee filters, cups with drainage holes, cups without drainage holes, syringes and graduated cylinders or some other volumetric measuring devices.

Suggested Use: The study of earth materials often includes the observation of various soil types and compositions. The ability of certain soils to retain or shed water makes them more desirable for particular applications. Another aspect of soil composition that has considerable import is the nutrients that are available for growing and maintaining healthy plants

Ties to Content: Noting the difference between soil and dirt is key to this issue; the former containing humus, the dark brown organic material made up of decomposed plant and animal remains. Humus is desirable in certain types of soil because it has excellent water-retaining properties as well as the necessary nutrients for plants.

Landscapers are well aware of the different types of soil, their drainage characteristics, and the most appropriate and economic uses for each type. In addition to containing water and air, soil is a heterogeneous mixture inorganic and organic materials. The inorganic materials vary in size from pebbles to clay. Plants, animals and decaying material compose the organic materials. The actual composition of soil can vary greatly from one place to another. Thus, composition and the water retaining characteristics determine its suitability for plants or other uses.

Possible Procedures(s): Students will be expected to craft a "fair test" for determining the most appropriate use for different soil types. These proposals need to be reviewed and approved prior to the students gathering materials. As the investigation progresses the students will need to collect and record accurate data for processing, displaying, and interpreting. At the conclusion of this challenge the students will be expected to craft a written report of their investigation with recommendations.

Should you want to extend this challenge, require the students to create a map of the proposed development plan complete with scale, color and identification keys. Students could also research this component by contacting local landscapers, school district maintenance personnel or landscaping "how to" books.

Precautions: Students will be expected to wear appropriate eye protection during this investigation.

While the problem solving techniques used by each team may be different, the diversity of thinking is beneficial for enhancing the problem solving repertoire of each student. Sharing is not only encouraged it is a strategy used throughout the program.

GROUND HOG DAY, GROUND HOG DAY, GROUND HOG DAY

> - Think critically and logically to make the relationships between evidence and explanations. *NSES*
> - Develop and evaluate inferences and predictions that re based on data. *NCTM*
> - Students use a variety of technological and information resources (e.g., libraries, databases, computer networks, video) to gather and synthesize information and to create and communicate knowledge. *NCTE*
> - Students adjust their use of spoken, written, and visual language (e.g., conventions, style, vocabulary) to communicate effectively with a variety of audiences and for different purposes. *NCTE*

The Context: Predicting the weather is a combination of interpreting previous records in conjunction with current data.

The Scenario: Weather is an integral part of our lives and affects us on a daily basis. The meteorologists have high speed computers that process both past and current data, radar to display immediate conditions, and satellites that provide weather information on a global scale. With all this technology you would think that relying on a rodent's behavior as a long range predictor of weather would be dismissed as ridiculous. But still, we persist to hang on to this folklore. How many other common weather myths continue to be part of our culture?

The Challenge: Your challenge is to select and research a weather myth to determine its country of origin or ethnic group association and determine if there is any scientific evidence that supports this bit of folklore.

The Limitations:
- Four class periods will be devoted to this challenge. One period will be divided over time into smaller segments for teams to meet and discuss at the discretion of the teacher. The other periods will be used as research and presentation sessions.
- Students must continue their work at home.
- Each team must craft a "fair test" procedure that could be used to test the accuracy of the prediction/predictions described in the myth.
- Depending on the weather myth selected, each team may also have to compare the conditions described in their weather myth with actual events (recorded or observed).

The Rules:
- Each research team must document all references in bibliographical form.
- Each team must interpret its weather myth and create a poster displaying this myth complete with appropriate illustrations.
- Conclusions regarding the accuracy of the myth must be supported by collected data and/or research.
- Each team must also construct its own weather saying based on the collection and/or the interpretation of the observable trends in the weather. The "new" folklore must be supported by evidence.
- Each team should refer to the *Team Presentation Rubric* for direction in crafting the oral presentation.

TEACHER NOTES

Suggested Materials: Teams are responsible for supplying all materials for this design challenge except for general classroom supplies. Students will need a copy of the *Team Presentation Rubric* as they craft their presentations.

Suggested Use: This design brief was written to accompany a unit on weather but could be used as a general research study on American folklore.

Ties to Content: Weather myths and folklore generally have a basis in the accumulated observations compiled by generations of humans. These usually rhymed sayings may have come about because of some meteorological consistencies associated with the behavior of animals or with changes in weather yet to come. While the use of these vernacular phrases as a predictive tool could be questioned from a scientific basis they did originate from observations much like the actual weather records that humans have been collecting for over a hundred years. As in the study of geology, we look to the past to see the future.

Possible Procedures(s): Unlike many design briefs, this challenge is completely researched based. It is anticipated that each student will complete the bulk of the assignment outside of class. This brief is a combination of individual and collaborative team effort. The students should be clear about what responsibilities they must shoulder themselves and those duties assigned to the team. An example of a proposed statement might be that when a low pressure system follows a high pressure system there is usually a change in the weather, and it is generally wet. The weather folklore might be…"When a low follows a high there's usually rain in the sky, but when a high follows a low the sun will show"

Precautions: No safety precautions are associated with this design brief.

While the problem solving techniques used by each team may be different, the diversity of thinking is beneficial for enhancing the problem solving repertoire of each student. Sharing is not only encouraged it is a strategy used throughout the program.

WEATHER MYTHS AND SAYINGS

- If the ground hog sees his shadow then we will have six more weeks of winter.
- Lightening only strikes good conductors.
- Crickets can predict the temperature.
- Red sky at morning, sailors take warning; Red sky at night, sailor's delight.
- When dew is on the grass, rain will never come to pass.
- When the swallow's nest is high, summer is dry.
- A cow with it's tail to the West makes the weather best,
- A cow with its tail to the East makes the weather least.
- When a cow lies down, bad weather is coming.
- Mackerel skies and mares' tails make ships carry lowered sails.
- The louder the frog, the more the rain.
- When pine cones close, bad weather is coming.
- If the oak is out before the ash then we are in for a splash,
- But if the ash is out before the oak we are in for a soak.
- Every wind has its weather.
- Wind in the East the fish bite the least,
- Wind in the West the fish bite the best.
- Rain on Easter Sunday, it will rain the next seven Sundays.
- Fog in January makes a wet Spring.
- February fog means a frost in May.

- If March comes in like a lamb, it will go out like a lion.

- A warm Christmas, a cold Easter.

- A ring around the moon is a sign there will be rain.
- When ants build high, rain will fall from the sky.
- Bees will not swarm before a storm.
- Rain before 7:00, clear before 11:00.
- When the comb crackles through the hair look for weather to be clear and fair.
- A Wooly Bear caterpillar with a wide band means a long winter.
- The last Sunday in the month indicates the weather for the next month.
- When there are lots of berries on the dogwood tree, it means a bad winter.
- If fleecy clouds cover the heavenly way, no rain should mar your plans that day.
- Smooth days in January will be paid for in February and March.
- Lightening never strikes the same place twice.
- The best place to be during a tornado is in the southwest corner of the building.
- If the leaves are turning up, a storm is brewing.
- Human joints can predict the weather.
- White, fluffy cumulus clouds bring good weather.
- When a pig carries sticks around in its mouth to build shelter, precipitation will come.
- A television set or an AM radio can be used as a tornado detector.

SURVIVAL

> - Design a solution to a problem. *NSES*
> - Implement a proposed design and evaluate completed technological designs or products. *NSES*
> - Apply and adapt a variety of appropriate strategies to solve problems. *NCTM*
> - Students adjust their use of spoken, written, and visual language (e.g., conventions, style, vocabulary) to communicate effectively with a variety of audiences and for different purposes. *NCTE*

The Context: Problems can sometimes be solved through the creative use of materials.

The Scenario: Your engineering team has decided to take a well deserved vacation in the South Pacific. Your plane is almost there when it develops engine trouble and is forced to perform a controlled belly landing in the shallow waters near a remote island. Everyone is safe and makes their way to dry land. By now, your energy turns to surviving, so your team conferences and takes stock of what the island can immediately provide. Materials to construct shelters seem plentiful since the island is covered with palm trees. Your other concern is for food and water. Searching the small island turns up food in the form of fruit trees and small crustaceans and fish in the shallows, but no fresh water is found.

The Challenge: You and your engineer friends are challenged to obtain fresh water for drinking. You return to the partly submerged plane and salvage as much material as you can before the plane disintegrates. Once safely back on shore you inventory your collection. This is all you have to work with and your thirst is already starting to become evident.

Collected Materials: black plastic bag , three meters of duct tape, three-one liter clear plastic soda bottles, one meter of aquarium tubing, a ball of clay, three plastic cups (drinking size), a small rock, a small ball of string, four sticks the size of paint stirrers, a one meter sheet of heavy duty aluminum foil and three large zip lock bags.

The Limitations:
- Each team will have the same materials with which to work. No other materials may be used.
- Each team will have the materials to examine as they make their plans.
- Each team will have three class periods to complete this challenge.
- Each team must craft an action plan and sketch or proposed system before beginning construction.
- Simulated ocean water will be available for teams to use.
- Water recovery systems must produce a sample of potable water.

The Rules:
- Students are strongly encouraged to conduct research outside of class.
- At the conclusion, each team must present and explain its water recovery systems including where and why any phase changes take place.
- Each team should refer to the *Team Presentation Rubric* for guidance in crafting the presentation.

TEACHER NOTES

Suggested Materials: In addition to general classroom supplies and common science equipment, each engineering team should receive the supplies noted in the design challenge. Feel free to add anything else that might find useful for completing this challenge. Have a supply of salty water ready for student use. Kosher salt could be used to create this simulated salt water as it will remain clear when in solution. Adding 150 grams of salt to one liter of water should be sufficient. It will be necessary to have access to the sun or domed utility lamps. Students should also have a copy of the *Team Presentation Rubric* for reference purposes.

Suggested Use: This design brief could be used with a unit on natural resources, an in depth investigation of water and water conservation, an application challenge associated with the change of state concept or a general design challenge. It could also be used in a physical science unit about mixture separation techniques. In any case, it will probably be necessary for students to research water desalination methods before they begin crafting an action plan and sketch. This research may take several days and should be done outside of class. It is suggested that students be given the assignment and time to discuss what steps they need to take first. The actual challenge should be scheduled to begin the following week.

Ties to Content: This design brief is most closely associated with the concepts of the water cycle, kinetic theory, phase change, evaporation, distillation and mixture separation. Water changes state with relative ease when compared to other materials. We experience this on a daily basis and probably never give it a thought. When liquid water is heated it changes to a gas through the process of evaporation. If cooled to zero degrees Celsius water will go through another phase change and turn to the solid we know as ice. Although the solid state of water appears to be relatively stable it is not as ice will also go through a change of state through the processes of melting or sublimation (changing directly to the gaseous state). Condensation could be considered to be the opposite process to evaporation. When water is in the gaseous form (water vapor) it will go through a change of state, becoming a liquid again if cooled to or below its boiling point, as represented in the water cycle. The changes of state can be explained by the kinetic theory of matter which states that all matter is made up of particles that are constantly in motion. The amount of energy needed to change a material from a solid to a liquid is known as the heat of fusion while the amount of energy needed to change a material from a liquid to a gas is called the heat of vaporization.

Possible Procedures(s): There are a number of ways to solve this dilemma using the equipment provided all of which use the processes of evaporation and condensation. The most rudimentary method for changing salt water into potable water involves placing the sample of salt water in a container that will get hot enough to quickly evaporate and condense the water in a separate "catch" container. If the container is relatively air tight, it will capture more potable condensate.

Precautions: Whenever students are involved in a construction project there is the possibility of a mishap, especially if tools, hot glue guns and other sharp objects are available. Students should be shown proper tool use and be expected to sign a safety contract. Students should wear safety glasses whenever working with sharp objects in close quarters. Appropriate safety contracts can be obtained from Flinn Scientific at www.flinnsci.com

While the problem solving techniques used by each team may be different, the diversity of thinking is beneficial for enhancing the problem solving repertoire of each student. Sharing is not only encouraged it is a strategy used throughout the program.

ENVIRONMENTAL SCIENCE

LET THE GAMES BEGIN

- Design a solution to a problem. *NSES*
- Implement a proposed design and evaluate completed technological designs or products. *NSES*
- Apply and adapt a variety of appropriate strategies to solve problems. *NCTM*
- Students use a variety of technological and information resources (e.g., libraries, databases, computer networks, video) to gather and synthesize information and to create and communicate knowledge. *NCTE*
- Students adjust their use of spoken, written, and visual language (e.g., conventions, style, vocabulary) to communicate effectively with a variety of audiences and for different purposes. *NCTE*

The Context: Many companies develop new products in an effort to increase profits and their share of the market.

The Scenario: The marketing department of the <u>Reality Game Company</u> predicts that products related to the environment will be big sellers during the next several years.

The Challenge: Your design team has been directed to meet this need by creating a board game that deals with current environmental issues and the roles that humans play in them.

The Limitations:
- Each team will have five class periods to complete this challenge at the discretion of the teacher.
- Team members are encouraged to work on this project at home.
- Each team must research existing board games as a comparative data gathering process.
- Each team must research current environmental issues to include on its board game.
- Each team must create, field test, revise, and produce a final version of an environmental board game.
- Each team must collaborate to craft criteria for game evaluation purposes.
- Detailed directions of the rules, including how to determine the order of play, must accompany the game.

The Rules:
- The game must have real life issues, environmental concepts, natural disasters, and human impact must be present in colorful illustrations and in the choices and decisions made by players.
- The game must provide some way of identifying each player.
- The game must have a way for players to advance (spinner, die, random drawing, etc.).
- The game must provide opportunities for the players to make choices on their own or have those choices made for them by virtue of rolling a die, choosing a directional card (choice, reward or consequence, for example) or some other random/chance method.
- The game should have a clearly marked route for the players to follow with a START location noted.
- The rewards must be equal to the consequences (see detailed notes for further explanation).
- Each team must play and evaluate the games of others teams.
- Students should refer to the *Team Presentation Rubric* as they prepare their presentations.

TEACHER NOTES

Suggested Materials: It is suggested that students be given an opportunity to compare and contrast a number of board games as a way to form an "idea bank" upon which to draw in constructing their own games. In addition to having access to general school supplies the students will also need copies of the *Team Presentation Rubric* for reference as they prepare their presentations.

Suggested Use: This design brief was written as a research and awareness lesson to accompany an environmental studies unit. This challenge requires the students to become familiar with current environmental issues (natural and human influenced), ways that humans mitigate environmental problems, and the reported results of these human efforts. As noted, the five days set aside for this challenge are at the discretion of the teacher and as such provide "wiggle room" to allow students sufficient time. These five days can be scatter throughout a marking period devoted to the study of the environment and ecology. It could also be used as a culminating activity for such. Be sure to set aside one day for the presentations.

Ties to Content: Environmental concerns occur naturally or as the result of human activities. In some cases, the extent of natural disasters has been amplified by the changes humans have made in the environment. In other cases, the mitigating adjustments humans have made to resolve one issue creates another. There are limited resources on earth to support the population that presently inhabits the earth. Increasing inhabitants also continues to deplete non-renewable resources.

A number of natural processes occur within ecosystems that influence humans. These processes include atmospheric quality, the water cycle, soil generation, energy flow, conservation, waste removal and recycling, to name a few. In turn, humans are influencing these cycles and processes; if these adverse affects are not stabilized the world's environments and ecosystems can be irreversibility affected. One of these unfavorable changes is the loss of diversity in the living and the nonliving environment. Other activities having adverse effects include overuse of land, pollution, obtaining ores and energy producing resources, and adding or removing specific organisms to local environments.

The choices and actions of individuals and societies can also contribute to alleviating some of the environmental problems. We must assess the risks, the costs, the benefits, and the trade-offs of continued expansion as well as the implementation of new technologies. Proposed improvements need to consider the human and the environmental impact of change.

Possible Procedures(s): There are several components associated with this design brief. Some challenge requirements are team oriented while others are designed for individuals. In either case the time students spend on each phase needs to be managed. It is suggested that a schedule be created and posted to help keep students on task. Initially, students will need to become familiar with the commonalities between board games, the methods that are used to identify the players, what determines the order and extent of player moves, the trade-offs associated with decision making and so on. This "game research" phase will also provide students with the background that they will find helpful in crafting scoring rubric to evaluate game boards. Once the structure of a board game has been clarified the students will then need to research environmental issues, the level of human impact and intervention as well as the results of this mitigation.

Precautions: No safety precautions are associated with this design brief.

While the problem solving techniques used by each team may be different, the diversity of thinking is beneficial for enhancing the problem solving repertoire of each student. Sharing is not only encouraged it is a strategy used throughout the program.

ENVIRONMENTAL GAME BOARD DETAILED NOTES AND OPTIONS

Risks and Consequences: Player risks should be comparable to player consequences. The greater the risk taken by a player the greater the potential gain or consequence. For example, if a shorter route is available to a desired location or reward, the probability of a major setback should also be present.

Reward and Probability: The size of a reward should be indirectly related to the probability that a player would be able to achieve that reward. For example, a large reward could be received only if the player, using three die, were lucky enough to roll the same number on all three die.

Environmental Concepts and Issues: The intent of the game is to highlight environmental concepts and issues including human impact on the environment. Concepts and issues may include such things as predator-prey relationships, food webs and chains, the interdependence of organisms, pollution, adaptation of living things, endangered species, hazardous wastes, renewable and non-renewable resources, recycling, watersheds and wetlands, land use and manufacturing…just to name a few.

Game Options:
- The opportunity for players to "barter" with each other might be part of the game.
- A timing device might be used in some way.
- Randomizing devices such as die and spinners might be used in combination.
- Drawing choice or consequence cards might be used.
- Players might be able to penalize each other in some way.
- If die are used, rolling doubles may be considered a positive occurrence or a negative one.
- A bag of different colored marbles could be used as a choice option. The color drawn by a player could then be a reward or punishment depending on the rules of the game.

MUDDY MESS

> • Design a solution to a problem. *NSES*
> • Implement a proposed design and evaluate completed technological designs or products. *NSES*
> • Apply and adapt a variety of appropriate strategies to solve problems. *NCTM*
> • Students adjust their use of spoken, written, and visual language (e.g., conventions, style, vocabulary) to communicate effectively with a variety of audiences and for different purposes. *NCTE*

The Context: Although water is a renewable resource, it is not always easily renewed.

The Scenario: The Incredibly Pure Water Company has been hit by a natural disaster that could potentially ruin its business. Three weeks of above average rainfall has caused massive flooding and erosion in the streams that are its main water source. The once tranquil, pristine streams are now a muddy mess.

The Challenge: Your environmental research team has been contacted by the bottling company to help design an advanced filtration system capable of converting the muddy water into the incredibly pure product that they require.

The Limitations:
- In order for a treatment system to be considered acceptable it must clean 300 ml of muddy water in five minutes.
- The water used for testing will be the same for each team and will consist of 1000 ml water, 50 grams of top soil, and 20 grams of powdered clay.
- Each team will be given three days, outside of class, to research this topic and gather the materials they deem necessary.
- Prior to construction, teams must present a detailed, colored sketch, with appropriate labeling.
- A materials list must also accompany the sketch.
- No coffee filters or paper towels may be used in purifying the water.
- All materials will be the responsibility of the environmental teams.
- Three additional class periods will be set aside for construction, testing, modification, and reporting.

The Rules:
- Each team will make up the test water for each other.
- Water clarity will first be determined by comparing all the samples against one another.
- The samples that appear to be the clearest will then be compared to tap water.

TEACHER NOTES

Suggested Materials: Most of the materials for this design brief are the responsibility of the student engineering teams. Students should have access to general science equipment, a supply of top soil, powdered clay (available at most craft stores), and standard school supplies.

Suggested Use: This design brief was written as an application lesson for an environmental unit or as an extension lesson on water purification techniques. It could also be used in a physical science lesson as a culminating activity on separation techniques, or differentiating between pure substances and mixtures.

Ties to Content: As part of the water cycle, precipitation falls to the earth. Of the water that lands on the ground, some soaks in directly, some runs along the surface before soaking in, and some runs along the surface and then into a lake, stream or other water source. The forests, fields and grasslands actually slow the movement of the water before it enters streams, lakes, and estuaries. Water also cleaned as it filters through rocks and soil where much of the solid particles are trapped. In addition, sunlight helps to kill bacteria and as water is splashed over rocks and waterfalls it is oxygenated. The introduction of oxygen encourages the development of living things. In addition, it helps to break down impurities. Algae in the water also absorb chemicals and soften the water.

Humans also treat water in specialized facilities called water treatment plants. These plants use a series of treatment stages, akin to the natural process, and consists to two major steps, primary and secondary treatment. In primary treatment, sand, grit, and the larger solids are separated from the liquid by using screens, settling tanks and skimming devices. After primary treatment is completed the water goes through a series of biological treatments in addition to aeration and filtering through sand filters. The filtered water is then disinfected to kill remaining bacteria and the water is discharged into a nearby water supply.

Possible Procedures(s): Following the introduction, and prior to the beginning of the initial research segment, it is suggested that the students discuss and chart research topics that might be helpful in acquiring background for this challenge. Students my use a combination of filtration techniques including separation funnels, settling, filtration through various sized particles, charcoal, aeration, etc. The actual combination of strategies will be team dependent, and not limited to those suggested here. In order to analyze the "clean" water, quantitative data regarding clarity can be obtained by using a light meter. Place the sample in front of a small enclosed light with the light meter on the opposite side. The cleaner the water, the more light will pass through it, and this will be quantitatively registered on the meter.

Precautions: Students will be expected to wear appropriate eye protection during this investigation. Care should be taken when using any chemical. Check the MSDS sheet for each chemical prior to use. Should these sheets not be available check the Flinn Scientific Catalog or the Flinn Scientific website, www.flinnsci.com. Click on the chemistry link and then the MSDS link.

While the problem solving techniques used by each team may be different, the diversity of thinking is beneficial for enhancing the problem solving repertoire of each student. Sharing is not only encouraged it is a strategy used throughout the program.

LET ME INTRODUCE YOU

- Think critically and logically to make the relationships between evidence and explanations. *NSES*
- Develop and evaluate inferences and predictions that re based on data. *NCTM*
- Create and use representations to organize, record, and communicate mathematical ideas. *NCTM*
- Students use a variety of technological and information resources (e.g., libraries, databases, computer networks, video) to gather and synthesize information and to create and communicate knowledge. *NCTE*
- Students adjust their use of spoken, written, and visual language (e.g., conventions, style, vocabulary) to communicate effectively with a variety of audiences and for different purposes. *NCTE*

The Context: Unwanted living things, can often spread rapidly into a new environment because there are few natural controls. These uninvited additions are said to be invasive.

The Scenario: Each year we discover that our earth is changing because of the spread of non-native living things. These unwanted species can invade a new area on their own, be inadvertently introduced by another animal (including humans), or be purposely established for some other reason. Once these organisms take hold, they can change the environment in ways that are generally unanticipated.

The Challenge: Your research team is being charged with compiling a detailed report for your state's Department of Environmental Protection. This overview should review the scope of the problem of a specific invasive species. The review should include:
- How the species became invasive.
- How the species has affected its new habitat and humans.
- What humans have done, if anything, to "manage" the invasive species.
- Suggestions as to how to eradicate the problem.
- What state and/or federal laws have been enacted because of this invasive species?

The Limitations:
- Each team will have two weeks to complete this research topic.
- Each team must research this topic as a group, sharing the information found. However, each team member must write an individual report.
- Each report must include at least one example of how humans successfully managed an invasive species or successfully introduced a non-native species that benefited humans and the environment.

The Rules:
- No class time will be devoted to this project except for the day of the presentations.
- Each group will have no more than five minutes for its presentation and each member of the group must participate.
- Students should refer to the *Team Presentation Rubric* in crafting their presentations.

TEACHER NOTES

Suggested Materials: This challenge is strictly a research assignment designed to help students become more aware of the problems incurred by the introduction of non-native species into the environment. Students should have copies of the *Team Presentation Rubric* for reference as they craft their presentations.

Suggested Use: This design brief was written as an application lesson for an environmental unit. Humans impact their environment in a variety of ways. This challenge requires students to become familiar with the environmental issue of invasive species, specifically local examples. It can be used in a life science, earth science, or environmental science context.

Ties to Content: Established ecosystems have their own natural balances and controls. The plants and animals within those systems find this balance suitable for survival. Non-native species, while harmless and beneficial in their natural surroundings, are not natural to all ecosystems to which they have been introduced and can cause major issues that can devastate a new environment. These species do this by reducing biodiversity, degrading habitats, altering native genetic diversity, transmitting exotic diseases to native species, and further jeopardizing endangered plants and animals.

Possible Procedures(s): This design brief is strictly a research based challenge to be completed outside of class. This challenge will require students to complete a number of components. Some challenge requirements are team oriented while others are designed for individual effort. In either case, the time students spend on each phase needs to be managed. It is suggested that a schedule be created and posted to help keep students on task. Be sure to set aside one class period for the presentations.

Precautions: There are no precautions associated with this design brief.

While the problem solving techniques used by each team may be different, the diversity of thinking is beneficial for enhancing the problem solving repertoire of each student. Sharing is not only encouraged it is a strategy used throughout the program.

CREATE–A–COASTLINE (PART 1)

- Design a solution to a problem. *NSES*
- Implement a proposed design and evaluate completed technological designs or products. *NSES*
- Apply and adapt a variety of appropriate strategies to solve problems. *NCTM*
- Students adjust their use of spoken, written, and visual language (e.g., conventions, style, vocabulary) to communicate effectively with a variety of audiences and for different purposes

---

The Context: Developing a piece of property is not always an easy proposition.

The Scenario: You and your partner have just won a plot of ocean front property in the New Jersey State Land Lottery. You would like to develop it but that may not be solely your decision. There were several rather odd stipulations attached to the distribution of these shoreline building plots. The New Jersey Zoning Board wanted a "planned community" to be developed to eliminate messy lawsuits over individual land use, so each of the plots was required to be developed in a pre-determined way. There was to be a business section, a place for municipal services, tourist accommodations and a residential area. Each land lottery winner was assigned a business and a plot of land that was to be developed accordingly. However, on the way to the meeting, Miss Take, the Zoning Board secretary, dropped the plot plans and they scattered all over the pavement. After retrieving the plans, and afraid for her job, she said nothing and went to the meeting and distributed the plot plans as if they were in the correct order. OOPS!

The Challenge: You and your must partner pick up a packet containing a description of your new occupation and the plot plan. Although the land is free, you must develop it in a specific way… that is one of the Zoning Board stipulations.

The Limitations:
- Each team will have four class periods, at the discretion of the teacher, to complete its plot development and present the development proposal.
- Plot plans must be held so that the red dot appears in the upper right hand corner. The lower half of the map is the beach and the top section is the ocean.
- Each team must develop the plot as described in its Occupation Description. Development should be dictated by research data or personal experience.
- Before beginning to build anything on this land, each team must provide a detailed plot plan of its ideas to the Zoning Board.
- Each team must present its development proposals to the Zoning Board during the third class period.

The Rules:
- All plot plans must be done in color.
- The occupation label must appear at the bottom of the plot plan.
- A map key must accompany each plot plan.
- Only symbols may appear on the map.
- All plot plans must be drawn showing the top view only.
- The scale for the plot plans is one centimeter is equal to 1.5 meters.
- Plot plans must be done to scale.
- Each team must document all research references.
- Each team member must individually complete one of the extension assignments.

TEACHER NOTES

Suggested Materials: Students should have access to general science equipment and standard school supplies. In addition they will also require a prepared section of coastline and a copy of the *Team Presentation Rubric* for reference purposes as they craft their presentations.

Prepare for this activity by drawing the coastline with a blue marker on tractor feed computer paper, or individual sheets lined up in that fashion. This line represents the water's edge and separates the ocean from the beach. Each section of coastline should be different. Create enough coastline papers for half your class, as the students will be working in two person teams for this activity. When the coastline is complete put a red dot in the upper right hand corner of each section to act as a reference point. Before you mix up the papers, turn them over and use a pencil to lightly number the sections in the upper left hand corner. These reference numbers will come in handy when the class reassembles this ocean coastline in the proper sequence. Shuffle the coastline sections so they are randomly ordered. Clip an *Occupation Label* and a corresponding *Occupation Description* to each of the coastline sections before distributing them to the students.

After the students have presented their proposed development plans have them turn their papers over, find the reference number on the back of their coastline section, and reassemble (tape) the entire coastline in the proper sequence.

Suggested Use: This design brief was written as an application lesson to accompany an environmental studies unit and addresses appropriate land use and human impact.

Ties to Content: Increasing human population numbers are putting great pressure on many of our limited resources, and at the same time are depleting those resources which can not be renewed. It is entirely possible that, within a half century, 50% to 90% of the world's land area may be significantly impacted by human activities. One needs to look no further than the encroachment that continues to occur along the nations coastlines. This will most likely result in a significant increase in the environmental problems.

Possible Procedures(s): This challenge will require students to complete a number of components. Some challenge requirements are team oriented while others are designed for individual effort. In either case the time students spend on each phase needs to be managed. It is suggested that a schedule be created and posted to help keep students on task. As noted, the four days set aside for this challenge are at the discretion of the teacher and as such provide "wiggle room" to allow students sufficient time.

Required Presentation Questions
- What benefits do you think your development provides to the community?
- What environmental problems do you think your development plan might create to the entire community?
- What problems might your development create for your immediate neighbors?
- If you could create an open space next to your property which side would you choose? Why would you select this side?
- If you could swap locations with another building plot which would you select. Explain.

Precautions: No safety precautions are associated with this design brief.

While the problem solving techniques used by each team may be different, the diversity of thinking is beneficial for enhancing the problem solving repertoire of each student. Sharing is not only encouraged it is a strategy used throughout the program.

SAMPLE COASTLINE

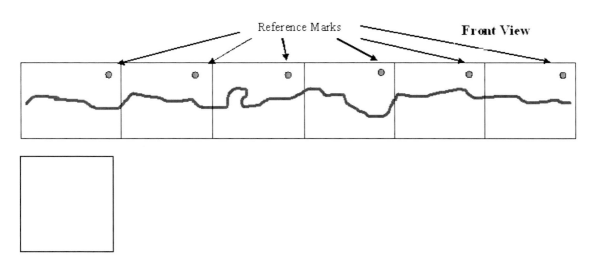

Create-A-Coastline Occupation Labels

Fishing Pier Owner	Electricity Power Plant	Vacation Home Owner
Amusement Park Owner	Wildlife Park Operator	Retirement Home Owner
Hotel Owner	Boardwalk Food Store	Coast Guard Captain
Sewage Treatment Plant	Boat Yard Operator	Theater Owner
Cafe Owner	Restaurant Owner	Campground Owner
Variety Store Owner	Miniature Golf Operator	Casino Operator

Extension Assignments for Create-A-Coastline:
- Write a letter to your neighbors convincing them that living or working next to you has some advantages.
- Write a report to the Town Council about the environmental and or social problems your business creates and how you plan to correct the problems.

- You are thinking of selling your business. Prepare a six-line advertisement describing the positive features of your business.
- Suppose you could redesign your coastline town and put the businesses anywhere you would like. Describe what you would move and why.
- Write a letter to your neighbors proposing how you could jointly solve the problems each of you creates.
- Is any land along the coastline still empty? If so, then what businesses do you think should be built there and why? What businesses should not be allowed to be developed and why?

CREATE-A-COASTLINE OCCUPATION DESCRIPTIONS

Fishing Pier: Your structure will stretch 20 meters into the ocean so that your customers can fish in deeper water. You intend to rent fishing and crabbing equipment and sell frozen bait wrapped in foil and paper. You also plan to have a snack bar. There will always be a strong fish odor around the pier but hopefully the ocean breeze will push it elsewhere.	**Amusement Park:** Your amusement park will take up most of your property along with enough space for parking 200 cars and storing a large trash dumpster. In addition to the many rides, you will also sell a variety of typical carnival foods. You plan to keep your park open until 1:00 A.M.
Seaside Hotel: Your hotel is to be a huge, 400 room structure that takes up one half of your property. Another quarter will be devoted to parking for approximately 200 cars. The rest of the property will remain as a private beach for registered guests. Those guests without on site parking will just have to put their cars elsewhere.	**Sewage Treatment Plant:** Your facility will be responsible for treating all the waste water for the shoreline community. Your property will contain two very large treatment buildings and ten open filtering tanks. Waste water is sprayed up into the air from the center of each tank and is then filtered as it passes down through layers of sand and small stones. A very strong sewage odor is always present.
Vacation Home: You plan to locate your home near the back of your property as far away from the water as possible as tides in this area tend to be rather high. You also plan to install a large jetty along the right border of your property. The jetty will help preserve your beach but will probably cause beach erosion for your neighbors on that side.	**Electricity Power Plant:** Your company will be responsible for making electricity for the entire shoreline community. Your facility will burn coal to heat water for the steam driven generators. The coal produces a lot of smoke and is always visible pouring out from the three tall smokestacks. The coal is delivered by a train which is also used to remove the coal ashes. The railroad tracks are on the right side of your property and end near the waterline.
Boardwalk Food Store: You plan to have an old fashioned boardwalk store just like you remember as a child. Your store will be located on the boardwalk with entrances on three sides. The rear of the property, behind the boardwalk, is reserved for customer parking, four leaking trash dumpsters left over from your other business, and about 15 shopping carts. You plan to be open 24 hours a day, seven days a week.	**Fins, Claws, Shells, and Smells Seafood Restaurant:** You plan to have a small but unique restaurant located directly on the boardwalk that runs across the back of your property opposite the shoreline. In addition to the regular eating facilities, you also plan to have outside tables on the boardwalk and a beach volleyball court. The rear of your property will be reserved for parking, deliveries and trash storage. Sea breezes tend to blow things from the tables.
Captain Bob's Boat Yard: You and your partner plan to develop Captain Bob's Boat Yard. You will be renting boat slips, boats and jet skis. All of your equipment will have gasoline powered engines and fuel spills will certainly be possible. Storing boats will take up most of the shoreline area except for your repair shop and office. There will also be many boats moored in the water in front of your property. You plan to have a large boat ramp leading from the street directly into the water.	**Gonzo's Great Golf:** You plan for this miniature golf course to take up most of your property. A large sea wall must be constructed to keep the water from washing away a few of the holes along the shore line. This wall will help you but will probably cause beach erosion for your neighbors. Large, very bright lights will allow your customers to play golf all night long.

Big Bucks Casino and Lodge: Your business will be located in the center of your property with an attached pier that will extend into the ocean for customers who choose to arrive by boat. Parking seems to be a problem for most shore line businesses so you have constructed a ten story parking facility next to Bug Bucks. You have plenty of parking but absolutely no beach for your guests to enjoy. The parking garage is cleaned each week of the oil and grease deposits.	**Coast Guard:** Your responsibility is to maintain safety on the waters for the entire community and all the boats and ships that enter and leave. Your facility is composed of three large buildings along the water, a lighthouse, and three boat piers that extend 7 meters into the water. Your seven different Coast Guard boats are moored to the piers. Your plans also include a heliport behind the buildings. All of your boats are gasoline powered and fuel spills and leaks will be likely.
Triple Plex, I-Max Theater: You plan to create a very unique place for your customers to view their favorite movies. Your facility will have a retractable roof and will be the only movie location capable of showing the new wide screen I-Max films. Opening the roof can draw in sea breezes strong enough to blow around any loose trash. In addition, the Dolby sound system is very, very loud.	**Wild Bill's Campground:** Yes, your facility will be the ultimate in camping pleasure… right on the ocean. Your entire property will be covered with tents, campers, RV's and converted buses. Since your business will probably be seasonal, you intend to cram in as many people into Wild Bill's as possible. There will be absolutely no room for beach activities and your sanitary system will probably not be large enough so you intend to rent a dozen Port-A-Potties. Thank goodness for the occasional wind.
Wildlife Park: You and your partner have decided that the best use for your plot of land will be to establish the Roadkill Wildlife Park. It will be a small facility compared to other theme parks but you will have a large variety of animals and intend to landscape with hundreds of plants and trees. Your park takes up most of your property, with the exception of a small office and a parking at the street line. Cleaning up after your animals and the many visitors is a continuous job and disposing of the waste is also a concern.	**Breezy Point Café:** You plan to be the proud owner of the only outside café in the community. The feature that makes your establishment unique is that it does not have a kitchen. Each outside table has its own charcoal grill that customers use to cook their own food to suit themselves. All tableware is disposable plastic or paper since you don't own a dishwasher either. The winds are very strong along this part of the shore line.
Boardwalk Variety Store: You plan to own and manage the only variety store in the community and business should be brisk. You will be open 24 hours a day, 7 days a week and often have unannounced specials on beach items like kites, blankets, sun glasses, lotion, rafts, balls, plastic shovels, buckets, skimmers and umbrellas. Everything you sell is packaged in lightweight plastic bags that display your store name and location. Inside each bag you intend to include 15 to 20 discount coupons for your customers to pass out to their friends on the beach.	**The Golden Years Retirement Village:** Your partner and you believe you have designed the ideal retirement community. Your facility will be a sprawling one story building that includes a gymnasium, pool, dining room, and private rooms for 100 wealthy senior citizens. Around the building will be lovely gardens and walking paths. To keep the morning sun from disturbing the old folks, you plan to install a four meter high fence the entire length of your property from the street to the ocean. The fence will block the sun, but structures like this tend to create sand dunes.

Big Bucks Casino and Lodge: Your business will be located in the center of your property with an attached pier that will extend into the ocean for customers who choose to arrive by boat. Parking seems to be a problem for most shore line businesses so you have constructed a ten story parking facility next to Bug Bucks. You have plenty of parking but absolutely no beach for your guests to enjoy. The parking garage is cleaned each week of the oil and grease deposits.	**Coast Guard:** Your responsibility is to maintain safety on the waters for the entire community and all the boats and ships that enter and leave. Your facility is composed of three large buildings along the water, a lighthouse, and three boat piers that extend 7 meters into the water. Your seven different Coast Guard boats are moored to the piers. Your plans also include a heliport behind the buildings. All of your boats are gasoline powered and fuel spills and leaks will be likely.

CREATE–A-COASTLINE (PART 2) *

Additional Design Challenge:
Now that you have seen the problematic results of haphazard community planning, it is time you lent a hand. Suppose you had the responsibility of planning the development of this shoreline community and were able to move the proposed 18 developments around in any order.

Occupation Labels

Fishing Pier Owner	Electricity Power Plant	Vacation Home Owner
Amusement Park Owner	Wildlife Park Operator	Retirement Home Owner
Hotel Owner	Boardwalk Food Store	Coast Guard Captain
Sewage Treatment Plant	Boat Yard Operator	Theater Owner
Cafe Owner	Restaurant Owner	Campground Owner
Variety Store Owner	Miniature Golf Operator	Casino Operator

On a large sheet of paper make a sketch of your Ideal Community. Attach the labels to your ideal community sketch where appropriate.

Once your team has completed the sketch of your Ideal Community each person on the team must prepare a written presentation to the Zoning Board. Each report should include:

- A justification for why your designed community is better for the social, economic and environmental reasons.

- A review of the problems that still exist and how you plan to fix them.

* Create-A-Coastline Parts I and II have been adapted from a lesson entitled "Dream-A-Stream", presented at the Schuylkill Valley Center for Environmental Education, 1973.

While the problem solving techniques used by each team may be different, the diversity of thinking is beneficial for enhancing the problem solving repertoire of each student. Sharing is not only encouraged it is a strategy used throughout the program.

DRILL THE WELL A LITTLE DEEPER

- Design a solution to a problem. *NSES*
- Implement a proposed design and evaluate completed technological designs or products. *NSES*
- Apply and adapt a variety of appropriate strategies to solve problems. *NCTM*
- Students adjust their use of spoken, written, and visual language (e.g., conventions, style, vocabulary) to communicate effectively with a variety of audiences and for different purposes. *NCTE*

The Context: As the population of a community increases so does the need for available resources.

The Scenario: Living in the southwestern part of the United States is becoming increasingly popular. While housing sales are at an all time high, water reserves and aquifers are at an all time low. This has been a growing problem and is compounded by the number of people who move into the area and bring high water usage habits with them.

The Challenge: The Flagstone Development Company has just landed a contract to design and construct 1000 new homes along the banks for the Colorado River. However, the Arizona Water Authority has stipulated that all new construction must be designed to conserve as much water as possible. In an effort to solve this problem your engineering team has been contacted by the Flagstaff Development Company to help them design a specific device that conserves water.

The Limitations:
- Each team will have a total of three weeks to complete this challenge. Students are expected to complete about half of the required work outside of class.
- During week one, each team must research the major uses of water and water conservation techniques. It must also conduct a water usage survey to assess water consumption at home. Individual surveys will be combined into a single document for general class use.
- Using the general survey, students must assess their families' water usage for the next two weeks.
- Each team must its survey data as a basis for making water conserving design changes and devices for the homes designed by the Flagstone Development Company.
- Each team must create a detailed, colorful, labeled sketch illustrating the water conservation plans designed for the new houses.
- Each team must build a working model of its specific conservation device, which may differ from those of other teams.
- Each team is responsible for the materials necessary to build its model.

The Rules:
- Each team member must write a report to the Flagstaff Development Corporation presenting its ideas for conserving water. Specific references must be made to the structural, behavioral, facility-related and aesthetic factors of water use, conservation or waste.
- Each team must also make suggestions as to conservation measures that could be undertaken by the community at large.

TEACHER NOTES

Suggested Materials: Students will need general school supplies to complete this design brief. Any additional materials are the responsibility of the actual design teams.

Suggested Use: This challenge was designed to compliment an environmental program that includes the conservation of natural resources. This design brief does not require the students to have prior knowledge but will provide an opportunity for the students to research water conservation practices and devices and to collect data regarding their own water usage. If the specificity of the water conservation device is determined ahead of time by the teacher, this activity could also be used as a physical science lesson about fluids (water flow), forces, energy, etc.

Ties to Content: This design challenge was created to help familiarize the students with common, real life water conservation measures. While water is a renewable resource it is increasingly becoming scarce in some communities because of increasing demands, the indiscriminate water usage and lack of conservation measures.

Possible Procedures(s): Given the extended time frame associated with this design challenge (three weeks), it is suggested that a completion schedule be posted for reference. The amount of class time, and the placement of those sessions, will be left up to the discretion of the teacher. The students will need one class period to analyze water use data based upon a one week survey. They will also need a class period to compile and analyze the remainder of the data and the any research they collect. Illustrating and communicating the water conservation measures in their new designs will take yet one more class period.

It is anticipated that students may include such water conservation measures as recycling the bath and kitchen water for landscaping purposes, installing cisterns to capture and store rain water, designing roof systems to direct rain water into a cistern system, using a limited number of native species of plants for landscaping, eliminating lawns, installing water saving shower devices and low flush toilets to name a few.

Precautions: Whenever students are involved in a construction project there is the possibility of a mishap, especially if tools, hot glue guns and other sharp objects are available. Students should be shown proper tool use and be expected to sign a safety contract. Students should wear safety glasses whenever working with sharp objects in close quarters. Appropriate safety contracts can be obtained from Flinn Scientific at www.flinnsci.com

While the problem solving techniques used by each team may be different, the diversity of thinking is beneficial for enhancing the problem solving repertoire of each student. Sharing is not only encouraged it is a strategy used throughout the program.

SAMPLE WATER SURVEY SHEET

Daily Water Use	Average Amount of Water Used in Gal.	Number of Times Per Week	Total Number of Gallons Used
Washing Clothes	35-60		
Flushing the Toilet	1.5-3.5		
Taking a Shower	25-40		
Washing Hands	2		
Brushing Teeth	2		
Washing the Car	5-10		
Watering the Lawn	5-10 per minute		
Washing the Dishes (machine)	10		
		Grand total for one weeks use	

WATER CONSERVATION/WASTE FACTORS

Structural: This category addresses the design of the human-made structures to capture or shed rain water.

Behavioral: This category reflects our use, or misuse, of water. These include the length of our showers, the frequency of hand washing, running the water while we brush our teeth, and so on. Our behaviors contribute a great deal to the amount of water we use or conserve.

Facility-Related: This category reflects the number of water using devices we have in and around our homes. These facilities can either conserve or waste water.

Aesthetic: This category focuses all things that grow and need water. Having landscaping does not necessarily mean that you have to use a lot of water.

ENVIRO-LAND

- Design a solution to a problem. *NSES*
- Apply and adapt a variety of appropriate strategies to solve problems. *NCTM*
- Students adjust their use of spoken, written, and visual language (e.g., conventions, style, vocabulary) to communicate effectively with a variety of audiences and for different purposes. *NCTE*
- Students apply knowledge of language structure, language conventions (e.g., spelling and punctuation), media techniques, figurative language, and genre to create, critique, and discuss print and non-print texts. *NCTE*

The Context: The success of a project is often determined by design specifications and environmental conditions.

The Scenario: A group of local investors is interested in building an amusement park in the old factory district along the river. The theme for the park, and all its attractions, will be environmental in nature (issues, problems, concepts or successful human intervention in the environment).

The Challenge: Your research and engineering team has been contacted to design the layout of the park including, the rides, the eating and vending facilities as well as all visitor accommodations.

The Limitations:
- Each team will have four class periods to complete its park design.
- Each design team must include the following items in its layout of the park: Parking lot, concession stands/restaurants, restrooms, rides (both adult and child appropriate), trash disposal facilities, picnic areas and walking paths and resting areas.
- Each team may also include security, first aid and in-park transportation systems.
- The park design should allow for the smooth flow of visitors from one place to another, keeping in mind that some rides are going to be more popular.
- The city has granted six blocks along the river for the creation of this park (3000 feet long and 500 feet wide.
- There is an interstate highway just outside the park boundary.
- Traffic flow in and out of the park is a major consideration as is visitor parking.
- Each team should consider the natural and human made features when designing the park.

The Rules:
- All park designs must:
  - Be drawn to scale. The scale used in the design must be noted.
  - Use color to highlight and identify park features
  - Use appropriate symbols for clarity
  - Include a legend
  - Be drawn using the top view only
- Each team must include a written description of its park and a rationale for the design features.
- Each team must present its park design to the other teams for consideration.
- Each team will use the Enviro-Land Design Rubric as a rating tool.

TEACHER NOTES

Suggested Materials: This design brief will only require basic school supplies and a metric ruler/meter stick for each design team. Students should be encouraged to supply some of their own materials whenever possible. Prior to the start of this assignment students should have a copy of the *Enviro-Land Design Rubric* and the *Team Presentation Rubric*.

Suggested Use: This design brief was developed as a general engineering brief but can be used for a variety of other purposes. For example, some students at the middle school level may still have difficulty in creating an overhead projection and as a result may have difficulty in reading and interpreting maps. An activity like this could prove helpful in identifying these students. Enviro-Land might also be used to reinforce the environmental issues the students have been studying as well as a venue for putting theory into practice when their parks are evaluated in respect to the earth friendly facilities and programs they have projected into their park design. Other applications center around art, measurement, conservation and blueprinting. Finally, it is expected that students present their park designs in an open forum. This provides a good opportunity for students to field questions and defend their designs.

Ties to Content: This design brief addresses the process skills, collaborative group structure, and the design relationships of form and function. Often applied to architecture, engineering, and industrial design *form follows function*. This tenet is true for the structure of living organisms as well as human designed structures. This design theory often becomes more noticeable when it is not properly applied that when it is. For example, the ergonomically correct placement of controls in a car is an expectation of form following function. When these controls are not correctly placed it is more than noticeable because it is an annoyance.

The smooth flow of pedestrian traffic is essential to the success of a theme park. The placement of the most popular amusements and strategically placed pathways of sufficient size are two of many considerations that have to be taken into account when planning such a park. It is suggested that students openly discuss these considerations as a large group prior to their small group deliberations and planning.

Possible Procedures(s): This challenge could be approached from a variety of perspectives. Some design teams may focus on pedestrian flow and transportation issues, others may begin with the types of attractions and their respective placement within the park, and still others may begin by addressing the environmental issues an amusement park might create. Regardless of how the students begin it will be essential that they refer to the *Enviro-Land Rubric* for guidance as they plan and design.

Precautions: There are no safety precautions associate with this design brief.

While the problem solving techniques used by each team may be different, the diversity of thinking is beneficial for enhancing the problem solving repertoire of each student. Sharing is not only encouraged it is a strategy used throughout the program.

ENVIRO-LAND RUBRIC

	4	3	2	1	Team Evaluation Score	Class Evaluation Score
Required Features	All required features included are present.	Most required features are present	Some required features are included.	None of the required features are represented.		
Optional Features	All the optional features are present. Creative additions have also been included.	All optional features have been noted but no creative additions are included.	Most of the optional features have been noted but no creative additions are included.	No optional features have been noted and no creative additions have been included.		
Use of Natural and Human Made Features	The natural and human made features have been incorporated into the park's design.	Some of the natural and human made features have been incorporated into the park's design.	There has been minimal attention paid to the natural and human made features in the park's design.	The natural and human made features were not included in the park's design.		
Visitor Accommodations	The park is designed to be user friendly for all groups regardless of age, size or special need.	The park is generally user friendly but has not accounted for all age groups.	The park design focuses on only one age group and is lacking in some accommodations	The park design is limited in its design and as such will only appeal to one healthy age group.		
Traffic Patterns	Visitors can expect many transition points into and out of the park and parking lot. The design of the park allows for easy access to all sections and crowded areas have been kept to a minimum.	Visitors will find only two transition points into and out of the park. The design of the park allows for access to most sections but bottlenecks have been created.	Visitors can expect some difficulty getting into and out of the park. The design of the park does not allow for access from everywhere. There are bottlenecks in many locations.	Visitors can expect to have difficulty with parking and access to the single park. The design of the park does not allow for access to most sections and crowded areas will be numerous.		
Map Requirements	All map requirements are present. The map legend/legends is/are easy to read with appropriate use of symbols, color and scale. The entire map is presented using the top view.	Most of the map requirements are present. The map legend/legends is/are in color and contain some symbols. Most of the map is presented using the top view.	Most of the map requirements are present. The map legend/legends is/use some color but symbols are not generally used. The map is presented using a variety of views.	Many of the map requirements are not present. The map legend/legends is/do not use color and symbols are not generally used. The map is presented using a variety of views.		
				Total Score		

FORCE AND MOTION

WHEELED WONDERS

- Design a solution to a problem. *NSES*
- Implement a proposed design and evaluate completed technological designs or products. *NSES*
- Apply and adapt a variety of appropriate strategies to solve problems. *NCTM*
- Students adjust their use of spoken, written, and visual language (e.g., conventions, style, vocabulary) to communicate effectively with a variety of audiences and for different purposes. *NCTE*
- Students apply knowledge of language structure, language conventions (e.g., spelling and punctuation), media techniques, figurative language, and genre to create, critique, and discuss print and non-print texts. *NCTE*

The Context: To stay competitive, manufacturers must produce products that are reliable and perform as advertised.

The Scenario: The Belchfire Automotive Group has been under attack from the public and the media regarding the performance of its cars.

The Challenge: Your engineering team has been hired to pull the Belchfire Automotive Group out of its problem. Your challenge is to design and construct a gravity powered vehicle capable of carrying 100 pennies and covering a distance of five meters in as straight a trip as possible.

The Limitations:
- Each team is responsible for supplying its own materials beyond regular classroom supplies.
- There are no limitations on the materials used.
- Car construction may only be done in class.
- All cars must fit through the "Size-O-Matic" calibrating device as if going headlong through a tunnel (a 15 cm by 15 cm square cut in the end of a box).
- Cars must carry at least 100 pennies and complete the five meter course.
- Three class periods are allotted for this challenge. Students are urged to be aware of the clock so as to have enough time to complete all phases of the challenge.

The Rules:
- The required five meter course will be measured from the bottom of the ramp.
- No adjustments to vehicles will be allowed once final testing begins.
- All cars that pass the strict size, weigh carrying, and distance requirements will pass on to the second elimination round where driving accuracy will be assessed.
- In the event of a tie during second elimination, total distance will determine the winner.
- Each team will be responsible for creating and presenting an advertising campaign (mini-poster, newspaper or magazine article, or a radio or television commercial that highlights the vehicle's features and or performance.
- Each group member must take part in the construction of the car, the advertising campaign and the project presentation.
- Students should refer to the *Project Assessment Rubric* for guidance when designing, constructing, testing and presenting their projects.
- Students should refer to the *Team Presentation Rubric* and the *Advertising Guidelines* for direction in crafting their presentations.

TEACHER NOTES

Suggested Materials: This construction project is best served if the students have a wide variety of materials from which to choose. General classroom supplies could include tape, staplers, paper clips, different kinds of paper, scissors, and rulers. In addition, large and small straws, cardboard, dowel sticks, and anything that could be used for wheels (plastic, wide mouth bottle lids, wheels and axles from old toys, white glue (hot glue if possible), string, scraps of wood and hand tools, if available. Students should be responsible for supplying some of their supplies. Commercial building materials, like K'Nex or Tinker Toys will reduce the time required to construct the vehicles. Students should have a better idea of what they can add to their team list of materials after they have seen what is available and the direction their plans are taking. A ramp should be set up to provide a starting point for the test, as well as to provide the energy needed to move the car. A scrap of 1/4 inch plywood or tempered hardboard, approximately 4 feet long and 10-12 inches wide, makes a good ramp. If more than one ramp is used, be sure that the raised ends are positioned at the same height. You will also need a supply of pre-sorted pennies. Please note that pennies minted prior to 1982 weigh approximately 3.1 grams. In 1982 the Federal Government changed the composition of the coins so they now weigh approximately 2.5 grams. Lastly, students will need copies of the *Project Assessment Rubric, Team Presentation Rubric*, and the *Advertising Guidelines*.

Suggested Use: This challenge is one of several associated with wheeled vehicles and the variables that affect vehicle performance. It would be to the students' advantage if they had some prior construction experience with other projects, preferably with other wheeled vehicles. This design brief addresses the identification and the manipulation of variables that affect the performance of gravity powered vehicles and the design process as a problem solving technique. Students will be expected to keep accurate records of their designs, the results, the modifications, the rationale for the changes, and any related questions that arise. Specific content areas that may align with this challenge include fluid motion, aerodynamics, Newton's Laws, gravitational force, speed, velocity and acceleration. This design brief also could also be classified as a general design challenge. As such, students will be expected to use the *Design Loop* and the *Project Assessment Rubric* as references in the planning, construction and testing of their vehicles. Students will be expected to use the *Team Presentation Rubric* and the *Advertising Guidelines* as they progress through these requirements.

Ties to Content: This challenge is focused on students successfully following the *Design Loop*, and using the appropriate process skills as they pursue the challenge. The identification and manipulation of the variables that affect vehicle performance are critical to the successful completion of this challenge. Once the students have completed a "basic car," which might be something as simple as a rectangle of cardboard and four wheels, they will be ready to begin "tweaking" or refining the vehicle to meet the specific requirements of this challenge. If they have some knowledge of forces and motion, Newton's Laws, velocity or acceleration, they will be able to make reasonable predictions for modifying their vehicles and testing them.

Possible Procedures(s): If the students have previously constructed a vehicle then this challenge would then be focused on modifying the vehicle. Crafting a vehicle that meets all required specifications is the primary directive and students should be urged not to tackle more than one of these requirements at a time. It is suggested that the problem solving process, illustrated by the *Design Loop*, be revisited with each separate vehicle specification. It is further suggested that a production and testing schedule be established for students in an attempt to keep all groups on pace.

Precautions: Whenever students are involved in a construction project there is the possibility of a mishap, especially if tools, hot glue guns and other sharp objects are available. Students should be shown proper tool use and be expected to sign a safety contract. Students should wear safety glasses whenever working with sharp objects in close quarters.

While the problem solving techniques used by each team may be different, the diversity of thinking is beneficial for enhancing the problem solving repertoire of each student. Sharing is not only encouraged it is a strategy used throughout the program.

VEHICLE CHALLENGE CARDS

These cards may be used as additional challenges for wheeled vehicles

Design a vehicle to repeatedly travel a distance between 300 and 315 cm as measured from the bottom of the ramp.	Design a vehicle to travel in a complete circle under its own power.
Design a vehicle to travel up a one meter ramp having a height of 15 cm.	Design a vehicle to travel around a cardboard box.
Design a vehicle to carry a load equal to the mass of the cart.	Design a vehicle to travel in a perfectly straight line.
Design a vehicle to travel with a wobble.	Design a vehicle to do a "wheelie".
Design a vehicle to produce a motor sound while moving.	Design a vehicle to pull a sled containing 50 pennies.
Design a vehicle to be amphibious.	Design a vehicle to travel forward, stop, and then back up a short distance.
Design a self-powered vehicle to travel a distance greater than five meters.	Design a vehicle to maneuver over rough terrain.
Design a four wheel drive vehicle.	Design a vehicle to turn left and then right.
Design a vehicle that will cover a distance of 3 meters in less than 10 seconds.	Design a vehicle that includes a "flywheel" which allows the vehicle to travel further.

ROLL-A-RAMA

- Design a solution to a problem. *NSES*
- Design and conduct a scientific investigation. *NSES*
- Implement a proposed design. *NSES*
- Apply and adapt a variety of appropriate strategies to solve problems. *NCTM*
- Students adjust their use of spoken, written, and visual language (e.g., conventions, style, vocabulary) to communicate effectively with a variety of audiences and for different purposes. *NCTE*

The Context: The solution to a problem often lies in understanding the variables causing the issue and recognizing ways to change them.

The Scenario: The Rancid Canned Goods Company has been in business for many years producing only its famous Aunt Clara's Creamy Lima Bean Soup (YUCK!). To stay competitive, the company recently decided to expand its product line to include other canned goods. Sales are starting to pick up, but the shipping department cannot keep up with all the orders. The packers need all of the canned goods to arrive at the same time so that shipping can be done in a timely fashion. However, the different products arrive from the warehouse at different times. So, the old delivery system needs to be changed. It consists of simple ramps leading directly from the factory to the warehouse, which is now delaying the packers. This is obviously a problem and the company is looking for help…FAST!

The Challenge: Your engineering team has been contacted to investigate and design a solution to this problem. A brief tour of the factory confirms your suspicions. All of the can goods are different in mass yet all of the ramps are the same in length and height. No wonder the all the cans do not arrive in the warehouse at the same time.

The Limitations:
- Each team must first meet to discuss, develop and record a plan of action.
- Each team will have access to the same materials but will probably have to share ramps and canned goods.
- Each team will work with four different canned goods.
- Each team will have two class periods to complete this part of the challenge.

The Rules:
- A data collecting format will have to be designed by each team.
- All collected data will be graphically displayed and accompanied by corresponding data tables.
- All measurements must be metric.
- Each team must demonstrate its revisions to the canned goods delivery system.
- Each team member must craft a data supported report to the Rancid Canned Goods Company about how the company can solve its can delivery problem.

TEACHER NOTES

Suggested Materials: Materials for this challenge include ramps (1/4 inch plywood, hardboard, reinforced cardboard), blocking materials that can be used to adjust the height of the ramps (pieces of wood or books), metric measuring tapes, stop watches, canned goods with the labels removed and a balance to measure mass. It is very important that the canned goods chosen vary significantly in consistency, from thin liquid to very thick or solid paste and everything in between. A dozen different cans should be sufficient. Remove the labels and number the cans with a permanent marker.

Suggested Use: This design brief could be used as a general design challenge or as a discrepant event for introducing the concept of inertia and Newton's laws. In any case, students will need to explore the rolling characteristics of each of the cans of soup as well as the other variables that affect their relative speeds. Given the mathematics background of the students, the formula $V = d/t$ could be used to compute the speed of each can (V = speed, d = distance and t = time).

Ties to Content: This design challenge provides an opportunity for students to identify and manipulate the variables associated with the inclined plane, as well as the concept of moment of inertia. An object's tendency to stay at rest, or to stay in motion, is called inertia. This is often referred to as a resistance to change in motion, and is measured in terms of mass (kilograms). When an object is rotating, its resistance to a change in its state of rotation is called rotational inertia, or moment of inertia. The variables related to the cans include the weight of the can, the size of the can and the consistency of the contents. These three factors affect each can's moment of inertia or the resistance of the can to move. Since an object's moment of inertia increases as its mass is moved further from its axis of rotation, hoops and rings represent a greater moment of inertia than solid cylinders. This concept can be applied to our cans. A can of solid material, like processed dog food, has a low moment of inertia when compared to an identically sized can of fruit cocktail that is more resistant to moving. When these two cans are rolled down a ramp the dog food will reach the bottom first. In general cans with loose chunks are slower because the mass accumulates on the periphery of the can, resulting in a higher moment of inertia.

Possible Procedures(s): Regardless of how the teams approaches this problem, they will all need to collect the same basic data including the mass and size of each can, its rolling characteristics and ramp speed. Teams will have to select four cans with which to work. Although student groups may have to share cans and ramps, this will encourage continuous and accurate record keeping. Students will need a period of time to explore the rolling characteristics of the selected canned goods and the effect that changing the ramp angle and/or the ramp length have on the speed of each can. Students will have to set a "benchmark" by selecting a can, a ramp angle, and a ramp length to serve as the standard for adjusting the rolling times of the other cans. The rolling characteristics of the other cans will be inherently different because each may have a different moment of inertia. The "rolling time" can be manipulated by changing the ramp angle or the ramp length. Remember, the challenge is to have all the cans arrive at the warehouse at the same time. To extend this challenge ask the students to design a can that will roll slower than the slowest can. Here the task is directly related to the contents of the can and its behavior within the can...everything else should remain the same.

Precautions: There are no precautions associated with this challenge.

While the problem solving techniques used by each team may be different, the diversity of thinking is beneficial for enhancing the problem solving repertoire of each student. Sharing is not only encouraged it is a strategy used throughout the program.

HUMPTY DUMPTY

> - Design a solution to a problem. *NSES*
> - As a result of activities in grades 5-8, all students should develop an understanding of transfer of energy. *NSES*
> - Develop descriptions, explanations, predictions, and models using evidence. *NSES*
> - Apply and adapt a variety of appropriate strategies to solve problems. *NCTM*
> - Students adjust their use of spoken, written, and visual language (e.g., conventions, style, vocabulary) to communicate effectively with a variety of audiences and for different purposes. *NCTE*

The Context: Among the many issues facing automobile manufacturers is the challenge to produce safer cars.

The Scenario: The National Highway Traffic and Safety Administration performs crash tests on cars every year and uses the results to assign safety ratings. The Binford Transportation Company received the inferior rating of "Not Safe At Any Speed Award" for all of its models.

The Challenge: As a member of Binford's crack engineering team you have been assigned the responsibility of improving the overall safety of its cars. Since your department budget has been slashed in half, you decide to use model cars rather than the real thing and a raw egg for the passenger since the crash dummy has just been promoted to vice president of marketing. When you have perfected the system with the models, you will move on to the actual cars. Until then, don't break any eggs!

The Limitations:
- A detailed action plan must be submitted before any construction begins.
- Each team will receive a model car to modify.
- Any additional materials are the responsibility of the team.
- Three class periods will be allotted for this challenge at the discretion of the teacher.
- Each team must budget its time accordingly and remain aware of the number of tasks.
- Plastic eggs will be used during the research and development phase.
- Raw eggs will be used for the final test.

The Rules:
- Each team will use the same ramp for testing. The angle of the ramp will also remain constant.
- Each team member will individually prepare a written report that describes the vehicle's safety features, the safety modifications made to the vehicle, the testing procedure and the final test results.
- Test Criteria:
    -Shell not cracked and yolk unbroken = alive and well (safety rating, excellent)
    -Shell cracked but yolk unbroken = a few broken bones (safety rating, good)
    -Shell not cracked but yolk broken = internal injuries (safety rating, poor)
    -Shell cracked, yolk broken = dead (safety rating, unsafe at any speed)
- Students should refer to the *Project Assessment Rubric* for guidance when designing, constructing, testing and presenting their projects.

TEACHER NOTES

Suggested Materials: A scrap of 1/4 inch plywood approximately 4 feet long and 10-12 inches wide makes a good ramp. Place the end about 30 cm from a wall (the crash site) with a ramp angle of about 30 degrees. It is suggested that plastic or wooden cars be purchased for this activity unless the students have already constructed cars prior to this. Remember that the cars have to be large enough to carry an egg and have sufficient room to make a variety of safety modifications. A "dollar store" is a great place to find inexpensive cars. Students should also have a copy of the *Project Assessment Rubric* for reference purposes as they progress through this challenge.

Suggested Use: This design brief was developed to be used as a real life application of Newton's first law of motion. This design brief also could be classified as a general design challenge. As such, students will be expected to use the *Design Loop* and the *Project Assessment Rubric* as guides in their planning, construction, testing and presentation phases. In addition to the foregoing, this challenge could be used as an opportunity for students to research the design of actual automobile restraint devices.

Ties to Content: The concepts of force and inertia are demonstrated in this investigation. According to Newton's first law of motion, an object in motion will remain in motion, or an object at rest will remain at rest, unless acted upon by an outside force. This is sometimes referred to as the law of inertia. Seatbelts and airbags are employed to protect the passengers in a moving car against sudden stops, i.e. sudden changes in inertia. During an accident passengers not wearing seatbelts continue to move forward (not a good thing) while passengers belted in generally remain in place because the seat belt exerts a force keeping them in place.

Possible Procedures(s): There are presently two major passenger protection devices, the seatbelt and the airbag. If students select the latter please remind them that air bags are not deployed until a crash occurs and their air bags must function in a similar manner. While it seems a simple matter of just belting in the egg passenger, students may find that the sudden stop of their vehicle hitting the wall, will still be enough to destroy the egg. Students may find that there needs to be a little flex, or give, in their restraint systems. Given the shape of the egg passenger, the design of the restraint system will also need to be considered. As students pursue this challenge they will be expected to select and appropriately apply the process skills associated with an investigation. Teachers should take this opportunity to continue the assessment of these important skills.

Precautions: Whenever students are involved in a construction project there is the possibility of a mishap, especially if tools, hot glue guns and other sharp objects are available. Students should be shown proper tool use and be expected to sign a safety contract. Students should wear safety glasses whenever working with sharp objects in close quarters.

While the problem solving techniques used by each team may be different, the diversity of thinking is beneficial for enhancing the problem solving repertoire of each student. Sharing is not only encouraged it is a strategy used throughout the program.

GONE WITH THE WIND

- Design a solution to a problem. *NSES*
- As a result of activities in grades 5-8, all students should develop an understanding of transfer of energy. *NSES*
- Apply and adapt a variety of appropriate strategies to solve problems. *NCTM*
- Students adjust their use of spoken, written, and visual language (e.g., conventions, style, vocabulary) to communicate effectively with a variety of audiences and for different purposes. *NCTE*

The Context: Energy costs are constantly rising and it is becoming more costly to travel. Inexpensive and alternative sources of energy need to be further investigated.

The Scenario: Your community of Dry Gulch is located in the southwestern part of the United States. Everyone in the town works in the borax mine. The area is very dry, flat, and contains little vegetation. Every product must be transported into and out of Dry Gulch by truck and is very costly. To make matters worse, there is a constant westerly wind blowing. As a member of the Town Council, your job is to somehow reduce the town's energy expenses.

The Challenge: You must design, build, and test a vehicle capable of taking advantage of the windy conditions that exist in Dry Gulch. In addition, this vehicle must also be able to carry 125 grams of material (a roll of pennies)

The Limitations:
- Each team will have a total of four days for this project. (One day to sketch and design, two days to construct your and modify the vehicle and one day to test and refine the design.)
- Teams may use any materials to construct their vehicles.
- All vehicles must fit through the opening "Deadman's Arch", a natural passageway through the mountains (a 30 centimeter square cut in a cardboard box).
- Vehicles must travel in a straight line.
- Vehicles must cover a distance of two meters in less than ten seconds powered only by the wind.
- Vehicles must de designed to carry a container of material weighing 125 grams.

The Rules:
- Each team member must keep an "Alternative Vehicle Journal," which contains all design changes, the test results of these changes, conclusions, and ideas for further alterations.
- There are no weight requirements for the vehicle.
- Each team will be responsible for supplying additional materials.
- All vehicles will be tested on the same track. Three trials will be made and the average time will be used to determine the fastest vehicle.
- The track will consist of two, three meter strips of tape attached to the floor, 24 centimeters apart.
- Should the vehicle stray off the track, a one second penalty will be added to the time for each centimeter the vehicle is completely off the road.

TEACHER NOTES

Suggested Materials: This construction project is best served if the students have a wide variety of materials from which to choose. General classroom supplies could include tape, staplers, paper clips, different kinds of paper, scissors, and rulers. In addition, large and small straws, cardboard, dowel sticks, and anything that could be used for wheels (plastic, wide mouth bottle lids, wheels and axles from old toys, white glue (hot glue if possible), string, scraps of wood and hand tools, if available. Students should be responsible for supplying some of their supplies. Commercial building materials, like K'Nex or Tinker Toys will reduce the time required to construct the vehicles. Students should have a better idea of what they can add to their team list of materials after they have seen what is available and the direction their plans are taking. The westerly wind mentioned in the design brief can be created with a common, three speed box window fan. You will also need a supply of pennies. (Please note that pennies minted prior to 1982 weigh approximately 3.1 grams. In 1982 the Federal Government changed the composition of the coins so they now weigh approximately 2.5 grams.) Of course, if you did not pre-sort the pennies and also did not tell the students about it, this discrepancy could serve as a real life problem for the students to pursue.

Suggested Use: This challenge is one of several associated with wheeled vehicles and the variables that affect vehicle performance. It would be to the students' advantage if they had some prior construction experience with other projects, preferably with other wheeled vehicles. These other vehicles could have been powered by rubber bands, electricity, solar energy, air pressure, tension springs or gravity. This challenge expects the vehicle to be wind powered.

Ties to Content: Specific content areas that may align with this challenge include fluid motion, aerodynamics, Newton's Laws, gravitational force, speed, velocity and acceleration. This design brief also could also be classified as a general design challenge. As such, students will be expected to use the *Design Loop* as a reference in the planning, construction and testing of their vehicles. The identification and manipulation of the variables that affect vehicle performance are critical to the successful completion of this challenge. Once the students have completed a "basic car", which might something as simple as a rectangle of cardboard and four wheels, they will be ready to begin "tweaking" or refining the vehicle to meet the specific requirements of this challenge. Will it fit through the 30cm hole in the box? Will it carry 125 grams of material? Can it travel the given distance in ten seconds? Will it travel in a straight line? And so on…

Possible Procedures(s): This challenge is one of several that involve wheeled vehicles. If the students have already constructed a vehicle, then this challenge would be focused on converting the machine to be powered by wind. Crafting a vehicle that meets all required specifications is the prime directive, so students should probably be urged not to tackle more than one of these requirements at a time. Once the basic vehicle is together, the team could split the remaining responsibilities. However, they should be frequently reminded of managing their time effectively.

Precautions: Whenever students are involved in a construction project there is the possibility of a mishap, especially if tools, hot glue guns and other sharp objects are available. Students should be shown proper tool use and be expected to sign a safety contract. Students should wear safety glasses whenever working with sharp objects in close quarters.

While the problem solving techniques used by each team may be different, the diversity of thinking is beneficial for enhancing the problem solving repertoire of each student. Sharing is not only encouraged it is a strategy used throughout the program.

WINGED WONDER

> - Design a solution to a problem. *NSES*
> - As a result of activities in grades 5-8, all students should develop an understanding of transfer of energy. *NSES*
> - Use appropriate tools, and techniques to gather, analyze, and interpret data. *NSES*
> - Apply and adapt a variety of appropriate strategies to solve problems. *NCTM*
> - Students adjust their use of spoken, written, and visual language (e.g., conventions, style, vocabulary) to communicate effectively with a variety of audiences and for different purposes. *NCTE*

The Context: Understanding the capabilities of a mechanical device and the variables that affect its behavior are essential elements in determining its performance.

The Scenario: Your air freight company makes daily flights from your distribution center to the metropolitan city of Hersheyberg, a distance of 475 centimeters. The sluggish economy has forced your company to begin carrying passengers as a way to increase profits. Adding people also adds weight and that means that more fuel is required to complete the trip. But, how much fuel needs to be added? If you add too much fuel the "Winged Wonder" will overshoot the runway and will be destroyed, too little fuel will result in a crash landing in the mountains, neither of which would be good for business.

The Challenge: Your flight crew has been given the responsibility of redesigning and fueling the "Winger Wonder" to fly to and successfully land in the city of Hersheyberg, 475 centimeters from the freight company hanger.

The Limitations:
- A plane must travel between 460 cm and 490 cm to be considered successful.
- Planes must complete <u>three successful flights in a row</u> in order to be considered successful and thus used as a model for a very lucrative government transportation contract.
- Each team will have two class periods to complete this challenge...Budget your time wisely.
- Planes must carry a load of five passengers (5 large paper clips).

The Rules:
- Each team must construct a format of some sort for recording its data (a data display).
- All experimental data must also be graphically displayed.
- All modifications to the original "Winged Wonder" must be noted and reasons for these changes explained. Additional modifications suggested by further tests need to be included in the data display.
- A successful plane will be considered a proto-type and each team will be required to manufacture and test a replica to prove the worthiness of its design.
- Students should refer to the *Project Assessment Rubric* for guidance when designing, constructing, testing and presenting their projects.

TEACHER NOTES

Suggested Materials: Aside from the actual vehicle, students will also need measuring tapes, large paper clips and zip lines (strings on which to hang the vehicles). It is suggested that brightly colored, braided nylon contractors' cord be used for this as it knots without difficulty. Also, it can be easily seen and is therefore considerably less hazardous than traditional fishing line. It can be found in hardware and home improvement stores. This challenge was designed to extend zip line vehicle experiences through the application and manipulation of the identified variables. The materials used in the construction of the original vehicles should be made available to the design teams including standard classroom materials like tape, scissors, glue, string, paper and so on. Students will also need a copy of the *Project Assessment Rubric* as a reference guide in developing and/or modifying their projects.

Suggested Use: A common way for students to experience identifying and manipulating variables is through the use of a zip line vehicle, powered by air pressure or rubber bands. This design brief is to be used as application of this concept but focuses on the manipulation of variables that affect the flight of the vehicle. Students are expected to keep accurate records of their designs, results, modifications, rationales for changes, and any related questions that arise. In addition, students must individually display and interpret the collected data. It is important that the students share their procedures and findings as this process enriches the background of all students and lends credibility to the concept that a problem often has more than one solution. This design brief also could also be classified as a general design challenge. As such, students will be expected to use the *Design Loop* and the *Project Assessment Rubric* as guides in the planning, construction, testing and presentation phases.

Ties to Content: This challenge is generally used as an application of Newton's third law of motion, which simply states: for every action there is an opposite but equal reaction. For example, when a zip line balloon rocket is inflated the air pressure inside the balloon is greater than the air pressure surrounding it. As long as the neck of the balloon is held tightly closed, or is tied in a knot, the forces inside the balloon are balanced in all directions. When the neck of the balloon is released, the forces inside and outside of the balloon are no longer equal. Thus, air escapes from the neck in one direction and pushes the balloon forward in the opposite direction. Greater pressure inside the balloon will result in greater the outward pressure (thrust) when the neck is released. Limiting the students to a specific distance will compel students to consider other variables that might be manipulated to increase the efficiency of their vehicles. If rubber bands are used as the energy source, questions regarding Hooke's Law might arise. Simply stated, in elastic materials, stress is proportional to strain. However, although rubber bands can store large amounts of energy, Hooke's Law does not apply to them, except for possibly a small range of motion in the middle range of the rubber band. So, if rubber bands are used as the energy source for this design brief, keep in mind that some winds or twists will add more elastic potential to a vehicle's system than others. This same caution applies to balloons. Perhaps having a large supply of similar rubber bands and/or balloons will assist in attempting to control these variables.

Possible Procedures(s): This challenge can be as open ended as students can handle. Time however, can be a critical factor. You may consider setting a schedule for each day of the project. The first day could be set aside for the development of the data display and initial construction. The second day could be devoted to vehicle testing, modifications and the construction or vehicle replicas. A logical extension of this challenge would be to set a time restraint for the flight. Since airlines have some "wiggle" room in their flight schedules, the same should be provided the students. Tell them that their flight should take no more than 3.8 seconds and no less than 3.0 seconds. A stop watch will be needed for this extension.

Precautions: Whenever students are involved in a construction project there is the possibility of a mishap, especially if tools, hot glue guns and other sharp objects are available. Students should be shown proper tool use and be expected to sign a safety contract. Students should wear safety glasses whenever working with sharp objects in close quarters.

While the problem solving techniques used by each team may be different, the diversity of thinking is beneficial for enhancing the problem solving repertoire of each student. Sharing is not only encouraged it is a strategy used throughout the program.

MORE BANG FOR THE BUCK

- Design a solution to a problem. *NSES*
- As a result of activities in grades 5-8, all students should develop an understanding of transfer of energy. *NSES*
- Use appropriate tools, and techniques to gather, analyze, and interpret data. *NSES*
- Apply and adapt a variety of appropriate strategies to solve problems. *NCTM*
- Apply appropriate techniques, tools, and formulas to determine measurements. *NCTM*
- Students adjust their use of spoken, written, and visual language (e.g., conventions, style, vocabulary) to communicate effectively with a variety of audiences and for different purposes. *NCTE*

The Context: The cost of energy is constantly rising and this causes changes in our daily lives.

The Scenario: You are a member of an engineering team for the Wrong Brothers Airplane Company. Fuel prices have doubled in the past year, the machinists' union is seeking additional health care benefits and your supplier has doubled the costs for your materials. In order for the company to stay in business it must seek ways to be more efficient.

The Challenge: As a member of the Wrong Brothers Research and Development committee you suggest that the perhaps, just perhaps, the 60 year old planes should be updated. Using additional material, or altered equipment, your team must redesign or modify a plane to increase its efficiency. The more efficient the plane, the further it will travel on a given amount of energy.

The Limitations:
- Each team will have two days to complete this design challenge.
- Each design team must submit a plan of action before starting construction. Each modification to the original design must be supported with a rationale.
- Each plane will receive the same amount of fuel (windings or thrusts from an air pump)
- Only one rubber band or balloon will be permitted per plane.
- Materials may be removed, changed, or added as determined by the design team.
- Each team will receive a new rubber band or balloon for the test...if they so desire.
- Testing may be conducted on any flight line but the competition will be conducted only on the official flight line.
- Each team may bring in additional materials for this project

The Rules:
- Results of each vehicle modification must be recorded and results noted.
- Efficiency will be determined by the distance each plane travels.
- Individualized Assignment: Based upon the design of the most efficient plane, write a letter to the president of the Wrong Brothers Airplane Company explaining the changes they need to make in their planes in order to increase efficiency. The use of data and illustrations will help the president of the company understand.
- Students should refer to the *Project Assessment Rubric* for guidance when designing, constructing, testing and presenting their projects.

TEACHER NOTES

Suggested Materials: Aside from the actual vehicle, students will also need measuring tapes, stop watches, and zip lines (strings on which to hang the vehicles). It is suggested that brightly colored, braided nylon contractors' cord be used for this as it knots without difficulty. Also, it can be easily seen and is therefore considerably less hazardous than traditional fishing line. It can be found in hardware and home improvement stores. This challenge was designed to extend zip line vehicle experiences through the application and manipulation of the identified variables. The materials used in the construction of the original vehicles should be made available to the design teams including standard classroom materials like tape, scissors, paper clips, glue, string, paper and so on. Students will also need a copy of the *Project Assessment Rubric* as a reference guide in developing and/or modifying their projects.

Suggested Use: A common way for students to experience identifying and manipulating variables is through the use of a zip line vehicle, powered by air pressure or rubber bands. This design brief is to be used as application of this concept but focuses on the manipulation of variables that affect the flight of the vehicle. Students are expected to keep accurate records of their designs, results, modifications, rationales for changes, and any related questions that arise. In addition, students must individually display and interpret the collected data. It is important that the students share their procedures and findings as this process enriches the background of all students and lends credibility to the concept that a problem often has more than one solution. This design brief also could also be classified as a general design challenge. As such, students will be expected to use the *Design Loop* and the *Project Assessment Rubric* as guides in the planning, construction, testing and presentation phases.

Ties to Content: This challenge is generally used as an application of Newton's third law of motion, which simply states: for every action there is an opposite but equal reaction. For example, when a zip line balloon rocket is inflated the air pressure inside the balloon is greater than the air pressure surrounding it. As long as the neck of the balloon is held tightly closed, or is tied in a knot, the forces inside the balloon are balanced in all directions. When the neck of the balloon is released, the forces inside and outside of the balloon are no longer equal. Thus, air escapes from the neck in one direction and pushes the balloon forward in the opposite direction. Greater pressure inside the balloon will result in greater the outward pressure (thrust) when the neck is released. Limiting the students to a specific distance will compel students to consider other variables that might be manipulated to increase the efficiency of their vehicles. If rubber bands are used as the energy source, questions regarding Hooke's Law might arise. Simply stated, in elastic materials, stress is proportional to strain. However, although rubber bands can store large amounts of energy, Hooke's Law does not apply to them, except for possibly a small range of motion in the middle range of the rubber band. So, if rubber bands are used as the energy source for this design brief, keep in mind that some winds or twists will add more elastic potential to a vehicle's system than others. This same caution applies to balloons. Perhaps having a large supply of similar rubber bands and/or balloons will assist in attempting to control these variables.

Possible Procedures(s): This challenge can be as open ended as students can handle. Time however, can be a critical factor. You may consider setting a schedule for each day of the project. The first day could include the action plan, the design and rationale and the initial construction and testing. The initial test results could also serve as the base line data for comparing future tests. The second day could be devoted to project modifications and continued testing, ending with the students writing their data supported recommendations to the Wrong Brothers Airplane Company.

Precautions: Whenever students are involved in a construction project there is the possibility of a mishap, especially if tools, hot glue guns and other sharp objects are available. Students should be shown proper tool use and be expected to sign a safety contract. Students should wear safety glasses whenever working with sharp objects in close quarters.

While the problem solving techniques used by each team may be different, the diversity of thinking is beneficial for enhancing the problem solving repertoire of each student. Sharing is not only encouraged it is a strategy used throughout the program.

THE X-PLANE

> - Design a solution to a problem. *NSES*
> - As a result of activities in grades 5-8, all students should develop an understanding of transfer of energy. *NSES*
> - Use appropriate tools, and techniques to gather, analyze, and interpret data. *NSES*
> - Apply and adapt a variety of appropriate strategies to solve problems. *NCTM*
> - Apply appropriate techniques, tools, and formulas to determine measurements. *NCTM*
> - Students adjust their use of spoken, written, and visual language (e.g., conventions, style, vocabulary) to communicate effectively with a variety of audiences and for different purposes. *NCTE*

The Context: Humans have always been obsessed by speed. As a result, they have created competitions to test and encourage the efforts of engineers, and those who pilot the craft, to push the limits.

The Scenario: The "Right Stuff" Aerospace Foundation has offered a 10 million dollar prize to any engineering group that can design and successfully fly a plane that is able to break the existing speed record of 78 meters per minute.

The Challenge: Your design team has decided to accept the challenge set forth by the "Right Stuff" Aerospace Foundation. You have been experimenting with the zip line vehicle long enough to understand that there are a number of variables that affect the speed and the distance the vehicle will travel. But, which of these changes, or combination of changes, will result in increasing the speed of the vehicle?

The Limitations:
- There are no design, material or testing restrictions.
- This challenge is limited to two class periods.
- Each team must submit a detailed, labeled drawing of their X-plane before testing.
- All work must be done in the room during scheduled class periods.
- No planes may be removed from the room at any time for any reason.
- Each team may also supply some of its own items as needed.
- Each team will be given two chances to break the speed record.

The Rules:
- Each team will be given one period to design and test their X-plane. An additional period will be reserved for modifications and final testing.
- Any modifications made to the plane must be recorded along with the reason these changes.
- All test results will be recorded in a data table and will show the mathematical calculations for determining the plane's speed.
- Testing may be done on any flight line. Final flights must be held on the "Right Stuff" Official Flight Line.
- No repairs, or modifications, may be made to the plane once final testing begins.
- Students should refer to the *Project Assessment Rubric* for guidance when designing, constructing, testing and presenting their projects.

TEACHER NOTES

Suggested Materials: Aside from the actual vehicle, students will also need measuring tapes, stop watches, and zip lines (strings on which to hang the vehicles). It is suggested that brightly colored, braided nylon contractors' cord be used for this as it knots without difficulty. Also, it can be easily seen and is therefore considerably less hazardous than traditional fishing line. It can be found in hardware and home improvement stores. This challenge was designed to extend zip line vehicle experiences through the application and manipulation of the identified variables. The materials used in the construction of the original vehicles should be made available to the design teams including standard classroom materials like tape, scissors, glue, paperclips, string, paper and so on. Students will also need a copy of the *Project Assessment Rubric* as a reference guide in developing and/or modifying their projects.

Suggested Use: A common way for students to experience identifying and manipulating variables is through the use of a zip line vehicle, powered by air pressure or rubber bands. This design brief is to be used as application of this concept but focuses on the manipulation of variables that affect the flight of the vehicle. Students are expected to keep accurate records of their designs, results, modifications, rationales for changes, and any related questions that arise. In addition, students must individually display and interpret the collected data. It is important that the students share their procedures and findings as this process enriches the background of all students and lends credibility to the concept that a problem often has more than one solution. This design brief also could also be classified as a general design challenge. As such, students will be expected to use the *Design Loop* and the *Project Assessment Rubric* as guides in the planning, construction, testing and presentation phases.

Ties to Content: This challenge is generally used as an application of Newton's third law of motion, which simply states: for every action there is an opposite but equal reaction. For example, when a zip line balloon rocket is inflated the air pressure inside the balloon is greater than the air pressure surrounding it. As long as the neck of the balloon is held tightly closed, or is tied in a knot, the forces inside the balloon are balanced in all directions. When the neck of the balloon is released, the forces inside and outside of the balloon are no longer equal. Thus, air escapes from the neck in one direction and pushes the balloon forward in the opposite direction. Greater pressure inside the balloon will result in greater the outward pressure (thrust) when the neck is released. Limiting the students to a specific distance will compel students to consider other variables that might be manipulated to increase the efficiency of their vehicles. If rubber bands are used as the energy source, questions regarding Hooke's Law might arise. Simply stated, in elastic materials, stress is proportional to strain. However, although rubber bands can store large amounts of energy, Hooke's Law does not apply to them, except for possibly a small range of motion in the middle range of the rubber band. So, if rubber bands are used as the energy source for this design brief, keep in mind that some winds or twists will add more elastic potential to a vehicle's system than others. This same caution applies to balloons. Perhaps having a large supply of similar rubber bands and/or balloons will assist in attempting to control these variables. In this challenge, students are expected manipulate the variables that affect the speed of their vehicles and compute the speed by applying the formula $V=d/t$ (Speed = Distance / Time).

Possible Procedures(s): This challenge can be as open ended as students can handle. Time, however, can be a critical factor. Consider setting a schedule for each day of the project. Day 1 could be set aside for the development of an action plan as well as the design, rationale and the initial construction. Day 2 could be devoted to vehicle testing, modifications. Day 3 could be used for the individual writing assignments, which could also be assigned as homework.

Precautions: Whenever students are involved in a construction project there is the possibility of a mishap, especially if tools, hot glue guns and other sharp objects are available. Students should be shown proper tool use and be expected to sign a safety contract. Students should wear safety glasses whenever working with sharp objects in close quarters.

While the problem solving techniques used by each team may be different, the diversity of thinking is beneficial for enhancing the problem solving repertoire of each student. Sharing is not only encouraged it is a strategy used throughout the program.

SPECIAL EFFECTS

> - Design a solution to a problem. *NSES*
> - Design and conduct a scientific investigation. *NSES*
> - Use appropriate tools, and techniques to gather, analyze, and interpret data. *NSES*
> - Apply appropriate techniques, tools, and formulas to determine measurements. *NCTM*
> - Students use spoken, written, and visual language to accomplish their own purposes (e.g., for learning, enjoyment, persuasion, and the exchange of information. *NCTE*

The Context: There is often a lot of science in science-fiction.

The Scenario: While working with a Hollywood studio your special effects team has been given the responsibility of figuring out two different, but related problems. The first quandary is to determine which organism, the mealworm or the isopod (pill bug) is the fastest. This challenge appears at first glance to be rather odd. However, when you read the following excerpt from the letter of request, it becomes apparent why your team has been given this job.

The Challenge: (Direct quote from the work letter)

In addition to finding out which critter is faster you must also determine if either of these organisms, if enlarged to human size through special effects, would theoretically be able to catch a human. The studio is almost out of money and we need to cut corners somewhere. These little organisms are inexpensive, readily available, and we don't have to pay them. The script has been rewritten and we expect this film to be the best yet in our "Invasion of the Monster (fill in the blank)" series.

Oh yes, one more thing. The animal rights groups will be watching so be sure to treat the organisms with respect. The Board of Directors must also be convinced that our film is scientifically accurate so it will be necessary to write them a report that includes your <u>procedure</u>, your <u>findings</u> (multiple trials and averages), your <u>interpretation of the data</u>, and your <u>conclusions</u>."

> *Sincerely,*
> *Maximus Minimus, CEO*
> *Gargantuan Films*

The Limitations:
- Each team must submit a detailed plan of how it proposes to meet this challenge.
- It will be the responsibility of the team to create a way to display collected data.
- Each team must show how it computed the relative speeds of the organisms tested.

The Rules:
- All animals must be handled with care and returned to their environments after experimental data has been collected.
- All team members must individually craft a report to the Board of Directors as requested by Maximus Minimus.

TEACHER NOTES

Suggested Materials: Your students will need metric tapes, and a timing device of some kind. If you cannot find isopods then any other crawling insects will suffice. This challenge could also be done with common mealworms, available at pet and bait stores. If available, "superworms" are more than double the size of the regular mealworms and are easier for students to work with.

Suggested Use: This challenge presents an opportunity for students to design and conduct a fair test investigation, to gather accurate data about the physical abilities of a living organism and to make reasonable interpretations of collected data. In addition, the students will also be expected to correctly apply the formula for computing speed and to develop a method for comparing the speed of the organism to that of a human.

Ties to Content: The change in position of objects is commonly referred to as motion, whereas speed is the time it takes for this change in position to occur. In general, the speed that an object travels is not constant. For example, during a short 14 mile trip to the store you slow down and speed up a number of times. Upon arriving home again you find the entire trip took 40 minutes. Since the speed of the vehicle varied we divide the total distance by the total time to find the average speed. Given the mathematics background of the students, the formula $V = d/t$ could be used to compute the speed of each organism (V = speed, d = distance and t = time).

Possible Procedures(s): There are a variety of ways students could pursue this challenge. One way would be to measure the length of the organism, create a course ten times larger, then measure the time it takes for the organism to complete the course. Using the formula $V = d/t$, students can then determine the organism's speed. This procedure should also be followed to determine the speed of a human. Comparing the organism's speed to that of a human would then be a matter of comparing the relative speeds of the two. That would work as long as the organism remained small but the design brief challenges students to figure out what would happen if the organism were enlarged to human size. Would it be able to catch a human? Let's suppose that organism is 2 cm long and can cover a 20 cm course in15 seconds. That would be a speed of 3 cm/second. A human, 170 cm tall covering a 1700 centimeter race course in 7 seconds would be traveling 243 cm/second. The human is 84 times larger than the organism. If the organism's size is increased 84 times and its speed increases accordingly would it be able to catch the human?

This design brief also could also be classified as a general design challenge. As such, students will be expected to use the *Design Loop* as a guide in their planning, construction, testing and presentation phases. As students pursue this challenge they will be expected to select and appropriately apply the process skills associated with an investigation. Teachers should take this opportunity to continue the assessment of these important skills.

Precautions: There are no precautions associated with this design brief. However, students will be working with living organisms and should, therefore, be reminded to treat the organisms with respect. Perhaps this could be a clause in the standard laboratory safety agreement which students sign at the beginning of the school year.

While the problem solving techniques used by each team may be different, the diversity of thinking is beneficial for enhancing the problem solving repertoire of each student. Sharing is not only encouraged it is a strategy used throughout the program.

OLD HANDS—NEW TOOLS

- Design a solution to a problem. *NSES*
- Develop an understanding of abilities of technological design and understandings about science and technology. *NSES*
- Apply and adapt a variety of appropriate strategies to solve problems. *NCTM*
- Students adjust their use of spoken, written, and visual language (e.g., conventions, style, vocabulary) to communicate effectively with a variety of audiences and for different purposes. *NCTE*

The Context: A tool can be defined as a device that helps us perform a task. Redesigned tools can sometimes make our work even easier to do.

The Scenario: The Wingnut Company is the largest manufacturer of hand tools in southern New Jersey. The company attributes its success to its crack research and development team and its innovative product designs. Recently, the advertising department decided that there existed an untapped market for tool sales with senior citizens. The problem is that seniors are not as strong as when they were young.

The Challenge: As a member of the R & D team you have been given the challenge of redesigning a standard hand tool so that it will be easier for someone to use.

The Limitations:
- All tools must be of the manual type. No power tools will be accepted.
- Each team will have two days to design, test and present the results of the challenge.
- Each team must create a detailed, labeled illustration of its design in color.
- Illustrations must also contain dimensions and show the location of the resistance and the effort.
- It will be necessary for each team to collect and display experimental data that demonstrates how its new design actually makes performing a task easier.
- In place of experimental data, students may demonstrate the increase in a tool's ideal mechanical advantage through the use of tool measurements and application of appropriate formulae.
- Each team must present and demonstrate its redesigned tool along with supporting data that the tool is easier to use.

The Rules:
- Each team is responsible for supplying all materials outside of general classroom supplies.
- Each team must create a working model of its redesigned tool or make modifications to an existing tool.
- Each member of the research team must prepare a rationale describing why changes in the tool design make performing a task easier.
- Experimental data must be quantitative. No subjective measures will be accepted.
- Students should refer to the *Project Assessment Rubric* for guidance when designing, constructing, testing and presenting their projects.
- Students should refer to the *Team Presentation Rubric* for direction in crafting their oral presentations.

TEACHER NOTES

Suggested Materials: Teams are responsible for supplying all materials for this design challenge except for general classroom supplies. Students will need a copy of the *Team Presentation Rubric* and the *Project Assessment Rubric* as reference guides.

Suggested Use: This design brief was developed as an application challenge for students following a unit on simple machines. Students will be expected to identify the location of the resistance and the effort on their selected tools, as well as a method to alter the tool, thereby increasing its mechanical advantage.

Ties to Content: Machines are found throughout out daily lives…from opening a door to cutting a string with a pair of scissors. Some machines are considered simple machines, devices that perform a task most with only one moving part. Other machines are more complex such as compound machines, two or more simple machines working together. In either case, machines make work easier by reducing the effort needed to perform a task. Actually, the same amount of work is done it just seems easier because of the distance trade off. For example, it is easier to move a rock by using a pry bar (first class lever), providing we move our hands as far from the fulcrum as possible. Depending on the position of the fulcrum, our hands will travel a greater distance than the rock but will require less effort than trying to move the rock without the pry bar.

The amount of effort force reduced by using simple or complex machines is called mechanical advantage (MA). The mechanical advantage of a machine is the ratio of the resistance force, that which opposes the effort, to the effort force, that which is applied to the machine. For example, if a 400 N object can be lifted by applying only 25 N of force, then the MA of the machine is 8. This means that the machine multiplies the effort force 8 times, or reduces the effort by a factor of 8. The mechanical advantage of a simple machine not only indicates how much the effort force is multiplied but how much the effort needs to be moved in relation to the resistance distance. Mechanical advantage should not be confused with mechanical efficiency (ME) which compares the work output with the work input.

Possible Procedures(s): At the conclusion of a unit on simple machines ask the students to review the machines (tools) they studied, what advantage each machine was to those who use it, and how the ideal mechanical advantage of the machine could be computed. The ability to identify those factors that influence the mechanical advantage of a machine or tool is a prerequisite for success with this challenge. Changing a tool to increase its mechanical advantage could be as easy as increasing the length of the handles on a pair of pliers, altering the size of the handle section of a screwdriver or moving the fulcrum on a pry bar. Students have the option of physically changing a tool, and creating a reliable way of testing the effort required to use it, or design one on paper and prove, through the use of formulas, their modifications resulted in an increase in mechanical advantage. In either case, the students are still held accountable for demonstrating that their changes in tool design result in a device with a greater ideal mechanical advantage.

Precautions: Whenever students are involved in a construction project there is the possibility of a mishap, especially if tools, hot glue guns and other sharp objects are available. Students should be shown proper tool use and be expected to sign a safety contract. Students should wear safety glasses whenever working with sharp objects in close quarters.

While the problem solving techniques used by each team may be different, the diversity of thinking is beneficial for enhancing the problem solving repertoire of each student. Sharing is not only encouraged it is a strategy used throughout the program.

WEIGHT LIFTING

- Design a solution to a problem. *NSES*
- As a result of activities in grades 5-8, all students should develop an understanding of transfer of energy. *NSES*
- Identify appropriate problems for technological design. *NSES*
- Design a solution to a problem. *NSES*
- Implement a proposed design. *NSES*
- Apply and adapt a variety of appropriate strategies to solve problems. *NCTM*

The Context: Simple machines are devices which provide humans some advantage when performing task and do work with one movement. They can decrease the effort used, change the direction of the effort or change the speed. Some simple machines can perform two of these functions at the same time but not all three.

The Scenario: You have built a very large tree house and are now ready to furnish your creation. Building the tree house was done a little at a time so the materials were easy to handle. However, the furniture, like the couch, refrigerator, and 65 inch projection television weigh more than you can lift alone.

The Challenge: You assume that this task can be accomplished by using one or more simple machines and your engineering team suggests building a model to test out that idea. It is decided that an acceptable simulation would be a model machine capable of lifting a mass of 480 grams while using an effort of no more than one Newton (N).

The Limitations:
- Each team will have two class periods to complete this challenge.
- A sketch of the model and a list of needed materials must be completed before any equipment is gathered.
- Each team may use only the materials they request.
- Design changes to the original sketch must be done in ink along with a written explanation, describing the reason for the modifications.
- Each team may redesign and test its weight lifting system as long as time permits.
- Each team must construct a data collection format and graphical display of testing results

The Rules:
- The working model must be presented, along with the investigative data.
- Each team will have <u>one chance only</u> to demonstrate its model.
- Completed devices only have to lift the load off the table high enough to get a reading on the scale.
- Students should refer to the *Project Assessment Rubric* for guidance when designing, constructing, testing and presenting their projects.

TEACHER NOTES

Suggested Materials: This challenge is best given at the conclusion of a unit on simple machines. The materials used while completing a unit on simple machines should be made available for student use. Common materials will include a variety of pulleys, string, spring scales, levers, inclined planes, different sized wheels and so on. In addition, general classroom supplies will also be needed. For reference purposes, students will need a copy of the *Project Assessment Rubric.*

Suggested Use: This design brief was developed to serve as an application of student understanding following a unit on simple machines. There are six basic simple machines (lever, wheel and axle, inclined plane, wedge, pulley, and screw) and, by definition, each of these devices reduces the amount of effort required to perform a task. It should be anticipated that student engineering teams will select different ways of solving this problem. Regardless of what simple machine groups select the goal remains the same…to raise a 480 gram mass with only a one Newton force.

Ties to Content: Machines are found throughout out daily lives…from opening a door to cutting a string with a pair of scissors. Some machines are considered simple machines, devices that perform a task most with only one moving part. Other machines are more complex such as compound machines, two or more simple machines working together. In either case, machines make work easier by reducing the effort needed to perform a task. Actually, the same amount of work is done it just seems easier because of the distance trade off. For example, it is easier to move a rock by using a pry bar (first class lever), providing we move our hands as far from the fulcrum as possible. Depending on the position of the fulcrum, our hands will travel a greater distance than the rock but will require less effort than trying to move the rock without the pry bar. The amount of effort force reduced by using simple or complex machines is called mechanical advantage (MA). The mechanical advantage of a machine is the ratio of the resistance force, that which opposes the effort, to the effort force, that which is applied to the machine. For example, if a 400 N object can be lifted by applying only 25 N of force, then the MA of the machine is 8. This means that the machine multiplies the effort force 8 times, or reduces the effort by a factor of 8. The mechanical advantage of a simple machine not only indicates how much the effort force is multiplied but how much the effort needs to be moved in relation to the resistance distance. Mechanical advantage should not be confused with mechanical efficiency (ME) which compares the work output with the work input.

Possible Procedures(s): At the conclusion of a unit on simple machines ask the students to review the machines they studied, what advantage each machine was to those who used it, and how the mechanical advantage of each machine could be changed. The ability of students to identify factors that influence the mechanical advantage of a machine is a prerequisite for success. This challenge raises the bar by expecting students to modify a machine to perform according to specified criteria. Teachers could further extend this challenge by asking the teams to re-design their systems to lift twice as much mass (960 g) using same amount of effort (1 Newton).

Precautions: Whenever students are involved in a construction project there is the possibility of a mishap, especially if tools, hot glue guns and other sharp objects are available. Students should be shown proper tool use and be expected to sign a safety contract. Students should wear safety glasses whenever working with sharp objects in close quarters.

While the problem solving techniques used by each team may be different, the diversity of thinking is beneficial for enhancing the problem solving repertoire of each student. Sharing is not only encouraged it is a strategy used throughout the program.

FORENSIC SCIENCE

CREATING A FORENSIC STANDARD

- Design a solution to a problem. *NSES*
- Understand meanings of operations and how they relate to each other. *NCTM*
- Create and use representations to organize, record, and communicate mathematical ideas. *NCTM*
- Apply and adapt a variety of appropriate strategies to solve problems. *NCTM*
- Students adjust their use of spoken, written, and visual language (e.g., conventions, style, vocabulary) to communicate effectively with a variety of audiences and for different purposes. *NCTE*

The Context: Forensic science techniques and procedures are generally used in the search for answers to crime related questions.

The Scenario: While working alone one night in your CSI lab you are startled by Police Inspector Brown. He presents you with a gift of sorts...several very old bones which you quickly identify as a femur (thigh), a tibia (lower leg), and a radius (forearm). The Inspector explains that these bones were found by a contracting crew during the demolition of Moldy's Food Store on the west side of town. "We think the bones might belong to Knuckles Malone." From the sketchy police records, you find that Knuckles was 188 centimeters tall. This is not much to go on, but you decide that using a forensic standard might provide some additional help. You measure the bones and find that the femur is 57 cm long, the tibia is 46 cm, and the radius is 31 cm in length. The reference book on forensic standards provides you with the following information for males.

Bone	Length	Multiplied by	Add		Height of Body
Femur	57 cm	1.89	80.35	**Equals**	
Tibia	46 cm	2.38	78.61	**Equals**	
Radius	31 cm	3.29	86.1	**Equals**	

The Challenge: Could these bones belong to Knuckles Malone? Crunch the numbers then write a brief, data supported letter to Inspector Brown informing him of your conclusions. Your CSI Team now wonders if similar relationships exist between other body parts. For example, "Is there is a relationship between the length of a person's foot in centimeters and their height in centimeters?"

The Limitations:
- Each team will have three classes to complete this challenge at the teacher's discretion.
- Each team must list ten possible body part relationships including the foot/height connection.
- Each team must collect data outside of class and create a data display of their findings.

The Rules:
- All measurements must be made in centimeters and any relationships reported as a percentage.
- Each team must measure a minimum of 50 different people for their data bank.
- Each team member is responsible for crafting a data supported, summary of the investigation.
- Each team must present its findings to the class during the third class period.
- All team members must actively participate in the presentation.
- Students should refer to the *Team Presentation Rubric* when constructing their presentation.
- Each team must demonstrate three examples from their research showing how the size of one body part can be used to predict the size of another body part.

TEACHER NOTES

Suggested Materials: The only materials students require for this investigation are metric measuring tapes. It is suggested that students work in same sex teams for this investigation and that they be cautioned about being discrete when measuring. Students should have a copy of the *Team Presentation Rubric* to use as reference.

Suggested Use: This challenge is one in a series of investigations that concentrates on forensic science and the process skills associated with pursuing such inquiries. This challenge will help students understand how and why scientists establish standards, as these benchmarks can be used to evaluate new information or predict the outcome of new investigations. Students should be made aware that accurate measurements are critical and that averaging data is a necessity. This challenge can also be used to evaluate the reasonableness of data supported interpretations.

Ties to Content: Using established scientific standards is a commonplace occurrence for researchers in all areas of scientific inquiry. For example, meteorologists use accumulated weather records as one predictor of future weather patterns. The creation of forensic standards began on or about 1870 when a French anthropologist developed a system for measuring and comparing the bones of the human body. Numerous such standards are in use today some of which ensure that forensic scientists have tools that yield accurate results that will hold up in court. Examples of such standards include such things as computer tools for validating software, reference indices for identifying glass, blood-and-breath alcohol analysis procedures and fire debris analysis standards.

Possible Procedures(s): Initially, students must compile a list of ten possible body part relationships that might be used as a standard. In the challenge section of this design brief a forensic standard is given as an example of the relationship between body parts (the length of one's foot compared to one's height). If 20 or more data entries are averaged the comparison of foot length to height will be approximately 15 percent.

Precautions: No safety precautions are associated with this design brief. Teachers should however, emphasize care when measuring.

While the problem solving techniques used by each team may be different, the diversity of thinking is beneficial for enhancing the problem solving repertoire of each student. Sharing is not only encouraged it is a strategy used throughout the program.

SLOPPY COPY

> - Design a solution to a problem. *NSES*
> - Implement a proposed design. *NSES*
> - Apply and adapt a variety of appropriate strategies to solve problems. *NCTM*
> - Students adjust their use of spoken, written, and visual language (e.g., conventions, style, vocabulary) to communicate effectively with a variety of audiences and for different purposes. *NCTE*

The Context: Forensic science techniques and procedures are generally used in the search for answers to crime related questions.

The Scenario: Halloween has come and gone but some of your candy supply remained in your school locker… until someone broke in and took the sweet treats. Determined to get to the bottom of this crime you grab a roll of clear, transparent tape and look for some clues in the many smudges that cover the locker. You find a place that contains a complete set of chocolaty fingerprints. From their position on the locker you conclude that they are most likely from the right hand of the guilty party and the thumb print is the clearest. Pressing a piece of your tape over the print you capture a clear image of the right thumb.

The Challenge: After you successfully "lift" the thumb print it becomes apparent that you have a few other problems. Perhaps your investigation team can help you resolve these issues. Fingerprints can be very detailed and making comparisons will be difficult unless you can find a way to enlarge the prints. The second problem is that there are hundreds of students in your school. Without help, and an efficient way of collecting, processing or eliminating fingerprints, you'll never solve the mystery.

The Limitations:
- Each team will have three class periods to complete this challenge at the discretion of the teacher.
- Each team must conduct any research regarding fingerprints and print making <u>on its own time.</u>
- Each team must craft an action plan of how they intend to collect their investigative data.
- Action plans must be approved before investigating may begin.
- Each team will be responsible for creating a data display.
- Each team must develop a way to enlarge its fingerprints so as to make more accurate print comparisons.

The Rules:
- No team will be permitted to use a copy machine for any purpose.
- Each team will receive a copy of the mystery fingerprint on a piece of clear plastic.
- Each team must present its fingerprint research and the results of the mystery print investigation during the last class meeting.
- Each team member must respond to the following prompt: "If you had to repeat this investigation what would you change to make it more efficient. Explain why you would be an improvement."

TEACHER NOTES

Suggested Materials: Each team must have a copy of the mystery thumb print on clear acetate. First make multiple copies of the original print and then place these on the staging glass of a copy machine. Make a copy of the multiple prints on a single transparency. The individual **EVIDENCE PRINTS** can then be cut out and distributed to the student teams. Any other materials are the responsibility of the students.

Suggested Use: This challenge is one in a series of investigations that concentrates on forensic science and the process skills associated with pursuing such inquiries. It should be noted that students may not find irrefutable evidence in this forensic investigation. It is for this reason that a variety of interpretations may be valid and should be accepted so long as these contentions are supported by data.

Ties to Content: The term fingerprint refers to the impressions that are transferred from the dermal ridges on the pads of the fingertips other surfaces. These ridge impressions are generally classified into three major categories, whorls, loops and arches and these patterns are different for every human, even identical twins. This unique characteristic prompted the use of fingerprints as a personal identification method. The use of fingerprints as an identifying characteristic however had its beginning in ancient Babylon and in China where they were used on clay tablets used to record business transactions. In the years that followed many scholars noted the difference in prints but it was not until 1856 that Sir William Herschel, Chief Magistrate of the Hooghly district in Jungipoor, India used fingerprinting as a means to insure a person's honesty on contracts. But, his use was based on superstitious beliefs and not scientific evidence.

In 1880 Dr. Henry Faulds published his first paper about fingerprints in a scientific journal but it took a few more years for this concept to be adopted as a viable method of personal identification.

Whorl fingerprints are characterized by lines that go in circles. All lines come back to the place where they started.

Loop fingerprints are characterized by lines that start at one side of the print, rise and then turn and exit on the same side.

Arch fingerprints are characterized by lines that start on one side of the print, rise, fall and exit on the opposite side of the print.

Possible Procedures(s): Obtaining the mystery print is the initial concern. It is suggested that colleague be asked to donate their fingerprint for this challenge as this will increase the level of difficulty. Students will probably not consider including teachers in their data collection until they are unsuccessful with the student data. Fingerprints are usually collected by the carbon transfer method. This entails briskly rubbing a #2 pencil on a piece of scrap paper and then rubbing the finger tip across the carbon deposit. This transfers the carbon to the finger tip. In the next step, clear transparent tape is use to "lift" the print from the finger. The tape can then be placed on a clean post-it, a 3X5 card or a transparency.

Students should first classify their collected prints by type and then more closely inspect those that are in the same category as the **EVIDENCE PRINT**. Fingerprints can be easily enlarged is by placing the transparency containing the print on overhead projector. Comparing the mystery print with "suspect prints" can be made side by side or by overlaying the prints. Prints can also be enlarged if they are made, in ink, directly on a white latex balloon. When the balloon is inflated the size of the fingerprint is automatically enlarged.

Precautions: No safety precautions are associated with this design brief.

While the problem solving techniques used by each team may be different, the diversity of thinking is beneficial for enhancing the problem solving repertoire of each student. Sharing is not only encouraged it is a strategy used throughout the program.

STRANGE CONCOCTION (PART 1)

> - Design and conduct a scientific investigation. *NSES*
> - Use appropriate tools, and techniques to gather, analyze, and interpret data. *NSES*
> - Develop descriptions, explanations, predictions, and models using evidence. *NSES*
> - Think critically and logically to make the relationships between evidence and explanations. *NSES*
> - Apply and adapt a variety of appropriate strategies to solve problems. *NCTM*
> - Students adjust their use of spoken, written, and visual language (e.g., conventions, style, vocabulary) to communicate effectively with a variety of audiences and for different purposes. *NCTE*

The Context: Forensic science techniques and procedures are generally used in the search for answers to crime related questions.

The Scenario: "**Kids Challenge**", a popular children's program designed around team building and tests of physical endurance, uses a risk reward system for their competitions. One of the risks associated with **not** successfully completing a task is that the entire team gets "*slimed*".

The show is about to enter it's second season and the production crew is frantic because the chemical company responsible for producing the slime has gone out of business leaving only a small sample of their unique, gooey, green product.

The Challenge: Your research team has been given the challenge of recreating the original slime for the television program. A review of the abandon chemical lab is not too helpful since the scientists took their notebooks with them. There are some liquids in bottles but conditions in the abandon chemical lab have caused the labels to deteriorate and fall off. You collect a sample of the six different liquids and label them #1 - #6.

You return to your research facility with the six liquids and a small sample of the original slime. Remember, your task is to duplicate the original slime. Could these different liquids hold the key to your success and will these liquids affect the slime?

The Limitations:
- Two class periods will be devoted to Part 1 of this investigation at the discretion of the teacher.
- Each team must design a plan of action before gathering any materials.
- Action plans must be approved before investigating may begin.
- Each team must design a data display to communicate its findings.
- Each team will receive the same materials. No other materials may be used.

The Rules:
- Each team member must keep a science journal that details each step of the investigation.
- Each team will receive only two tablespoons of slime. Extra slime will not be available.
- Each team must present its investigative results during the second class meeting.
- Students should refer to the *Team Presentation Rubric* and as they prepare their presentations.

TEACHER NOTES

Suggested Materials: Each team of students should receive a sample of slime, a set of the bottled liquids (labeled #1-#6), waxed paper or freezer paper and a supply of mixing sticks. Additional items would include hand lenses, safety glasses and paper towels. The six liquids include water, alcohol, dilute ammonia, vinegar, iodine and a mixture of water with 15 drops of green food coloring. The slime used in this challenge is not a new concoction and is basically cornstarch, water and food coloring commonly known as Oobleck. Our slime mixture varies slightly in that we suggest using equal amounts of cornstarch and baking soda. This mixture will react with the iodine (starch reaction – turns black) as well as with the vinegar (chemical reaction producing bubbles of CO_2). This bubbling is often a subtle difference for many students and helps teachers identify the best observers. To make the slime, just add water and a few drops of food coloring to a 50-50 mixture of cornstarch and baking soda until it is uniform in color, has the consistency of soft serve ice cream and stiffens when pressure is applied. If the mixture gets too runny simply add more cornstarch and baking soda until the desired consistency is obtained. Students should have a copy of the *Team Presentation Rubric* to use as reference.

Suggested Use: This challenge is one in a series of investigations that concentrates on forensic science and the process skills associated with pursuing such inquiries. This investigation presents an opportunity for students to develop a reasonable procedure for testing the affect unknown liquids have on an unknown semi-solid (slime). Students should be cautioned about making any assumptions about the materials with which they will work. It is also critical that they make and record accurate observations and draw reasonable inferences. It should be noted, the need for creating an accurate record of all procedures and observations will become abundantly clear during the second part of this challenge. It is during this phase that students are expected to apply the collected data as they continue analyzing the slime. It should also be noted that students may not find irrefutable evidence in this forensic investigation. It is for this reason that a variety of interpretations may be valid and should be accepted so long as these contentions are supported by data.

Ties to Content: This challenge is tied more closely to the process skills than it is to any specific content. To be certain, there is a connection to analytical chemistry, but in a more global sense, the basic process skills of observing, inferring, classifying and communicating are absolutely critical to the successful completion of the challenge.

Possible Procedures(s): The procedures devised by students will probably vary greatly because of the open ended nature of this challenge. Regardless, it is a requirement that each testing procedure be reasonable and well thought out. Haphazardly mixing "things" together is unacceptable. Students will also be required to collect accurate data and create appropriate data displays. It should also be noted that while the procedure, the testing and the data collection/displays are the responsibility of the "team", the processing and the interpretation should be the responsibility of each individual student.

Precautions: Students will be expected to wear appropriate eye protection during this investigation. Care should be taken when using any chemical. Check the MSDS sheet for each chemical prior to use. Should these sheets not be available check the Flinn Scientific Catalog or the Flinn Scientific website, www.flinnsci.com.

While the problem solving techniques used by each team may be different, the diversity of thinking is beneficial for enhancing the problem solving repertoire of each student. Sharing is not only encouraged it is a strategy used throughout the program.

STRANGE CONCOCTION (PART 2)

> - Design and conduct a scientific investigation. *NSES*
> - Use appropriate tools, and techniques to gather, analyze, and interpret data. *NSES*
> - Develop descriptions, explanations, predictions, and models using evidence. *NSES*
> - Think critically and logically to make the relationships between evidence and explanations. *NSES*
> - Apply and adapt a variety of appropriate strategies to solve problems. *NCTM*
> - Students adjust their use of spoken, written, and visual language (e.g., conventions, style, vocabulary) to communicate effectively with a variety of audiences and for different purposes. *NCTE*

The Context: Forensic science techniques and procedures are generally used in the search for answers to crime related questions.

The Scenario: Your research team just conducted an exhaustive survey of the original slime and the six unknown liquids found at the abandon chemical laboratory. You have gathered many observations but have not solved the mystery. You decide that there must be something missing and you return to the lab to look for additional clues.

The Challenge: After searching for most of the day one member of your team locates a wall safe behind a picture. A locksmith is called in and within a few minutes cracks open the safe. Inside you find five unlabeled containers, each holding a white powder. "Great! More unknowns", you exclaim. But, at least you have something to work with. You label the containers A-E and return to your research facility to continue the quest of developing slime.

The Limitations:
- Two class periods will be devoted to Part 2 of this investigation at the discretion of the teacher.
- Each team must design a plan of action before gathering any materials.
- Action plans must be approved before investigating may begin.
- Each team must design a data display to communicate their findings.
- Each team will receive the same materials. No other materials may be used.

The Rules:
- Each team member must continue detailed journaling of each step taken by the team in the attempts to recreate the slime.
- Each team will again receive two tablespoons of slime. Extra slime will not be available.
- Each team will be expected to share its data supported conclusions with other researchers during a presentation in the second class meeting.
- Students should refer to the *Team Presentation Rubric* and as they prepare their presentations.
- Each team member must write a <u>data supported</u> letter to the production crew of "**Kids Challenge**" describing the formula for creating slime.

TEACHER NOTES

Suggested Materials: The materials for Strange Concoction (Part 2) are the same as in Strange Concoction (Part 1) with the addition of the five unknown white powders labeled A-E. Prepare these powders for bulk distribution with an appropriately labeled plastic spoon in each. While most of these powders can vary based upon availability, the two essential powders, the cornstarch and the baking soda, must be present. The other powders could be such things as baby powder, flour, Plaster of Paris, diatomaceous earth, powdered clay, powdered chalk, powdered sugar and so on. Students should have a copy of the *Team Presentation Rubric* to use as reference.

Suggested Use: This challenge is one in a series of investigations that concentrates on forensic science and the process skills associated with pursuing such inquiries. This investigation presents an opportunity for students to develop a reasonable procedure for testing the affect unknown liquids have on an unknown semi-solid (slime). Students should be cautioned about making any assumptions about the materials with which they will work. It is also critical that they make and record accurate observations and draw reasonable inferences. It should be noted that the need for creating an accurate record of all procedures and observations will become abundantly clear during the second part of this challenge. It is during this phase that students are expected to apply the data as they continue analyzing the slime. It should also be noted that students may not find irrefutable evidence in this forensic investigation. It is for this reason that a variety of interpretations may be valid and should be accepted so long as they are supported by data.

Ties to Content: This challenge is tied more closely to the process skills more that it is to any specific content. To be certain, there is a connection to analytical chemistry, but in a more global sense, the basic and integrated process skills are absolutely critical to the successful or justifiable completion of the challenge. Of particular importance are the students' abilities to apply the information gathered during part one of this two part challenge. It is most important that their conclusions are supported by the data they collected. Hopefully, there will be differences of opinion regarding the formulation of slime as this presents a wonderful opportunity for students to revisit, reprocess and evaluate their data as well as the data of other teams. Student discussions such as these should be encouraged as learning occurs through such discrepancies.

Possible Procedures(s): The procedures devised by students will, in all likelihood, vary greatly because of the open ended nature of this challenge. Regardless, it is a requirement that each testing procedure be reasonable and well thought out. Haphazardly mixing "things" together is unacceptable. Students will also be required to collect accurate data and create appropriate data displays. It should also be noted that while the procedure, the testing and the data collection/displays are the responsibility of the "team", the processing and the interpretation should be the responsibility of each individual student.

Precautions: Students will be expected to wear appropriate eye protection during this investigation. Care should be taken when using any chemical. Check the MSDS sheet for each chemical prior to use. Should these sheets not be available check the Flinn Scientific Catalog or the Flinn Scientific website, www.flinnsci.com.

Extension Activity: Students are probably going to make some inferences about the origin of the powders and the liquids. Challenge the students to pursue their inferences by creating slime at home from what they "think" are the essential components. They could then bring in their sample and compare it to the original. It is strongly suggested that student created procedures and formula be checked for potential safety issues prior to giving them permission to continue.

While the problem solving techniques used by each team may be different, the diversity of thinking is beneficial for enhancing the problem solving repertoire of each student. Sharing is not only encouraged it is a strategy used throughout the program.

TOOTH TROUBLE

> - Design a solution to a problem. *NSES*
> - Implement a proposed design. *NSES*
> - Apply and adapt a variety of appropriate strategies to solve problems. *NCTM*
> - Students adjust their use of spoken, written, and visual language (e.g., conventions, style, vocabulary) to communicate effectively with a variety of audiences and for different purposes. *NCTE*

The Context: Forensic science techniques and procedures are generally used in the search for answers to crime related questions.

The Scenario: Lunchtime! Finally! It was a very long morning and Justin was famished. Sitting down at the table he opened his brown bag and removed the delicious contents one item at a time. A ham and cheese sandwich (his favorite), a zip lock bag of carrots, two cream-filled cupcakes, and a big red apple…**WITH A BIG BITE OUT OF IT!!!!** This was the last straw. Two weeks ago his cherry pie was half gone and last Tuesday his cheese stick was chomped in the middle. He needed to get to the bottom of this and he had to do it now.

The Challenge: You gather your forensic research team together and tell them about Justin's problem. "There must be a way to identify the culprit", you comment. "But how?" In true CSI fashion your team decides to "follow the evidence" which leads directly to the mouth of the problem. Could teeth marks be a personal identifier like fingerprints?

The Limitations:
- Each team will be allowed three class periods to complete this challenge at the discretion of the teacher.
- Each team is completely responsible for its own materials.
- Each team must create an action plan, and have that plan approved, before starting the investigation.
- Each team must conduct research on this topic and note all references in a bibliography.
- Each team must design a "process" to collect and compare teeth prints.
- Teams must also craft a "fair test" procedure for verifying that teeth prints are, or are not, personal identifiers like fingerprints.

The Rules:
- Each team must present a process for teeth comparison, a "fair test" procedure and an interpretation of the results to the remainder of the class during the third class meeting.
- Students should refer to the *Team Presentation Rubric* as they design their presentations.
- Each team member must write a brief, <u>data supported</u> letter to Justin explaining what the research team did, what was found, and how he might lay a trap to catch the culprit who has been eating part of his lunch.

TEACHER NOTES

Suggested Materials: There are no teacher supplied materials associated with this design brief. Students should have a copy of the *Team Presentation Rubric* to use as reference.

Suggested Use: This challenge is one in a series of investigations that concentrates on forensic science and the process skills associated with pursuing such inquiries. This challenge presents an opportunity for students to develop a reliable procedure for gathering data then continues by asking students to verify if the human attribute being observed could be used as a personal identifier. It is also anticipated that students will make and record accurate observations and draw reasonable inferences.

It should be noted that students may not find irrefutable evidence in this forensic investigation. It is for this reason that a variety of interpretations may be valid and should be accepted so long as these contentions are supported by data.

Ties to Content: Humans are supplied with two sets of teeth. The first set, the deciduous or primary set, are present in early childhood. As we age these deciduous teeth are pushed out and replaced by the permanent set.

Much like fingerprints, the arrangement of the permanent teeth in adults is unique to each individual and can be used as a personal identifier. About eight percent of the time teeth impressions are used by forensic dentists to identify unknown victims.

Possible Procedures(s): The procedures devised by students will, in all likelihood, vary greatly because of the open ended nature of this challenge. This challenge is in two related sections. In part one students need to research and develop a way to capture teeth impressions such as biting a thick candy bar or making these impressions in a ball of clay or plasticine. For sanitary purposes, it is suggested that if the latter procedure is used that the clay or plasticine be contained in a clean plastic bag.

Once this impression process has been developed the students then need to develop a way to verify that this human characteristic can be used as a forensic tool. It is suggested that students be given a sufficient amount of time to discuss their procedures and their findings. Additional time may also be needed for students to gather research related to this human characteristic.

Precautions: There are no safety predictions associated with this design brief.

While the problem solving techniques used by each team may be different, the diversity of thinking is beneficial for enhancing the problem solving repertoire of each student. Sharing is not only encouraged it is a strategy used throughout the program.

HAIRY SCARY

> - Design a solution to a problem. *NSES*
> - Use appropriate tools, and techniques to gather, analyze, and interpret data. *NSES*
> - Apply and adapt a variety of appropriate strategies to solve problems. *NCTM*
> - Students adjust their use of spoken, written, and visual language (e.g., conventions, style, vocabulary) to communicate effectively with a variety of audiences and for different purposes. *NCTE*

The Context: Forensic science techniques and procedures are generally used in the search for answers to crime related questions.

The Scenario: Mr. Garfield was unceremoniously handcuffed and lead away to the police station. His wife was missing and he was the prime suspect. After obtaining a warrant, the crime lab carefully searched the entire house collecting and documenting a number of items considered to be trace evidence. All of the forensic samples were immediately taken to the laboratory in sealed containers including a number of different hair samples lifted from Mr. Garfield's car and his blue business suit.

The Challenge: You are a member of an intern team working in the forensic science laboratory. A number of crime scene items have been delivered for analysis and your group has been assigned the task of determining the origin of the hair samples.

The Limitations:
- Each team will have two class periods to complete this challenge at the discretion of the teacher.
- Each team must research this aspect of forensic science and document the resources in bibliographical form.
- Each team will have access to the same number and type of hair samples.
- Each team will be responsible for selecting or supplying any materials it deems necessary.

The Rules:
- Each team must create a poster displaying its hair research and hair investigation.
- Each team must craft a presentation of its research, laboratory procedures and investigative findings.
- Students should refer to the *Team Presentation Rubric* as they design their presentations.
- Each team member must write a data supported letter to the Chief of Police reporting the results of the trace evidence investigation.

TEACHER NOTES

Suggested Materials: Teachers will need to supply a variety of hair samples for the students to use. It is suggested that these samples be labeled, **EVIDENCE** and kept in separate plastic bags. Hair samples should be light in color (if possible) and include: dog hair, cat hair and two different samples of human hair. In addition to the Evidence Samples, each student team will need a set of labeled, permanent hair samples slides for comparative purposes. The permanent slides should be labeled for the animal of origin (DOG, CAT, HUMAN) and are easy to create. Place a hair sample on a glass or plastic slide, cover it with a light coating of five minute epoxy and cover with another slide. If possible, these Evidence Samples should be from different sources than the trace evidence.

Students should have access to general laboratory equipment, microscopes and related supplies in particular. In addition, students should have a copy of the *Team Presentation Rubric* to use as reference.

Suggested Use: This challenge was crafted as an application activity for a unit on microscope study or as a research/problem solving quest with a forensic twist. It should be noted that students may not find irrefutable evidence in this forensic investigation. It is for this reason that a variety of interpretations may be valid and should be accepted so long as these contentions are supported by data.

Ties to Content: Hair can present itself as indirect or circumstantial evidence in a court of law. This evidence would be used in conjunction with other forensic evidence. A forensic scientist could say that two hairs are similar but not the same unless the hair root was present and the DNA analysis could be performed.

- hair has a tough, outer scale structure and the scales point towards the tip or the hair
- the scales vary between animals
- hair has a rigid intermediate cortex structure that provides shape and color to the hair
- There are cells in the center of the hair called the medulla
- The medulla varies between animals
- There are four types of medullas, continuous, interrupted, fragmented, and absent.
- The shape of the hair can be straight, curly, or kinky. This depends on its roundness.

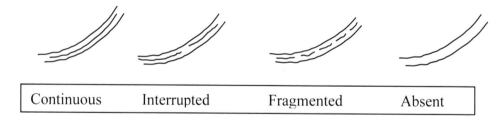

| Continuous | Interrupted | Fragmented | Absent |

Possible Procedures(s): This challenge, as noted, is an application lab for a unit in microscope study. As such, students need to be conversant with the use of the microscope and with the preparation of wet mount slides. Students should begin their challenge by researching hair as an aspect of forensic investigations. Once students have documented how to identify different hair samples they can turn their attention to comparing the prepared hair samples with the crime scene trace evidence.

Precautions: Students will be expected to wear appropriate eye protection during this investigation. Care should be taken when using any chemical. Check the MSDS sheet for each chemical prior to use. Should these sheets not be available check the Flinn Scientific Catalog or the Flinn Scientific website, www.flinnsci.com.

While the problem solving techniques used by each team may be different, the diversity of thinking is beneficial for enhancing the problem solving repertoire of each student. Sharing is not only encouraged it is a strategy used throughout the program.

I'M IMPRESSED

- Design a solution to a problem. *NSES*
- Use appropriate tools, and techniques to gather, analyze, and interpret data. *NSES*
- Apply and adapt a variety of appropriate strategies to solve problems. *NCTM*
- Students adjust their use of spoken, written, and visual language (e.g., conventions, style, vocabulary) to communicate effectively with a variety of audiences and for different purposes. *NCTE*

The Context: Forensic science techniques and procedures are generally used in the search for answers to crime related questions.

The Scenario: The vending machine at your school was broken into during the weekend and the all the money and peanut butter cups were taken.

The Challenge: Your investigation team has been given the responsibility of finding the perpetrator of the crime. A preliminary investigation revealed the following:

- The machine was refilled late Friday afternoon by the custodian, Mr. Grimis, an older fellow who is suspected of having a gambling problem.
- Mr. Secondplace, the custodian's temporary assistant reported the incident to the principal at 7:15 this morning.
- The school is undergoing some minor renovations and much of the work occurs after hours and during the weekend by a construction crew consisting of three workers and a foreman.
- The main control arm of the machine appears to have been gripped with a tool of some kind and twisted off.
- The broken control arm shaft was lying on the floor next to the machine.

The Limitations:
- Each team will have two class periods to complete this challenge at the discretion of the teacher.
- All teams must share the science equipment.
- Each team must supply any additional materials needed.
- Each team must have an approved action plan prior gathering any materials.

The Rules:
- Each team will have access to a variety of tools that could have been used in the break-in.
- Each team must create a display of some kind to communicate their findings.
- Each team member is responsible for writing a brief, illustrated report to the police detailing the investigative findings.

TEACHER NOTES

Suggested Materials: In preparation of this challenge teachers will need to gather a variety of different pliers, or other tools, that could have been used in the commission of this crime. Each tool should be labeled with the name of the owner. These names can come directly from the scenario or could be assumed to be part of that story, such as the contractors and the foreman.

In addition to the tools a supply of ½ wooden dowels approximately 2 inches long need to be supplied as well. Each student team will need one dowel for each tool examined. Small rolls of clay or plasticine, wrapped in plastic to prevent the tools from sticking to the material, might be used in place of the wooden test dowels. Soft wax is also a viable substitution to wooden dowels.

Prior to the start of the lab select one of the tools, place a wooden dowel in the inner jaw location (as close to the pivot point as possible) and squeeze down hard creating a tool impression on the surface of the dowel. Label this dowel as **EVIDENCE**. This dowel will represent the control arm shaft from the soda machine.

Students will also need access to general science equipment, including hand lenses and dissection microscopes if available.

Suggested Use: This challenge is one in a series of investigations that concentrates on forensic science and the process skills associated with pursuing such inquiries. This challenge presents an opportunity for students to develop a reasonable procedure for creating and comparing tool impressions. It is anticipated that students will make and record accurate observations, draw reasonable inferences and craft data supported conclusions. It should be noted that students may not find irrefutable evidence in this forensic investigation. It is for this reason that a variety of interpretations may be valid and should be accepted so long as these contentions are supported by data.

Ties to Content: Hand tools, generally made of iron or steel, often leave marks behind after their use. Forensic scientists have classified these marks into three categories:

- *cut marks,* like those that would be created by a saw, knife or wire cutters.
- *impressions*, such as those left by a hammer, crowbar or pliers.
- *scratch marks*, which could be made by a large variety of things being dragged across a softer surface.

Tool marks, like other forensic trace evidence, can provide investigators with possible links to suspects.

Possible Procedures(s): Carefully comparing the **EVIDENCE** with the impressions created by the variety of suspect tools is the most straight forward approach to this investigation.

Precautions: Whenever students are involved in a construction project there is the possibility of a mishap, especially if tools or other sharp objects are available. Students should be shown proper tool use and be expected to sign a safety contract. Students should wear safety glasses whenever working with sharp objects in close quarters. Appropriate safety contracts can be obtained from Flinn Scientific at www.flinnsci.com

While the problem solving techniques used by each team may be different, the diversity of thinking is beneficial for enhancing the problem solving repertoire of each student. Sharing is not only encouraged it is a strategy used throughout the program.

LIP SERVICE

> - Design a solution to a problem. *NSES*
> - Implement a proposed design. *NSES*
> - Use appropriate tools, and techniques to gather, analyze, and interpret data. *NSES*
> - Apply and adapt a variety of appropriate strategies to solve problems. *NCTM*
> - Students adjust their use of spoken, written, and visual language (e.g., conventions, style, vocabulary) to communicate effectively with a variety of audiences and for different purposes. *NCTE*

The Context: Forensic science techniques and procedures are generally used in the search for answers to crime related questions.

The Scenario: A businessman was hosting a dinner party for prospective clients in the private dining room of *Laura's*, a local restaurant. The Governor's wife returned from the rest room to report that her wallet was missing from her handbag which she had placed on the counter top near the sink. She stated that she heard someone enter the rest room, spend about a minute there and then leave, possibly with her wallet.

      The police found a tissue on the counter with lipstick stains on it. The victim remembered that the tissue was not there when she placed her handbag on the counter, as she had noticed the cleanliness of the room.

The Challenge: Your intern CSI team just received an emergency call from the police asking that you come to the *Laura's* ASAP. No guests have been allowed to leave and the only trace evidence, the lipstick stained tissue, has not been moved.

      On the short drive to the restaurant you wonder how you are supposed to solve this crime. Could lip prints be personal identifiers like fingerprints or teeth impressions?

The Limitations:
- Each team will be allowed three class periods to complete this challenge at the discretion of the teacher.
- Each team must create an action plan, and have that plan approved, before starting the investigation.
- Each team must design a process to collect and compare lip prints.
- Each team must conduct research on this topic and note all references in a bibliography.
- Teams must also craft a "fair test" procedure for verifying that lip prints are, or are not, personal identifiers like fingerprints.

The Rules:
- Each team must present its lip print investigation and interpretation of results to the remainder of the class.
- Students should refer to the *Team Presentation Rubric* as they design their presentations.
- Each team member must write a brief, <u>data supported,</u> illustrated letter to the police that contains a review of the research and the results of the investigation.
- Each team must speculate about what additional tests could be done to help narrow the search for the culprit or verify current suspicions.

TEACHER NOTES

Suggested Materials: The materials for this challenge include lipstick, cotton swabs, Post-Its, wipes or cold cream to help remove lipstick and paper toweling. Students will also require a copy of the *Team Presentation Rubric* for reference purposes. An **EVIDENCE PRINT** needs to be made and copies distributed to each student team. One way this can be accomplished is to have a student secretly create a lip print and then copy that print for distribution.

Suggested Use: This challenge is one in a series of investigations that concentrates on forensic science and the process skills associated with pursuing such inquiries. This challenge presents an opportunity for students to develop a reasonable procedure for creating and comparing lip prints. It is anticipated that students will make and record accurate observations, draw reasonable inferences and craft data supported conclusions. It should be noted that students may not find irrefutable evidence in this forensic investigation. It is for this reason that a variety of interpretations may be valid and should be accepted so long as these contentions are supported by data.

Ties to Content: The human body has a number of individual identifiers such as DNA, fingerprints, retina patterns and teeth impressions. Lip prints can also be helpful in forensic investigations but they are not as definitive as other identifiers and can only be used as a preliminary screening method.

There are five common lip print patterns in the area of cheilocopy (lip print study). These patterns include: diamond groves, branching groves, rectangular groves, short vertical groves and long vertical groves. These patterns do not change during a person's life but, to this point, have not yet been established as a credible way to identify a specific individual. For the present, lip prints can only be used to classify an individual into one of five possible groups. If an individual's lip print happens to be in the same group as the crime scene evidence then the only reasonable conclusion that can be drawn is that the individual is a "possible suspect" and nothing more.

Possible Procedures(s): Generally the procedure followed in this challenge is a simple comparison between the trace evidence collected at the crime scene and lip prints from all the individuals at the restaurant (everyone in the class). Only those who's lip print pattern is similar to that of the evidence will considered a suspect.

Enlist the help of the female students in your class. To create a lip print the students will need to first apply lipstick to their lips using a clean cotton swab. They then need press their lips together in a back and forth motion to evenly distribute the lipstick. The lips are then blotted in a single, quick motion on a folded Post-It. Ask students to print their names on their lip print so that it can be identified during the comparative investigation.

Precautions: For sanitary reasons students should use a cotton swab to apply lipstick. In addition, they should be cautioned to not "double swipe" but use a clean cotton swab if they need to apply more lipstick. Students should also be given the option of using their own lipstick.

While the problem solving techniques used by each team may be different, the diversity of thinking is beneficial for enhancing the problem solving repertoire of each student. Sharing is not only encouraged it is a strategy used throughout the program.

SUSPICIOUS SALINE

- Design a solution to a problem. *NSES*
- Implement a proposed design. *NSES*
- Use appropriate tools, and techniques to gather, analyze, and interpret data. *NSES*
- Apply and adapt a variety of appropriate strategies to solve problems. *NCTM*
- Students adjust their use of spoken, written, and visual language (e.g., conventions, style, vocabulary) to communicate effectively with a variety of audiences and for different purposes. *NCTE*

The Context: Forensic science techniques and procedures are generally used in the search for answers to crime related questions.

The Scenario: Inspector Goodling of the Maine CSI Unit was called to the Ocean Point Municipal Building early on a Sunday morning. Outside the rear entrance, in a tidal pool not far from the building, lie Bob Guessberg, the president of Ocean Point's Municipal Union and an avid scuba diver. Bob was dressed in his diving outfit complete with tanks, flippers, spear gun and mask...and dead as a door nail.

Inspector Goodling was immediately suspicious, since Bob never went diving alone. She ordered a complete investigation including an autopsy, which the medical examiner began as soon as the body was delivered to the morgue. The cause of death was determined to be drowning, since water was found in Guessberg's lungs. What kind of water was it?

The Challenge: Inspector Goodling was suspicious and suspected foul play since inside the Municipal Building were three large tanks containing brine (salt solution) for use on the county roads during the winter season. Each tank contained a different brine concentration. Samples of ocean water, brine (three different concentrations) and water from Guessberg's lungs were sent to your CSI lab. Inspector Goodling is relying on your expertise to provide help with this investigation.

The Limitations:
- Each team will be allowed two class periods to complete this challenge at the discretion of the teacher.
- Each team will have access to the five different solutions collected at the crime scene as well as distilled or bottled spring water.
- Each team will have access to all science equipment.
- Each team must craft a "fair test" procedure, and have that procedure approved, prior to gathering materials.
- Each team must develop appropriate data displays to communicate its findings.

The Rules:
- Each team must present its "fair test" procedure and findings to the other CSI teams.
- Students should refer to the *Team Presentation Rubric* as they design their presentations.
- Each team member must write a brief, <u>data supported,</u> report to Inspector Goodling that contains a review of the research, the results of laboratory investigation and a probable cause of death.
- Each team must speculate about what additional tests might be done to develop stronger evidence.

TEACHER NOTES

Suggested Materials: This investigation will require five different salt solutions, bottled water, graduated cylinders, several syringes, a pan balance and gram weights, an electronic balance (if available) and an eye dropper.

The various salt solutions should be made with kosher salt as this produces a clear solution regardless of the concentration. For ease of distribution and cost it is suggested that old water bottles be used to store the different solutions. These bottles should be labeled: **LUNG WATER, BRINE SOLUTION #1, BRINE SOLUTION #2, BRINE SOLUTION #3, OCEAN WATER** and **DISTILLED WATER**. The lung water should be the same concentration as one of the other samples. It is not important which solution is chosen since the CSI report is data based and is dependent upon the accuracy of student laboratory work.

Students will also require a copy of the *Team Presentation Rubric* for reference purposes.

Suggested Use: This challenge is one in a series of investigations that concentrates on forensic science and the process skills associated with pursuing such inquiries. This challenge presents an opportunity for students to develop a reasonable procedure for ascertaining the salt concentration in a variety of solutions. It is anticipated that students will make and record accurate observations, draw reasonable inferences and craft data supported conclusions. It should be noted that students may not find irrefutable evidence in this forensic investigation. It is for this reason that a variety of interpretations may be valid and should be accepted so long as these contentions are supported by data.

Ties to Content: Solutions can be solids, liquids, gases, or combinations thereof. They are homogeneous mixtures in which the solute particles are evenly distributed throughout the solvent particles. In this challenge, the salt water solution is composed of salt (solute) and water (solvent). The salt is an ionic compound which dissociates in water, meaning that it breaks down into positive and negative ions. This occurs partly because of the polar nature of water, meaning that the molecules have a slightly positive end and a slightly negative end. The positive end of the water molecule attracts the negative ions of the salt, and the negative end of the water molecule attracts the positive ions of the salt, causing the salt to dissociate.

The concentration of a solution can be indicated in a variety of ways, including percent by mass, which is a ratio of the mass of the solute to the mass of the solution (mass of solute/mass of solution X 100). As the concentration of a solution increases so does its density.

Possible Procedures(s): There are several ways that students could determine the most concentrated salt solution but weighing may be the most straight forward. Using pure water as the standard (1 ml = 1 cc = 1 g) students could weigh out equal volumes of the two salt solutions, the heavier of the two would be the most concentrated.

Precautions: Students will be expected to wear appropriate eye protection during this investigation. Care should be taken when using any chemical. Check the MSDS sheet for each chemical prior to use. Should these sheets not be available check the Flinn Scientific Catalog or the Flinn Scientific website, www.flinnsci.com. Click on the chemistry link and then the MSDS link.

While the problem solving techniques used by each team may be different, the diversity of thinking is beneficial for enhancing the problem solving repertoire of each student. Sharing is not only encouraged it is a strategy used throughout the program.

SO, WHAT'S BUGGIN' YOU?

- Develop descriptions, explanations, predictions, and models using evidence. *NSES*
- Think critically and logically to make the relationships between evidence and explanations. *NSES*
- Use appropriate tools, and techniques to gather, analyze, and interpret data. *NSES*
- Apply and adapt a variety of appropriate strategies to solve problems. *NCTM*
- Students adjust their use of spoken, written, and visual language (e.g., conventions, style, vocabulary) to communicate effectively with a variety of audiences and for different purposes. *NCTE*

The Context: Forensic science techniques and procedures are generally used in the search for answers to crime related questions.

The Scenario: A body has been found near a sheltered watering hole in the Australian outback. By the time you arrive most of the Blowflies have come and gone, but many other insects are busy with the body. One of your colleagues notices Hide Beetles and Carcass Beetles. These creatures prefer their food source slightly dried, a condition quickly accomplished in the outback.

Although dead, the body seems almost alive with activity as much of the surface appears to be moving. Your eyes are drawn toward the numerous glitters of deep red. You lean in closer and immediately identify these miniature stop signs to be the heads of dead Rove Beetles. The Rove Beetles arrived early in the decomposition cycle but their larvae do not appear until a few weeks into decomposition cycle. These numerous larvae not only feed on the corpse but serve as a food supply for the Carcass Beetles as well

It started to look like this body had been near the watering hole for some time. Additional evidence for this contention is provided by the presence of a Hairy Maggot Blowfly. Cheese Skipper Larvae and Black Soldier Fly Larvae are also present both in the third instar.

The Challenge: You, and your investigation team, have been called in to determine the approximate age of the corpse.

The Limitations:
- Each team will have two class periods to complete this challenge at the discretion of the teacher.
- Each team must conduct research on this topic and note all references in a bibliography.
- Each team must devise an illustrated data display to communicate the results of its investigation.

The Rules:
- Each team must use the information from the scenario and the Forensic Entomology Cards to make a reasonable estimate of how long the body has been dead.
- The concluding statement must make reference to the collected data.
- Students should refer to the *Team Presentation Rubric* as they design their presentations.

TEACHER NOTES

Suggested Materials: The only materials associated with this challenge is a copy of the entomology cards for each research team. The time allotment for this challenge can be reduced by eliminating the research component. Since students still need this information to proceed, it is suggested that copies of the content section, found below, be made for each student team. In addition, students should have a copy of the *Team Presentation Rubric* to use as reference.

Suggested Use: This challenge is one in a series of investigations that concentrates on forensic science and the process skills associated with pursuing such inquiries. It is anticipated that students will make and record accurate observations, draw reasonable inferences and craft data supported conclusions. It should be noted that students may not find irrefutable evidence in this forensic investigation. It is for this reason that a variety of interpretations may be valid and should be accepted so long as these contentions are supported by data.

Ties to Content: Forensic entomology uses the presence of insects, and insect stages, on the human corpse to determine how long the body has been dead. Most cases using this technique are at least 72 hours old. Prior to 72 hours other techniques are more accurate than insect evidence. However, after three days, insect evidence is often the most accurate and sometimes the only method of determining elapsed time since death. An entomologist will always estimate a *range* of time for the death or *PMI* (post-mortem interval). This *PMI* will vary from a few hours for bodies that have been dead for a day or two, to perhaps several months for bodies that have been dead for several years.

The first method of using insects, noting the succession of different species, is based upon the fact that the human body evolves from the fresh state to dry bones in a matter of weeks or months depending on geographic region. During this decomposition, the remains go through rapid physical, biological, and chemical changes, and the different stages of decomposition are attractive to different species of insects.

The second method, using the age and development of specific insect larvae, can give an approximate PMI to a day or less and is used in the first few weeks after death. The insects like Blowflies, are those that arrive first on the corpse. They are attracted to the corpse soon after death and lay their eggs on the corpse, usually in a wound or a body opening like the mouth, nose, or ears. The development of the eggs and other stages follows a set, predictable cycle.

Possible Procedures(s): This challenge focuses on the process skill of interpreting data. To reiterate, there may be more than one reasonable answer based upon how the data is interpreted.

Precautions: No safety precautions are associated with this design brief.

While the problem solving techniques used by each team may be different, the diversity of thinking is beneficial for enhancing the problem solving repertoire of each student. Sharing is not only encouraged it is a strategy used throughout the program.

FORENSIC ENTOMOLOGY CARDS

Pictures for insertion on these cards can be found at
http://www.deathonline.net/decomposition/corpse_fauna/beetles/carcass.htm.

Carcass Beetles:

Carcass beetles are very large beetles and inhabit the carcass between two and four months. The tough exoskeleton and uniform dark color provide camouflage as the beetles feast on the dried remains of hair, skin and ligaments. The larvae of the Carcass Beetle live in vertical burrows underneath the carcass.

Rove Beetles:

The Rove Beetle can easily be identified by it's elongated body, small wings, large jaws and bright red head. The adults usually arrive early to a corpse but their eggs develop very slowly in comparison to other organisms. The larvae of the Rove Beetle develop through only three instars and the final stage usually does not appear until late in the decomposition process.

Cheese Skipper Flies:

The adult Cheese Skippers generally arrive within the first week after death but it takes two months before their larvae appear. It is from the behavior of the larvae that organisms derive part of their name. When the young larvae are disturbed that can jump in a skipping-like manner 15 cm into the air. The other part of their name refers to the "cheesy" odor that bodies produce in the later stages of decomposition.

Blowflies:

The Blowfly, brightly colored, metallic green in and rather large in size, can detect a rotting corpse 20 km away. Once it find a corpse it lays its eggs that develop into larvae within 16 hours. The first molt takes about 24 hours, the second a few hours less and the third about 4-5 days. The complete life cycle takes somewhere around 16 days.
The maggots of the Blowflies take two forms, smooth and hairy. The former eat only on the corpse while that latter will also feed on the smooth maggots.

Hide Beetles:

During the final stages of carcass decomposition the Hide Beetles are considered a very important organism. These beetles feed only on dried skin, tendons, bone and ligaments. These specialized insects have an enzyme that breaks down the keratin in human hair. The Hide Beetle and the Carcass Beetle are often found on the same corpse.

<u>**Black Soldier Fly**</u>:

The adult forms of this insect resemble wasps but are without a stinger. These harmless insects, usually about 1.5 cm in length, generally arrive three to four weeks after the time of death. As with most insects, the adults lay eggs that pass through three instars each lasting about two days.

<u>**Carrion Beetles**</u>:

The Carrion Beetle makes its home underneath the decomposing corpse. Although the beetle eats its share of carrion it must also supplement its diet by eating maggots as well. Generally, they arrive during the second week or decomposition and will remain "on the job" so long as their food source is plentiful. In general terms the Carrion Beetle will stay with a corpse between 33 and 45 days. At this point there is usually nothing left but hair and bones.

HEAT

LET THE SUNSHINE IN (PART 1)

- Design a solution to a problem. *NSES*
- Develop descriptions, explanations, predictions, and models using evidence. *NSES*
- Apply and adapt a variety of appropriate strategies to solve problems. *NCTM*
- Students adjust their use of spoken, written, and visual language (e.g., conventions, style, vocabulary) to communicate effectively with a variety of audiences and for different purposes. *NCTE*

The Context: Because energy costs continue to rise, there is continued interest in alternative energy sources.

The Scenario: Capturing the sun's energy for home heating purposes is the goal of Thermo - Sun Contracting, Inc. The company has been successful in building a house that can be heated by the sun to a minimum temperature of 35° C during the day but maintaining the temperature at an acceptable level during the nighttime hours has proved problematic.

The Challenge: Solving the problem of the overnight energy loss is the challenge presented to your engineering team. You suspect that the design of the house might be part of the problem so your first step is to research, redesign, construct and test your modified version of a model solar house based on Thermo-Sun specifications.

The Limitations:
- Each team must present a detailed sketch, with metric measurements, prior to construction. This document will become part of the team's Project Journal.
- Each team will have access to the general supply of materials. Teams may supply some of their own materials.
- Styrofoam or fiberglass products <u>may not be used.</u>
- Each team has the option of working on this project at home.
- Each team will have three class periods, at the discretion of the teacher, to construct and test their model houses
- The volume of model houses must be between 5,500 and 6,000 cubic centimeters.

The Rules:
- All research references must appear in the journal bibliographical form.
- In order for a house to be considered for testing it must start with an inside temperature of approximately 20^{0} C and achieve an inside temperature of at least 35° C in two hours.
- All houses that reach an inside temperature of at least 35° C will be placed in a closet to test the heat retaining capabilities.
- If the temperature of any house drops more than more than 5° C per hour the house will be considered unacceptable.
- Each team must conduct multiple tests of their design, construct a data table of results and graphically display the averages obtained.
- Each team must also identify the types of heat transfer demonstrated by their model.
- In the event that two or more houses maintain an acceptable decrease, testing will continued for an additional hour. The house that has the smallest decrease in temperature will be considered the most efficient.

TEACHER NOTES

Suggested Materials: Students should have access to general laboratory equipment. Materials for general supply could include, construction paper of different colors, aluminum foil, small containers for water, clear plastic wrap, colored plastic wrap or cellophane (if available) newspaper, cardboard, thermometers, metric tapes, masking or clear transparent tape, a stapler, white glue, rubber bands, timing device, and several heat lamps with aluminum hoods (alternative light/heat source in case of cloudy days). Teams can also provide some of their own materials.

Suggested Use: This design brief is an application of heat transfer through the process of radiation and or a combination of radiation and conduction.

Ties to Content: Heat energy travels from areas of higher temperature to areas of lower temperature and does so in one of three different, but related ways. When heat is transferred through matter by the direct contact of particles the process is referred to as conduction. This principle is most commonly demonstrated by metals.

Liquids and gases differ from solids in a number of ways and one of these characteristics is the ability of the liquid or gas to flow. This moving material is how thermal energy is transferred in the process called convection.

The third type of heat transfer is known as radiation. In radiation, the heat energy moves in the form of waves. Our sun is the major source of heat for the earth and its energy reaches us in the form of radiant energy. Some of this energy is absorbed and some is reflected. Whatever energy is absorbed it is changed into heat energy.

Possible Procedures(s): Students are required to submit an action plan prior to gathering their equipment and testing their design. At the time of submission be sure to carefully review each procedure for safety issues. Each team may approach this problem in a different manner and this is to be expected. Students should be reminded of the Design Loop and how it functions especially in regard to modifying the design of their project as a result of testing. When the students are finished their construction and testing they are responsible for identifying the different types of heat transfer.

Precautions: Whenever students are involved in a construction project there is the possibility of a mishap, especially if tools, hot glue guns and other sharp objects are available. Students should be shown proper tool use and be expected to sign a safety contract. Students should wear safety glasses whenever working with sharp objects in close quarters. Appropriate safety contracts can be obtained from Flinn Scientific at www.flinnsci.com

While the problem solving techniques used by each team may be different, the diversity of thinking is beneficial for enhancing the problem solving repertoire of each student. Sharing is not only encouraged it is a strategy used throughout the program.

LET THE SUNSHINE IN (PART 2)

- Design a solution to a problem. *NSES*
- Develop descriptions, explanations, predictions, and models using evidence. *NSES*
- Apply and adapt a variety of appropriate strategies to solve problems. *NCTM*
- Students adjust their use of spoken, written, and visual language (e.g., conventions, style, vocabulary) to communicate effectively with a variety of audiences and for different purposes. *NCTE*

The Context: Because energy costs continue to rise, there is continued interest in alternative energy sources.

The Scenario: The Thermo-Sun Company has been successful in building a house that can be heated by the sun to a minimum temperature of 35° C during the day. The house can also maintain its temperature within 5° Celsius for the first hour of the evening. Now one of their customers wants to heat a detached garage next to his house but does not want to install a separate heating system.

The Challenge: Once again, your engineering group has been pressed into action to solve this dilemma. Your challenge is to modify, construct, and test the existing system to accommodate and successfully heat the detached garage. Your scale model of this structure has have a volume of between 2500 and 2700 cubic centimeters and be located 12-15 centimeters from the house. The garage must also have a window.

The Limitations:
- Each team may use their house from the previous design brief.
- Prior to construction, each team must submit a plan, including a top view sketch to scale, which details the proposed method of heat transfer to the garage.
- The home owner has stipulated that the garage must be within 10° C of the main house temperature after three hours of operation.
- Each team will be given three class periods at the discretion of the teacher to construct their heat transfer systems.
- The results of preliminary testing must be documented and displayed in some way.
- On the presentation day, teams must set up their models and check them after three hours.

The Rules:
- All research and related resources must be appropriately documented.
- No modifications of the models will be allowed on the day of the presentation.
- Any team with a garage that is not within the required 10° C temperature differential will be asked to submit a written evaluation and suggestions for further modifications.

TEACHER NOTES

Suggested Materials: Students should have access to general laboratory equipment. Materials for general supply could include, construction paper of different colors, aluminum foil, small containers for water, clear plastic wrap, colored plastic wrap or cellophane (if available) newspaper, cardboard, thermometers, metric tapes, masking or clear transparent tape, a stapler, white glue, rubber bands, timing device, and several utility lamps with aluminum hoods (alternative light/heat source in case of cloudy days). Teams can also provide some of their own materials.

Suggested Use: This design brief is an application of heat transfer through the process of radiation and or a combination of radiation and conduction.

Ties to Content: Heat energy travels from areas of higher temperature to areas of lower temperature and does so in one of three different, but related ways. When heat is transferred through matter by the direct contact of particles the process is referred to as conduction. This principle is most commonly demonstrated by metals.

Liquids and gases differ from solids in a number of ways and one of these characteristics is the ability of the liquid or gas to flow. This moving material is how thermal energy is transferred in the process called convection.

The third type of heat transfer is known as radiation. In radiation, the heat energy moves in the form of waves. Our sun is the major source of heat for the earth and its energy reaches us in the form of radiant energy. Some of this energy is absorbed and some is reflected. Whatever energy is absorbed it is changed into heat energy.

Possible Procedures(s): Students are required to submit an action plan prior to gathering their equipment and testing their design. At the time of submission be sure to carefully review each procedure for safety issues. Each team may approach this problem in a different manner and this is to be expected. Students should be reminded of the Design Loop and how it functions especially in regard to modifying the design of their project as a result of testing. When the students are finished their construction and testing they are responsible for identifying the different types of heat transfer.

Precautions: Whenever students are involved in a construction project there is the possibility of a mishap, especially if tools, hot glue guns and other sharp objects are available. Students should be shown proper tool use and be expected to sign a safety contract. Students should wear safety glasses whenever working with sharp objects in close quarters. Appropriate safety contracts can be obtained from Flinn Scientific at www.flinnsci.com

While the problem solving techniques used by each team may be different, the diversity of thinking is beneficial for enhancing the problem solving repertoire of each student. Sharing is not only encouraged it is a strategy used throughout the program.

ORGAN DONOR

> - Design a solution to a problem. *NSES*
> - Develop descriptions, explanations, predictions, and models using evidence. *NSES*
> - Apply and adapt a variety of appropriate strategies to solve problems. *NCTM*
> - Students adjust their use of spoken, written, and visual language (e.g., conventions, style, vocabulary) to communicate effectively with a variety of audiences and for different purposes. *NCTE*

The Context: Transplanting human organs has become a viable way of extending the lives of those in need.

The Scenario: Your local medical center is starting an organ replacement department. They have the skilled surgeons, the support staff and the up to date technology at the facility. What they lack is a way to safely transport donated organs in a timely fashion.

The Challenge: Time and temperature are the two issues that have been placed in the lap of your engineering team. The hospital has requested your help in designing, constructing and testing a container that can be used to transport live human organs to their facility. Transported organs must be kept between 0° to 5° Celsius and remain at this temperature range for up to four hours. Because of the physical properties of water, your team decides that building a container to house an ice cube would be a good way to simulate this project, since working with real organs is not an option at this point.

The Limitations:
- An action plan and detailed sketch, with metric measurements, must be provided before construction begins.
- Each team is responsible for providing their materials except for general laboratory supplies.
- Styrofoam and fiberglass are not acceptable materials for this project.
- Organ containers may not exceed an external volume of 1300 cubic centimeters.
- Simulated organ containers must contain an observation window to monitor the status of the ice cube.
- The ice cube must be enclosed inside a quart size zip lock bag.
- At the discretion of the teacher, three class periods will be allotted for product planning, and construction.
- Testing will occur after all organ containers have been completed and turned in.

The Rules:
- All containers will be refrigerated prior to testing.
- Ice cubes must be massed before testing begins.
- Containers may only be opened at the conclusion of testing.
- If a tie exists after four hours the ice that remains will be massed. The ice cube that has lost the smallest amount of its original mass will indicate the most efficient container.

TEACHER NOTES

Suggested Materials: The students should have access to general laboratory equipment as well as a supply of zip lock bags. In addition, access to ice cubes and mass measuring devices will be needed.

Suggested Use: This design brief is a real life application addressing the concept of heat and heat loss through the use of insulating materials.

Ties to Content: Heat energy travels from areas of higher temperature to areas of lower temperature and does so in one of three different, but related ways. When heat is transferred through matter by the direct contact of particles the process is referred to as conduction. This principle is most commonly demonstrated by metals.

Liquids and gases differ from solids in a number of ways and one of these characteristics is the ability of the liquid or gas to flow. This moving material is how thermal energy is transferred in the process called convection.

The third type of heat transfer is known as radiation. In radiation, the heat energy moves in the form of waves. Our sun is the major source of heat for the earth and its energy reaches us in the form of radiant energy. Some of this energy is absorbed and some is reflected. Whatever energy is absorbed it is changed into heat energy.

Insulators are a group of materials that resist the flow of energy. In a real life respect, they slow down the transfer of heat from one place to another. In general, materials that trap air are excellent insulators. In a house, the insulation prevents heat from easily moving to the outside during the winter and from moving into the house during the summer.

Possible Procedures(s): The students have three class periods, at the discretion of the teacher, to complete this challenge and should be encouraged to work on this project at home. Students will find it helpful to research the concept of insulation prior to crafting a design for their organ container.

The time students spend on each phase needs to be managed. It is suggested that a schedule be created and posted to help keep students on task. As noted, the three class periods days set aside for this challenge are at the discretion of the teacher and as such provide "wiggle room" to allow students sufficient time. Be sure to set aside one day for final testing.

Precautions: Whenever students are involved in a construction project there is the possibility of a mishap, especially if tools, hot glue guns and other sharp objects are available. Students should be shown proper tool use and be expected to sign a safety contract. Students should wear safety glasses whenever working with sharp objects in close quarters. Appropriate safety contracts can be obtained from Flinn Scientific at www.flinnsci.com

While the problem solving techniques used by each team may be different, the diversity of thinking is beneficial for enhancing the problem solving repertoire of each student. Sharing is not only encouraged it is a strategy used throughout the program.

THE PRICE OF DOWN IS UP

> - Design a solution to a problem. *NSES*
> - Develop descriptions, explanations, predictions, and models using evidence. *NSES*
> - Apply and adapt a variety of appropriate strategies to solve problems. *NCTM*
> - Students adjust their use of spoken, written, and visual language (e.g., conventions, style, vocabulary) to communicate effectively with a variety of audiences and for different purposes. *NCTE*

The Context: A rise in the cost of raw materials often prompts alternative materials to be used.

The Scenario: The Thermo Company has been a world leader in warm winter apparel. Thermo has prided itself on using nothing but natural goose down as its primary insulating material. However, a bird influenza has infected their flock of geese and all the birds had to be destroyed. With its supply of goose down gone the company will have to close its doors unless it can find another natural insulating material to use as a replacement.

The Challenge: Your engineering team has become aware of Thermo's plight and decides to help the company find another natural insulator.

The Limitations:
- Each team will have four class periods to complete this challenge.
- Each team must craft and submit an action plan prior to the start of construction and testing.
- All insulating materials will be the responsibility of the team. No Styrofoam, fiberglass bubble wrap or any other human made insulation may be used.
- General science equipment will be available for team use.
- The insulating material will be used inside winter clothing so softness and weight are important issues.

The Rules:
- To test the effectiveness of their natural insulating material, all teams must measure the heat loss of 100 ml of water over a 30 minute period. Standard Heat Loss Devices can be obtained from your teacher.
- Insulating materials may only be placed in between the outside of the metal can and the inside of the plastic bottle.
- The height of the insulating material may not exceed the top of the metal soup can.
- Each team will get three trials to modify and investigate their natural insulator/insulators.
- Each time a team modifies its material or procedure they must provide a written description noting that change and the reasons for the change.
- Each team must create their own data collection and display formats.
- Each team member must craft a written report to the Thermo Company describing the investigation along with data supported results. Recommendations as to what measures the company should take should also be included.

TEACHER NOTES

Suggested Materials: Standard Heat Loss Devices consist of a metal soup can placed inside half a one liter plastic soda bottle cut to the same height as the soup can. The space between the can and the bottle will be where the insulating material will be placed. Each team of students will also need at least one thermometer. It is also suggested that circular lids be crafted from cardboard and placed over the top of each metal can as the lids will help maintain the heat in the water. Make a small slit in the center of lid so that the thermometer can be inserted.

Metal soup can 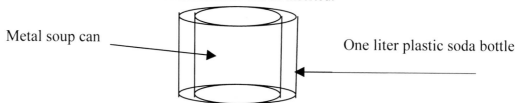 One liter plastic soda bottle

Suggested Use: This design brief is a real life application addressing the concept of heat and heat loss through the use of insulating materials. While fiberglass and Styrofoam are common insulating materials they are not appropriate materials for clothing. In this challenge students are expected to research and test alternative insulating materials to use in clothing.

Ties to Content: Heat energy travels from areas of higher temperature to areas of lower temperature and does so in one of three different, but related ways. When heat is transferred through matter by the direct contact of particles the process is referred to as conduction. This principle is most commonly demonstrated by metals.

Liquids and gases differ from solids in a number of ways and one of these characteristics is the ability of the liquid or gas to flow. This moving material is how thermal energy is transferred in the process called convection.

The third type of heat transfer is known as radiation. In radiation, the heat energy moves in the form of waves. Our sun is the major source of heat for the earth and its energy reaches us in the form of radiant energy. Some of this energy is absorbed and some is reflected. Whatever energy is absorbed it is changed into heat energy.

Insulators are a group of materials that resist the flow of energy. In a real life respect, they slow down the transfer of heat from one place to another. In general, materials that trap air are excellent insulators. In a house, the insulation prevents heat from easily moving to the outside during the winter and from moving into the house during the summer.

Possible Procedures(s): The procedure associated with this design brief is fairly well spelled out. Students will be using the Standard Heat Loss Devices to test possible insulating materials. The students have three days to complete this challenge and it is suggested that, since the equipment and process is already established, a third of the time be devoted to researching naturally occurring insulators.

Precautions: Students will be expected to wear appropriate eye protection during this investigation. Care should be taken when using any chemical. Check the MSDS sheet for each chemical prior to use. Should these sheets not be available check the Flinn Scientific Catalog or the Flinn Scientific website, www.flinnsci.com. Click on the chemistry link and then the MSDS link.

While the problem solving techniques used by each team may be different, the diversity of thinking is beneficial for enhancing the problem solving repertoire of each student. Sharing is not only encouraged it is a strategy used throughout the program.

HEAT TRANSFER

- Design a solution to a problem. *NSES*
- Develop descriptions, explanations, predictions, and models using evidence. *NSES*
- Apply and adapt a variety of appropriate strategies to solve problems. *NCTM*
- Students adjust their use of spoken, written, and visual language (e.g., conventions, style, vocabulary) to communicate effectively with a variety of audiences and for different purposes. *NCTE*

The Context: The solution to a problem may be found in using available materials in a unique way.

The Scenario: The liquid product that your company makes is <u>very cold</u> when it comes off the manufacturing line and must be warmed up to exactly 25° C before it can be packed for shipment. In another section of the building, there is a large supply of very hot waste water <u>but it is salty and deep red in color.</u>

The Challenge: Your team decides to pursue this idea just the same. Your challenge is to design a system that uses the hot, salty, deep red water to raise the temperature of the clean, cold liquid product without causing any contamination.

The Limitations:
- Each team must submit a design before gathering materials.
- Each team will have two class periods to complete this challenge. One period for planning and construction and one period for testing and interpreting data.
- Each team may supply some of their own materials.
- 50 ml of the product must be raised to a temperature of exactly 30° C in no more than 15 minutes.
- Each team may not use more than 125 ml of the hot, salty, deep red waste water.

The Rules:
- The clean, cold liquid product and the hot, salty, red water must not mix at any time.
- Each team must chart and graph all investigative data.
- Each team member must process test results and craft their own interpretation.
- Product temperature will be taken (judged) at the discretion of the design team.

TEACHER NOTES

Suggested Materials: Students should have access to general laboratory equipment. Teams can also provide some of their own materials. Teachers will need to supply the hot, red, salty water for the student teams. It is suggested that a microwave or a coffee pot be used of that purpose.

Suggested Use: This design brief is an application of heat transfer through the process of conduction.

Ties to Content: Heat energy travels from areas of higher temperature to areas of lower temperature and does so in one of three different, but related ways. When heat is transferred through matter by the direct contact of particles the process is referred to as conduction. This principle is most commonly demonstrated by metals.

Liquids and gases differ from solids in a number of ways and one of these characteristics is the ability of the liquid or gas to flow. This moving material is how thermal energy is transferred in the process called convection.

The third type of heat transfer is known as radiation. In radiation, the heat energy moves in the form of waves. Our sun is the major source of heat for the earth and its energy reaches us in the form of radiant energy. Some of this energy is absorbed and some is reflected. Whatever energy is absorbed it is changed into heat energy.

Possible Procedures(s): Students are required to submit an action plan prior to gathering their equipment and testing their design. At the time of submission be sure to carefully review each procedure for safety issues. Each team may approach this problem in a different manner. However, since transferring the heat from the hot, salty, red water to the clear water has to be done by the process of conduction, the student designs submitted should be similar. The most expedient method of transferring the heat would be to place the clear water in a small container with a thermometer. This container can then be carefully immersed into a container of hot, salty, red water without letting the two waters mix. The heat from the hot, salty, red water will transfer through the immersed container and then on to the clear water.

Precautions: Take precautions when using hot water. It is suggested that a coffee pot, or microwave, are relatively quick ways to produce hot water for classroom use. The water should be between 50° and 60° C. The teacher must be in charge of distributing the water when the students are ready. Add red food coloring for effect. There is no reason to add salt as tasting is not a recommended procedure. Safety glasses must be worn during the course of this challenge. In addition to the hot water the students will need a supply of ice water, Celsius thermometers, and glass containers.

While the problem solving techniques used by each team may be different, the diversity of thinking is beneficial for enhancing the problem solving repertoire of each student. Sharing is not only encouraged it is a strategy used throughout the program.

THE COOL POOL

- Design a solution to a problem. *NSES*
- Develop descriptions, explanations, predictions, and models using evidence. *NSES*
- Apply and adapt a variety of appropriate strategies to solve problems. *NCTM*
- Students adjust their use of spoken, written, and visual language (e.g., conventions, style, vocabulary) to communicate effectively with a variety of audiences and for different purposes. *NCTE*

The Context: Different materials conduct heat/transfer energy at different rates.

The Scenario: The temperature this spring has been abnormally warm, so the Floater family has decided to open their swimming pool early this year. After cutting the grass, sweeping the deck clear, removing the pool cover, and treating the water, all appeared ready for the upcoming weekend. There was just one problem… the temperature of the water was only 17° Celsius.

The Challenge: You have been contacted by the Floaters to help them with their problem. As one of the invited guests to their gala "Spring Fling Wind Ding" you feel not only a sense of honor but one of responsibility as well. Your challenge is to design a way to raise the temperature of the pool water 10° Celsius in time for their party. Scaling down the project to a manageable size will allow you to simulate a heat transfer system. If your model can raise the temperature of a gallon of water 10° degrees Celsius in a six hour period then a large scale version might just work on the actual pool.

The Limitations:
- Each team will have three class periods, at the discretion of the teacher, to complete this project.
- Heat transfer systems must be of the passive design type.
- Teams must submit illustrated plans of their design and a written description of how they think their system will increase the temperature of the water.
- All research must be noted and documented in bibliographical form.
- Each team will receive the same size container, same amount of water, and two thermometers.
- Each team will have access to standard laboratory equipment.
- Each team is responsible for any other materials or equipment that they deem necessary.
- A data collection and display format must be created by each team.

The Rules:
- Each team must start with the same temperature water.
- All containers will be placed in the same location for the six hour test. The temperature of all containers will be compared to a "control" container of water.
- No adjustments or modifications may be made to designs once the timing begins.
- Each team member must individually craft their own report to the Floater family describing the heating system and how it functions. The report must be supported by data.

TEACHER NOTES

Suggested Materials: The students should have access to general laboratory equipment. The students will also need a supply of containers to simulate swimming pools. If kitty litter pans are not readily available then plastic wash basins, plastic shoe boxes, or similar storage containers will suffice. All containers should be the same. Students will need two thermometers per group and two additional thermometers will be required for the control water container.

Suggested Use: This design brief is a real life application addressing the concept of heat and heat transfer.

Ties to Content: Heat energy travels from areas of higher temperature to areas of lower temperature and does so in one of three different, but related ways. When heat is transferred through matter by the direct contact of particles the process is referred to as conduction. This principle is most commonly demonstrated by metals.

Liquids and gases differ from solids in a number of ways and one of these characteristics is the ability of the liquid or gas to flow. This moving material is how thermal energy is transferred in the process called convection.

The third type of heat transfer is known as radiation. In radiation, the heat energy moves in the form of waves. Our sun is the major source of heat for the earth and its energy reaches us in the form of radiant energy. Some of this energy is absorbed and some is reflected. Whatever energy is absorbed it is changed into heat energy.

Possible Procedures(s): The students have three class periods, at the discretion of the teacher, to complete this challenge and should be encouraged to work on this project at home. Students will find it helpful to research the concept of heat transfer especially the processes of conduction and convection.

The time students spend on each phase needs to be managed. Following the research phase, teams must craft a design of their system and provide a rationale for how this system will work. It is suggested that a schedule be created and posted to help keep students on task. As noted, the three class periods days set aside for this challenge are at the discretion of the teacher and as such provide "wiggle room" to allow students sufficient time. Be sure to set aside one period for final testing.

Precautions: Whenever students are involved in a construction project there is the possibility of a mishap, especially if tools, hot glue guns and other sharp objects are available. Students should be shown proper tool use and be expected to sign a safety contract. Students should wear safety glasses whenever working with sharp objects in close quarters. Appropriate safety contracts can be obtained from Flinn Scientific at www.flinnsci.com

While the problem solving techniques used by each team may be different, the diversity of thinking is beneficial for enhancing the problem solving repertoire of each student. Sharing is not only encouraged it is a strategy used throughout the program.

LIFE SCIENCE

CELLULAR SCENES

- Design a solution to a problem. *NSES*
- Develop descriptions, explanations, predictions, and models using evidence. *NSES*
- Students should develop an understanding of the structure and function in living systems. *NSES*
- Apply and adapt a variety of appropriate strategies to solve problems. *NCTM*
- Students adjust their use of spoken, written, and visual language (e.g., conventions, style, vocabulary) to communicate effectively with a variety of audiences and for different purposes. *NCTE*

The Context: Science museums do not develop all of their own displays but share exhibits with similar facilities as a cost saving measure.

The Scenario: The Imagination Science Museum has decided to expand its traveling "Miniworlds" exhibit to include large scale models of plant and animal cells, each designed around a different theme. Due to an ongoing expansion project, the museum's design department is swamped with work and needs to sub-contract the development of these cell models to outside companies.

The Challenge: Your research and design company is aware of the museum's need for help and has decided to submit a cell model for consideration.

The Limitations:
- Three class periods will be provided to complete this project at the discretion of the teacher.
- Each team must choose a "theme" for its model and all displayed cell parts must be related to this theme. For example, if a team chooses to use "food items" then all the parts of the cell must be represented by such things as noodles, beans, cookies, candy, etc.
- The model must be three dimensional.
- Each team must present a preliminary theme and cell plan before construction begins.
- Each team must be responsible for all the materials used in the model and all materials must be related to the theme.

The Rules:
- No food items may be used since this was used as an example.
- The theme of the model and type of cell must be displayed on the finished product.
- Teams must accurately and clearly label the parts of their cell model.
- Each team may change its theme based upon the availability of materials or collaborative group decisions.
- An identification key must be designed to explain the function of each cell part.
- Each team must present its project, explain the various parts of the model and describe how these parts function.
- All team members must actively participate in the presentation.
- Students should refer to the *Team Presentation Rubric* for guidance in constructing their presentations.

TEACHER NOTES

Suggested Materials: Student teams are responsible for all materials used in this design challenge.

Suggested Use: This design brief was developed to serve as a content application for the study of plant and animal cells. Students will have to demonstrate a working knowledge of cellular structure and function by crafting and presenting a thematic model of a plant of animal cell.

Ties to Content: Cell theory states that all organisms are made of cells, all cells are generated from other cells and the cell is the basic unit of structure and function regardless of the organism. All cells can be divided into two large groups, eukaryotic cells and the prokaryotic cells. Both types of cells contain DNA and/or RNA, as well as cytoplasm. However, eukaryotic cells also have nuclei and other membrane-bound organelles. The organelles can be considered as small compartments that enable the cell to function by releasing energy, maintaining homeostasis and participating in cellular reproduction.

Plant cells are different than animal cells in that they have a cell wall, which is a rigid structure that surrounds the cell, giving it shape, support and protection. They also contain vacuoles that serve as storage areas for plant digestion, secretion or excretion. Additionally, plants contain chloroplasts, which are organelles that enable the plant to convert carbon dioxide in the air, water and sunlight into sugar through the process of photosynthesis.

Possible Procedures(s): Scheduling the time for this challenge is the only procedural consideration for this challenge. It is suggested that teachers post a completion schedule for each phase of this project as a means of keeping the students on pace.

Precautions: There are no precautions associated with this challenge except for the reminder that no food items should be used with the thematic models…unless you want the project to evolve into an investigation of mold variety.

While the problem solving techniques used by each team may be different, the diversity of thinking is beneficial for enhancing the problem solving repertoire of each student. Sharing is not only encouraged it is a strategy used throughout the program.

LIMITATIONS

> - Design a solution to a problem. *NSES*
> - Implement a proposed design and evaluate completed technological designs or products. *NSES*
> - Apply and adapt a variety of appropriate strategies to solve problems. *NCTM*
> - Students apply knowledge of language structure, language conventions (e.g., spelling and punctuation), media techniques, figurative language, and genre to create, critique, and discuss print and non-print texts. *NCTE*

The Context: The environmental factors of light, moisture and temperature generally determine the species of organisms that can survive in a particular area.

The Scenario: Seed companies are always searching for new varieties of seeds to expand their product lines. The new seeds, however, must be thoroughly tested so that the company can determine the optimum conditions under which these plants will grow in order to market them properly. The Green Valley Company (GVC) recently received a shipment of grass seeds from their field operation in Alabama. GVC needs help in creating and conducting the tests for this new variety of seeds.

The Challenge: Your research facility has been approached to test the seeds. Due to the time constraints placed on you by GVC, this challenge will require the help of every research team available. The Green Valley Company is interested in determining the best conditions for germinating the seeds.

The Limitations:
- Each team will have three weeks to complete this project. The amount of actual class time will be at the discretion of the teacher.
- Each team will randomly select the variable its team will test.
- Each team may only use the seeds supplied by the Green Valley Company.
- The criteria for evaluating the plants at the end of the testing cycle must be established before testing begins.
- Each team must submit a "fair test" action plan for approval prior to starting any experimentation, including a list of the conditions (variables) that will be held constant.
- Each team will have access to the general planting and standard laboratory equipment.
- Each team may supply additional materials if so desired.
- Each team must create a way to collect and display its data.

The Rules:
- Each team member must submit a detailed data supported report of its findings.
- Each team must create a poster that shows a thumbnail review (the steps) of its entire project.
- Individual class members will be responsible for using the data compiled from all posters to craft a set of consumer instructions for the back of the seed package.

TEACHER NOTES

Suggested Materials: Any variety of grass seeds will be appropriate for this investigation. Transfer the seeds to plain bags or containers so the students do not get any clues regarding the type of seed or the recommended planting/cultivating conditions. Other materials may include plant pots or planting flats, crushed aspirin and baking soda for adjusting the pH of the soil, sand, clay and top soil for making different planting media, plant fertilizer, thermometers, centimeter rulers, graduated cylinders, and a supply of paper towels.

Suggested Use: As students progress through most units on plants they will usually be asked to investigate the effects of changing environmental factors on the growth of plants. Such is the case with this design brief. However, unlike the traditional lessons, this challenge requires students to work in a variety of different sized groups from full class involvement to individualized assignments. The focus of this design brief is for students to develop and implement a procedure for testing one of the environmental factors that might affect the growth of grass plants. Students are then expected to conduct their investigations and share their data with others. Processing this data will be the responsibility of each student as they are then required to craft a data supported investigation overview in the form of a letter. Team responsibilities then continue with the creation of a data driven information label for their grass seeds. This challenge could be extended to test the use of commercial fertilizer or naturally occurring fertilizer.

Ties to Content: An ecosystem can be defined as the interaction of the abiotic and biotic factors in the environment. Basically, abiotic factors are non-living factors that affect the plants, whereas biotic factors are living factors that affect the plants. Abiotic factors include light, temperature, sunlight, and availability of nutrients. They can determine the growth rate and condition of plants, as well as if plants are able to live in a certain environment. Plants have a range of conditions under which they will survive and this range can vary for each species of plant. The focus of this design brief is to determine the optimum environmental conditions for common grass seeds.

Possible Procedures(s): Students will be expected to craft a "fair test" investigation for one of the abiotic variables that might affect the growth of grass seeds. These proposals need to be reviewed and approved prior to the students gathering materials. Each research team will be asked to design and conduct a different test, the data from which can be combined as a final "company proposal." Some conditions may include: depth of planting, distribution (crowded or not crowded conditions), optimum amount of water, optimum amount of sunlight, optimum range of temperature at soil surface, optimum range of temperature below soil surface, type of soil, pH of the soil, and so on. As the investigation progresses the students will need to collect and record accurate data for processing, displaying, and interpreting. The final segments of this challenge include a data supported overview and the creation of data based planting instructions.

Precautions: Students will be expected to wear appropriate eye protection during this investigation. Care should be taken when using any chemical. Check the MSDS sheet for each chemical prior to use. Should these sheets not be available check the Flinn Scientific Catalog or the Flinn Scientific website, www.flinnsci.com. Click on the chemistry link and then the MSDS link.

While the problem solving techniques used by each team may be different, the diversity of thinking is beneficial for enhancing the problem solving repertoire of each student. Sharing is not only encouraged it is a strategy used throughout the program.

PLANTING BY NUMBER (PART 1)

- Design a solution to a problem. *NSES*
- Implement a proposed design and evaluate completed technological designs or products. *NSES*
- Apply and adapt a variety of appropriate strategies to solve problems. *NCTM*

The Context: A graduating class traditionally provides a "Class Gift" to its alma mater at commencement. Because it is a long term benefit, and is often too expensive for schools to do themselves, graduates often propose donations of "living gifts" to enhance the school grounds.

The Scenario: An analysis of the soil is generally conducted prior to planting flowers and shrubbery as a measure of insuring the health of the plants. This is done because optimum soil conditions, including pH level, vary between plant species. Your school grounds contain areas that have been backfilled with soil from other parts of the county in addition to areas that have never been excavated. This makes local soil maps outdated and completely worthless.

The Challenge: Your survey team has been hired to determine the correct locations for a variety of plant species based on pH tests of the soil from different places around the school. Once you have completed your research you will be expected to analyze the data and make recommendations to the board of directors regarding the placement, and/or the selection of, a variety of plant types.

The Limitations:
- This research is limited to two class periods.
- Each team must develop and submit a written procedure prior to testing.
- Independent and dependent variables must be identified.
- Each team may only use the materials provided in the research lab.
- It will be necessary for teams to create a way of storing and displaying their data.

The Rules:
- Each team must leave the research station as they found it. CLEAN UP!
- Each team is responsible for testing at least four different soil samples.
- Each team is encouraged to share data.
- At home, each team member will be responsible for writing a letter to the college trustees explaining what was found and recommendations regarding the placement of particular plant species. These recommendations must be supported with data.

TEACHER NOTES

Suggested Materials: Provide students with a variety of soil samples that they actually collect from the school grounds or bring in samples from home. General lab equipment should be available, along with filter paper, pH paper, or another means to measure pH such as 1% phenolphthalein. There is a reference page included that shows common plants and their ideal soil pH ranges.

Suggested Use: This design brief was initially created to serve as real life application lab for identifying the strength of acids and bases. Prior to this challenge, students should have had experience with the use of wide range litmus paper or universal indicator, have knowledge of common acids and bases and the pH scale.

Ties to Content: Acids are sour to the taste, react with metals, break down proteins and can conduct electricity when dissolved in water. Many plants are slightly acidic, as are most vegetables and fruits. Other common acids include vinegar, carbonated beverages, orange juice, aspirin, eyewash solutions and gastric juice (stomach acid). The strength of an acid is determined by its extent of dissociation, or formation of the hydronium ion (H_3O^+) when it dissolves in water. Acids that dissociate completely are considered strong, while those that do not dissociate completely are considered weak. Bases are another group of special compounds and are chemically quite different from acids. While acids dissociate in water to produce hydronium ions, bases dissociate in water to produce hydroxide ions (OH^-). Most bases are crystalline solids. They have a bitter taste, are slippery to the touch and conduct electricity when dissolved in water. Strong bases are just as dangerous and corrosive as strong acids. Common bases include ammonia, many soaps, deodorants, antacids and drain cleaner. In order to compare the concentration of hydronium ions (in solution) of different compounds a pH scale was developed. This scale ranges from 0 to 14. Solutions below 7 are considered acidic, the lower the number the stronger the acid. Those solutions over 7 are considered basic and the higher the number the stronger the base. An indicator is often used to identify the specific pH of an acidic or basic solution. Indicators are special chemicals that change colors in the presence of acids or bases. Litmus, phenolphthalein and methyl orange are some examples of indicators.

Possible Procedures(s): Students could determine the pH of their soil samples by using wide range pH paper. If the students add distilled or spring water to a soil sample and filter the mixture they will be able to test the filtrate with wide range filter paper and compare the resultant filtrate color to a comparison chart. Another method would be to add a universal indicator to the filtrate and then use a color comparison chart to determine the pH of the filtrate. Coffee filters may be slightly acidic and could alter the results. Soil pH may vary and it is suggested that the samples be tested prior to use so as to determine the variation in pH. Should the soil samples not show a wide range some of the samples be "spiked" to raise of lower their pH. Adding a few grams of powdered aspirin will lower the pH of a sample while a few ground up antacid tablets will raise the pH of a sample. The students do not have to know that you have "adjusted" the soil samples.

Precautions: Students will be expected to wear appropriate eye protection during this investigation. Care should be taken when using any chemical. Check the MSDS sheet for each chemical prior to use. Should these sheets not be available check the Flinn Scientific Catalog or the Flinn Scientific website, www.flinnsci.com.

While the problem solving techniques used by each team may be different, the diversity of thinking is beneficial for enhancing the problem solving repertoire of each student. Sharing is not only encouraged it is a strategy used throughout the program.

REFERENCE LIST OF POTENTIAL PLANTS FOR THE GIFT

Name of Plant	Range of pH
Blue Spruce	4.0-5.0
Kalmia	4.5-5.5
Azalea	4.5-6.0
Rhododendron	4.5-6.0
Arnica	5.6-6.0
Magnolia	5.0-6.0
Virginia Creeper	6.0-7.5
Zinnia	5.5-7.5
Hawthorn	6.0-7.0
Acacia	6.0-8.0
Asphodoline	6.0-8.0
Day Lilly	6.0-8.0
Forget Me Not	6.0-8.0
Pampas Grass	6.0-8.0

CAMPUS MAP... NUMBERS SHOW THE 10 SOIL COLLECTION SITES.

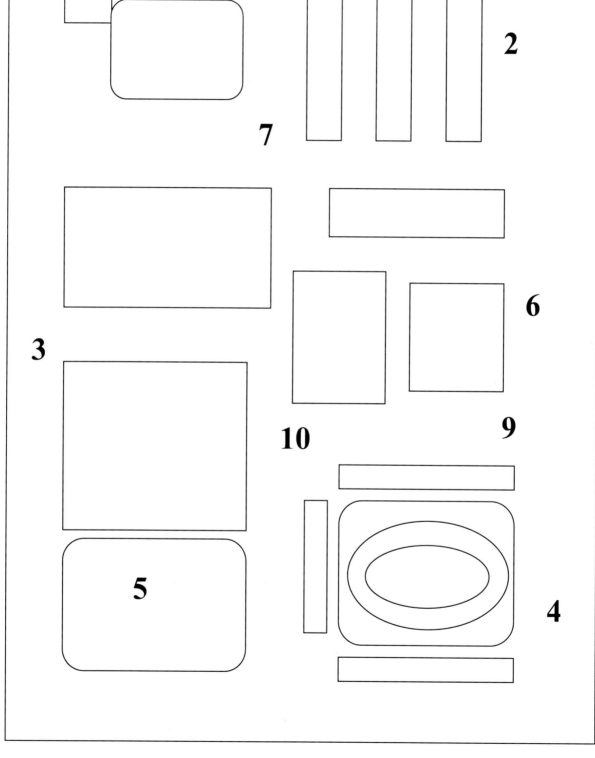

PLANTING BY NUMBER (PART 2)

> - Design a solution to a problem. *NSES*
> - Implement a proposed design and evaluate completed technological designs or products. *NSES*
> - Apply and adapt a variety of appropriate strategies to solve problems. *NCTM*
> - Students adjust their use of spoken, written, and visual language (e.g., conventions, style, vocabulary) to communicate effectively with a variety of audiences and for different purposes. *NCTE*

The Context: A graduating class traditionally provides a "Class Gift" to its alma mater upon commencement from the institution. Because it is a long term benefit, and is often too expensive for schools to do themselves, graduates often propose donations of "living gifts" to enhance the school grounds.

The Scenario: An analysis of the soil is generally conducted prior to planting flowers and shrubbery as a measure of insuring the health of the plants. In preparation for the living gifts the grounds crew of your institute has tested the soil in a number of locations and found that the pH of all the samples was between 5.0 and 5.5. The problem with these findings is that the Board of Directors has selected plants that require more basic or more acidic soil conditions. The selected plants include: Blue Spruce (4.0-5.0) Arborvitae (6.5-7.5) and English Ivy (6.5-7.0). In addition, the Board is concerned about possible contamination to the three campus lakes and has also stipulated that only natural materials may be used in adjusting the pH of any soil samples.

The Challenge: Your agricultural research team hears of this dilemma and decides to take up the challenge of finding a natural way of adjusting the pH of the soil to better match the requirements of the selected plants.

The Limitations:
- Each team has three class periods to complete this challenge.
- Each team must research the natural materials needed to adjust the pH of the soil.
- Each team must submit an action plan of its procedure and list of needed materials for approval prior to testing.
- Basic laboratory equipment and soil samples will be made available for use.
- Only natural materials may be used to adjust the soil condition of the soil samples.
- Each team will be required to supply any natural soil additives.

The Rules:
- Each team must provide both data collection and data display formats.
- Individual team members must construct a data supported report to the board of directors as to how the soil conditions could be altered to better match the growing requirements of the selected plants.
- Each team must also suggest ways in which the Board could acquire the large quantities of natural materials needed to make pH adjustments in the soil.

TEACHER NOTES

Suggested Materials: Provide students with a variety of soil samples that they actually collect from the school grounds or bring in samples from home. General lab equipment should be available, along with filter paper, pH paper, or another means to measure pH such as 1% phenolphthalein. There is a reference page included that shows common plants and ideal pH ranges for their soil.

Suggested Use: This challenge can be conducted as a separate investigation or as an extension activity of **Planting by Numbers (Part 1),** especially if the samples tested do not show a wide range of pH readings. Be sure to allow sufficient time for the students to complete their research. Prior to this challenge, students should have had experience with the use of wide range litmus paper or universal indicator, have knowledge of common acids and bases and the pH scale.

Ties to Content: Acids are sour to the taste, react with metals, break down proteins and can conduct electricity when dissolved in water. Many plants are slightly acidic, as are most vegetables and fruits. Other common acids include vinegar, carbonated beverages, orange juice, aspirin, eyewash solutions and gastric juice (stomach acid). The strength of an acid is determined by its extent of dissociation, or formation of the hydronium ion (H_3O^+) when it dissolves in water. Acids that dissociate completely are considered strong, while those that do not dissociate completely are considered weak. Bases are another group of special compounds and are chemically quite different from acids. While acids dissociate in water to produce hydronium ions, bases dissociate in water to produce hydroxide ions (OH^-). Most bases are crystalline solids. They have a bitter taste, are slippery to the touch and conduct electricity when dissolved in water. Strong bases are just as dangerous and corrosive as strong acids. Common bases include ammonia, many soaps, deodorants, antacids and drain cleaner. In order to compare the concentration of hydronium ions (in solution) of different compounds a pH scale was developed. This scale ranges from 0 to 14. Solutions below 7 are considered acidic, the lower the number the stronger the acid. Those solutions over 7 are considered basic and the higher the number the stronger the base. An indicator is often used to identify the specific pH of an acidic or basic solution. Indicators are special chemicals that change colors in the presence of acids or bases. Litmus, phenolphthalein and methyl orange are some examples of indicators.

Possible Procedures(s): Students could determine the pH of their soil samples by using wide range pH paper. If the students add distilled or spring water to a soil sample and filter the mixture they will be able to test the filtrate with wide range filter paper and compare the resultant filtrate color to a comparison chart. Another method would be to add a universal indicator to the filtrate and then use a color comparison chart to determine the pH of the filtrate. Coffee filters may be slightly acidic and could alter the results. Once students have determined the pH of their soil samples they need to "adjust" the sample by adding an appropriate base or acid to the sample. Landscapers "adjust" the pH of acidic soils by spreading pulverized limestone on lawns to "sweeten" the soil.

Precautions: Students will be expected to wear appropriate eye protection during this investigation. Care should be taken when using any chemical. Check the MSDS sheet for each chemical prior to use. Should these sheets not be available check the Flinn Scientific Catalog or the Flinn Scientific website, www.flinnsci.com.

While the problem solving techniques used by each team may be different, the diversity of thinking is beneficial for enhancing the problem solving repertoire of each student. Sharing is not only encouraged it is a strategy used throughout the program.

GOOD KING ZUCCHINI AND THE MYSTICAL LIMA BEAN SNAKE PLANT DREAM

- Design a solution to a problem. *NSES*
- Implement a proposed design and evaluate completed technological designs or products. *NSES*
- Apply and adapt a variety of appropriate strategies to solve problems. *NCTM*
- Students adjust their use of spoken, written, and visual language (e.g., conventions, style, vocabulary) to communicate effectively with a variety of audiences and for different purposes. *NCTE*

The Context: Successfully replicating an investigation is often done to verify the process.

The Scenario: Good King Zucchini had just awakened from a 10 year spell that was cast on him by the wicked Queen Sarnoff for not having the moat cleaned and Sterno the Dragon's nails clipped (She's really a tough one). Anyway, after he got himself cleaned up from ten years without a bath, a haircut, and a shave, he called his court together to tell them about the wonderful things he recalled from his ten year sleep including the very odd, mystical lima bean snake plants. "These plants were all over the place", the King replied. "Lima bean plants that looked like snakes," he continued, "Some were coiled round and round like a Slinky while others were bent back and forth in an "S" shape like a moving serpent. It would be wonderful if my kingdom could boast of such marvelous plants." Guards, go summon the Royal Wizards they will find an answer or I will feed them to the 12 headed lizard formally known as Prince."

The Challenge: The Royal Wizards were lead into the Royal Throne Room and told about their latest challenge. "I command you to find a way to grow lima bean plants so that they will look like Slinkys or snakes. No one really likes lima beans and perhaps if you can successfully grow such novel plants they will encourage the people in my kingdom to consume more beans" (not really a pleasant thought).

The Limitations:
- Each team will have three weeks to complete the royal request.
- Two class periods will be devoted to planning and one to student presentations. All other work will be done outside of class.
- Each team will be responsible for keeping an up to date account of its investigation including procedures, problems, modifications, observations, sketches and summaries.

The Rules:
- Each team will be responsible for planning and presenting but each member must conduct this investigation at home. In this way teams will have more than one sample of the same investigation and every team member will be directly involved.
- Each team must present its findings to the Royal Court at the end of three weeks. Each member of the team must take part in the presentation.
- All student wizards must individually write out a detailed, illustrated procedure describing the steps the townspeople could take for growing their own mystical lima bean snake plants.
- Each team must also identify the scientific reason/reasons that it was able to successfully create a mystical lima bean snake plant.
- Students should refer to the *Team Presentation Rubric* for guidance as they craft their presentations.

TEACHER NOTES

Suggested Materials: The only teacher supplied materials are a bag of lima beans. All other materials are the responsibility of the student teams. Students will need a copy of the *Team Presentation Rubric* as reference as they craft their presentation.

Suggested Use: This design brief would best fit as an application challenge following a unit on plants and the affect of abiotic environmental factors like light, moisture, and gravity on plant growth and plant response to stimuli. As students grow and observe plants they will become familiar with the behavior of roots growing down in response to gravity (geotropism) or growing toward a source of moisture (hydrotropism) and to stems growing toward a light source (phototropism). This challenge provides students an opportunity to investigate the factors that often control the growth and appearance of plants, as well as to manipulate them.

Ties to Content: Plants can be trained to grow in a variety of ways. In most cases, a plant's growth pattern is caused by plant hormones called auxins but can be regulated through mechanical means such as continuously re-positioning the plant to influence plant growth or by using wire restraints to shape plant growth. The plant hormones are generated in response to environmental abiotic stimuli like light, gravity, or moisture. In addition, chemicals such as the gibberellins encourage stem elongation by stimulating cell division and elongation. They can also cause plants to grow in prescribed ways. Ethylene has been used to hasten the ripening of fruit.

Possible Procedures(s): The most common method for producing a snake-like plant relies on the a plant's response to light called photoperiodism (growing toward the source of light). Once a plant begins to grow a mailing tube, or other cylinder, should be placed between the plant and its light source. As the plant continues to grow it should be continuously turned away from the light and this will encourage the plant to bend toward the light around the tube. The mailing tube blocks the light on the inside of the plant stem and encourages the auxins to elongate the cells on the outside of the plant stem. This differentiated growth pattern drives the stem around the tube in a Slinky-like manner. Once the plant is established, the tube should be removed.

Precautions: Allergic reactions to latex and food products may also be an issue. Be sure to obtain parental permission to check student medical records for such adverse reactions.

While the problem solving techniques used by each team may be different, the diversity of thinking is beneficial for enhancing the problem solving repertoire of each student. Sharing is not only encouraged it is a strategy used throughout the program.

SEED SCHEME

- Design a solution to a problem. *NSES*
- Develop descriptions, explanations, predictions, and models using evidence. *NSES*
- As a result of activities in grades 5-8, all students should develop an understanding of the structure and function in living systems. *NSES*
- Students adjust their use of spoken, written, and visual language (e.g., conventions, style, vocabulary) to communicate effectively with a variety of audiences and for different purposes. *NCTE*
- Students use a variety of technological and information resources (e.g., libraries, databases, computer networks, video) to gather and synthesize information and to create and communicate knowledge. *NCTE*

The Context: Classification systems rely on accurate observations and precise descriptions.

The Scenario: Your botanical research group has just returned from an expedition to the tropical rainforest. The purpose of your venture was to gather and identify new species of monocot and dicot specimens. The collecting phase went rather well but identifying these plants has become a real problem. To help you in classifying you decide to visit to your local Museum of Natural History only to find that its monocot/dicot display simply does not exist as funds ran out before the display could be created.

The Challenge: While speaking to the museum director, you expressed your dismay that the display was not in order. She suggested that your research group design and construct a display showing the variety of ways that monocots and dicots can be identified.

The Limitations:
- Each team will have five class periods to complete this project. The class periods are at the discretion of the teacher.
- Each team is solely responsible for researching this subject and is expected to include a bibliography of its sources.
- General school supplies like paper, scissors, tape, glue, crayons, markers, etc. may be supplied. All other materials will be the responsibility of the research group.

The Rules:
- Each team must design a way to display and communicate the research findings and bibliography to the museum visitors.
- Displays should be colorful, neat, informative and be easy to follow.
- Each team must present and explain its display.
- Students should refer to the *Team Presentation Rubric* as they craft their presentations.

TEACHER NOTES

Suggested Materials: Students will need general school supplies for this project. In addition, cardboard, poster board or tri-fold boards could also be made available or could be the responsibility of the students. The students will also need copies of the *Team Presentation Rubric* for reference.

Suggested Use: This design brief should be used with a unit on plant study. Plants can be classified in a variety of ways and separating them by their seed structure is a common procedure.

Ties to Content: Flowering plants (angiosperms) can be classified into two major categories: monocotyledons (monocots) and dicotyledons (dicots). Monocots have seeds that contain embryos with single cotyledons, or seed leafs, whereas, dicots have seeds containing embryos with two cotyledons. Besides the differences already noted, monocots and dicots also differ in the vein pattern of their respective leaves, the structure of their flowers, their root structures, the presence of secondary growth, and the arrangement of the vascular bundles. Monocots include such plants as lilies, palms, grasses (wheat, corn rye, barley) and orchids. Dicots include many of the common flowering plants, shrubs and cactuses.

Possible Procedure(s): The three class periods of this challenge are at the discretion of the teacher. It is suggested that you schedule this challenge in manageable parts to include project research, project display construction and project presentation. The establishment of a reasonable time line is essential for keeping children on task.

Precautions: There are no precautions directly associated with this challenge.

While the problem solving techniques used by each team may be different, the diversity of thinking is beneficial for enhancing the problem solving repertoire of each student. Sharing is not only encouraged it is a strategy used throughout the program.

DISTRIBUTION SOLUTION

- Design a solution to a problem. *NSES*
- Develop descriptions, explanations, predictions, and models using evidence. *NSES*
- Students should develop an understanding of the structure and function in living systems. *NSES*
- Apply and adapt a variety of appropriate strategies to solve problems. *NCTM*
- Students adjust their use of spoken, written, and visual language (e.g., conventions, style, vocabulary) to communicate effectively with a variety of audiences and for different purposes. *NCTE*

The Context: The process of spreading out from a single location is called dispersal. For example, young plants often benefit from being some distance from the parent plant because they do not have to compete with the more mature members of the species for food, water, and sunlight. Members of the plant kingdom demonstrate a variety of ways to disperse their seeds.

The Scenario: You work in the Model Fabrication Division of a metropolitan science museum and as such you are often asked to produce unique items that can be used as props in museum exhibits.

The Challenge: Your team has just been given the assignment of designing and constructing an exhibit that contains both a plant and a seed model for a display about prehistoric vegetation.

The Limitations:
- Each team will have to supply all of its own materials.
- Each team will have three class periods for this challenge. Budget your time and personnel.
- Each plant and seed model must be to scale (the seed cannot be larger than the prehistoric plant part that produced it).
- The prehistoric plant/seed must accurately show one or two methods of dispersal.
- Real plants and seeds, or their parts, may not be used.

The Rules:
- The plant must have a descriptive name.
- Each team must document how many seed dispersal methods it found in researching the topic.
- Research references must appear in bibliographical form.
- Each team must create a title for the exhibit along with an attractive poster or illustrated newspaper/magazine advertisement announcing the opening of the exhibit.
- This presentation should include:
  - The materials used in crafting the models and how they were put together.
  - How the plant name was selected and the one or two methods of seed dispersal demonstrated by this plant or seed.
  - A review of the poster or newspaper/magazine advertisement.
  - The reason/reasons that the museum director should select your model over the other designs.
- Students should refer to the *Team Presentation Rubric* in crafting their presentations.

TEACHER NOTES

Suggested Materials: Students should have access to general classroom supplies in crafting their plant and seed models. In addition they should also have copies of the *Team Presentation Rubric* in crafting their presentations.

Suggested Use: This design brief will give students an opportunity to translate the various methods of seed dispersal into a three dimensional model. Students will also be responsible for designing and crafting plant and corresponding seed models.

Ties to Content: The dispersal of seeds reduces the competition between parent plants and offspring, hopefully ensuring survival of a species. Additionally, it reduces overcrowding and provides opportunities for plants to spread to new locations. Seeds are dispersed in five different ways. These include wind dispersal, water dispersal, animal dispersal, explosive release, and fire. Wind dispersal occurs when the structure of the seed is able to catch air currents, thereby transporting the seed away from the parent plant Dandelions have seeds that disperse in this fashion. Other seeds like the maple employ a wing structure that act like a helicopter to carry the heavy seed away. Seeds can also be dispersed by water. In this case, seeds of fruit are dropped from the plant into water. Generally, the seeds float and are dispersed via the water currents. Animals can disperse seeds by carrying them on the outside of their bodies via hooks or burrs. They can also eat a fruit and then pass the seeds out through their droppings.

Plants can also disperse their seeds through mechanical means. For example, the seed pods of the Impatient plant contain a spring like device that is activated when the seeds are ripe and the turgor (water) pressure in the plant is high. When the seed pods are disturbed they split open and the spring throws the seeds away from the parent plant. Similarly, pea and bean plants keep their seeds in a pod. When the seeds are ripe and the pod has dried, the pod bursts open and the peas and beans are scattered.

The last way plants disperse their seeds is by fire. Trees like the Lodgepole pine and Jack pine are dependant on fire for seed dispersal. The cones of these trees require heat to open them allowing for seed dispersal. Other plant species that require heat for seed dispersal are rice grass, reed grass, deer bush and pine grass.

Possible Procedures(s): This design challenge requires students to research and apply information about the various methods of seed dispersal. After gathering data about the different methods of seed dispersal, the student teams may pursue different directions from there. This challenge contains a variety of components and student groups should be encouraged to assign responsibilities and manage the allotted time appropriately. To assist in this process, it is suggested that a time schedule be created to help keep students on task.

Precautions: Students will be expected to wear appropriate eye protection during this investigation.

While the problem solving techniques used by each team may be different, the diversity of thinking is beneficial for enhancing the problem solving repertoire of each student. Sharing is not only encouraged it is a strategy used throughout the program.

A GROWING CONCERN

- Design a solution to a problem. *NSES*
- Implement a proposed design and evaluate completed technological designs or products. *NSES*
- Apply and adapt a variety of appropriate strategies to solve problems. *NCTM*
- Students adjust their use of spoken, written, and visual language (e.g., conventions, style, vocabulary) to communicate effectively with a variety of audiences and for different purposes. *NCTE*

The Context: The results of our actions are not always immediately understood.

The Scenario: The Johnson Brothers have a seasonal lawn care business and want to expand it to include late fall and winter services. They have tons of equipment including a salt spreader that would evenly distribute any ice melting product. As winter approaches, they need to purchase something to help prevent ice on the sidewalks and driveways. But what should they buy?

The Challenge: Your research team has been contacted by the Johnson Brothers to help them with their dilemma. They have three questions that need to be answered: *Which ice melting product will work the fastest? Which will last the longest? Will these ice-melting products damage the grass plants that boarder the driveways and walks?*

The Limitations:
- Three class periods for researching, designing and presenting will be devoted to this design brief at the discretion of the teacher.
- As living things will be used in this challenge, research teams will also have 3-4 weeks to collect and process data regarding the three questions noted in the challenge.
- Each team must submit a detailed plan of action as to how they intend to address the questions before they begin.
- All variables for each of the three questions must be noted on the plan.
- No team will be permitted to proceed unless its plan has been approved.

The Rules:
- Each team must create data collecting and data display formats.
- Each individual in the research team must write a report to the Johnson Brothers detailing what steps were taken to answer their three questions, the results of each study, the conclusions, and recommendations.
- Conclusions and recommendations must be supported by experimental data.

TEACHER NOTES

Suggested Materials: The class will need at least two different ice melting products, three would be better. They will also need a freezer (unless it is cold enough outside), aluminum pans in which to freeze the water, planting pots, potting soil and grass seed. Research teams should be encouraged to supply some of their own materials as well.

Suggested Use: This design brief could be used with a unit on environmental studies or plant study. It could also be used in physical science lessons involving physical change, solutions, or melting point depression. The focus of this design brief is that the students to develop a "fair test" procedure to answer three separate, but related questions. Processing this data will be the responsibility of each student in that each is required to craft a data supported report with recommendations.

Ties to Content: Using ice melting compounds to clear snow and ice from sidewalks and driveways is virtually a universal practice today. There are more than 100 brands of ice-melters available. While products can carry labeling which specifies contents, there may be erroneous or misleading claims made about the products' abilities. This results in confusion about the benefits and limitations of such products.

Of the materials available, rock salt and calcium chloride are most extensively used. Rock salt, calcium chloride, potassium chloride, and magnesium chloride are naturally occurring salts. Urea, ammonium nitrate, and ammonium sulfate are synthetic materials which find their most common applications as fertilizers. Generally, all ice-melters work in the same way. They depress the freezing point of ice or snow and turn the mixture into a liquid or semi-liquid slush. Fertilizer products work in much the same manner, though they do not form a brine. All are soluble in water and the resulting solutions ac by depressing the freezing point of snow and ice. Ice-melters vary in how fast they work, the quantity of material required, and the duration of melting action. Their environmental friendliness is also an important consideration.

Possible Procedures(s): In order to evaluate the effectiveness of ice melting products, students will need to control the amount of the products used. Usually, the recommended use is determined by volume. Spreading the product might also be an issue. A sieve would work well for this distribution purposes. As the investigation progresses the students will need to collect and record accurate data for processing, displaying, and interpreting. At the conclusion of this challenge the students will be expected to craft written reports of their investigations with recommendations.

Precautions: Students will be expected to wear appropriate eye protection during this investigation. Care should be taken when using any chemical. Check the MSDS sheet for each chemical prior to use. Should these sheets not be available check the Flinn Scientific Catalog or the Flinn Scientific website, www.flinnsci.com. Click on the chemistry link and then the MSDS link.

While the problem solving techniques used by each team may be different, the diversity of thinking is beneficial for enhancing the problem solving repertoire of each student. Sharing is not only encouraged it is a strategy used throughout the program.

GROWING LIKE A WEED

> - Design a solution to a problem. *NSES*
> - Implement a proposed design and evaluate completed technological designs or products. *NSES*
> - Apply and adapt a variety of appropriate strategies to solve problems. *NCTM*
> - Students adjust their use of spoken, written, and visual language (e.g., conventions, style, vocabulary) to communicate effectively with a variety of audiences and for different purposes. *NCTE*

The Context: Growing things can be somewhat controlled by manipulating the factors that affect development.

The Scenario: The "Flower Power Boutique and Plant Emporium" has decided to cut the middle man out of its costs by building its own nursery and growing its own plants. While this idea is economically sound, completing this improvement project in time to have enough inventory for the annual Mother's Day Plant Sale is going to be close to impossible unless the growth rate of the plants can somehow be increased.

The Challenge: Your research lab has been asked by the boutique to develop and test a procedure for growing plants faster.

The Limitations:
- Each team will have three weeks to complete this project. The amount of actual class time will be at the discretion of the teacher.
- All research teams must prepare a "fair test" action plan before they gather any materials and begin setting up their investigation.
- Variables must be identified as dependent (responding) or independent (controlled)
- Each team will have access to the general planting and standard laboratory equipment.
- Each team may supply additional materials if so desired.
- Each team must create a way to collect and display its data

The Rules:
- As a whole, the class must determine the criteria for what is meant by "increasing growth" prior to the start of the investigations.
- All plants will be evaluated three weeks after planting.
- Each researcher must maintain a notebook containing observations, dates, sketches, collected data and formats, modifications, summary statements and questions that arise from the investigation.
- Each researcher must craft a report to the boutique containing a brief summary of the investigation and data supported recommendations.

TEACHER NOTES

Suggested Materials: The materials needed for this investigation could be as varied as the number of groups you have in the classroom. General planting materials such as pots, potting soil, sand, water, small stones or shard, plastic wrap, thermometers, fertilizer, and centimeter rulers would be a good start. Research teams should be encouraged to supply some of their own materials as well. Additionally, several packets of fresh flower seeds would need to be purchased for this investigation. When buying the seeds be sure to check the packet for planting and germination information as this would be helpful in scheduling.

Suggested Use: As students progress through most units on plants they will usually be asked to investigate the affect of changing environmental factors of the growth of plants. Such is the case with this design brief. The focus of this design brief is that the students develop a "fair test" procedure for optimizing the environmental conditions that affect the growth of flowering plants. Students are then expected to conduct their investigations and share their data with others. Processing this data will be the responsibility of each student as they are then required to craft a data supported letter with recommendations.

Ties to Content: After a seed has germinated, the new plant has certain requirements that must be met. All plants require water, a sufficient amount of sunlight for the process of photosynthesis, carbon dioxide as a chemical building block, nutrients that promote stem, root, leaf, and flower growth and a specific temperature range. Commercial nurseries must often "force" their plants to grow faster and to bloom at a certain time. Nurseries generally do this by adjusting the amount of light. Soil and air temperature are also critical considerations, as well as the humidity, the amount of water a plant receives and the specific nutrients made available. Each plant species has its own specific requirements in regards to the environmental limiting factors. Optimum conditions for most plants can be found in reference books and on the informational tags that come with plants.

Possible Procedures(s): Students will be expected to craft a "fair test" investigation for optimizing the environmental factors that might affect the growth of flowering plants. These proposals need to be reviewed and approved prior to the students gathering materials. As the investigation progresses the students will need to collect and record accurate data for processing, displaying, and interpreting. At the conclusion of this challenge the students will be expected to craft a written report of their investigations with recommendations.

Precautions: Students will be expected to wear appropriate eye protection during this investigation. Care should be taken when using any chemical. Check the MSDS sheet for each chemical prior to use. Should these sheets not be available check the Flinn Scientific Catalog or the Flinn Scientific website, www.flinnsci.com. Click on the chemistry link and then the MSDS link.

While the problem solving techniques used by each team may be different, the diversity of thinking is beneficial for enhancing the problem solving repertoire of each student. Sharing is not only encouraged it is a strategy used throughout the program.

MAGNETISM AND ELECTRICITY

MIGHTY MAGNETS

- Design a solution to a problem. *NSES*
- As a result of activities in grades 5-8, all students should develop an understanding of transfer of energy. *NSES*
- Apply and adapt a variety of appropriate strategies to solve problems. *NCTM*
- Students employ a wide range of strategies as they write and use different writing process elements appropriately to communicate with different audiences for a variety of purposes. *NCTE*

The Context: Measuring quantities can be done in a variety of ways even without standardized measuring equipment.

The Scenario: The Marketing Department at the Stickem Up Magnet Company, Inc. has just been given the responsibility of increasing company profits and they conceive of a very simple, but effective concept…the stronger the magnet the more it should cost. But, how will they determine a magnet's strength? Measuring is usually a quantitative process, which suggests that the answer needs to be in numerical form and that is the problem. How can the strength of a magnet be quantitatively measured?

The Challenge: Your challenge as a member of the research and development team is to develop, and verify, at least two different ways of measuring the relative strengths for a variety of magnets.

The Limitations:
- Each team is responsible for gathering its own materials from the general supplies in the room.
- All results must be numerical regardless of which methods are chosen.
- Two class periods will be devoted to this investigation
- Each team must create a data table for recording experimental results.
- Each team must conduct three or more trials with each selected method.
- Data must be averaged.

The Rules:
- Each team member must create a graph which illustrates the results of the investigations.
- Each team member must write a report describing the methods used to determine the relative strength of each magnet and the comparison of the rankings using each testing method.

TEACHER NOTES

Suggested Materials: The materials needed for this challenge are large and small paper clips, 3 X 5 cards, magnetic compasses, metric tapes, small steel washers, spring scales, several containers of water and other general school supplies as needed.

Suggested Use: This design brief can be used after the students have had some experience with magnets. A logical question to raise about magnets refers to their relative strengths. Students can offer their subjective opinions regarding the relative strengths of different magnets, but this challenge asks them to find a way to quantify that difference.

Ties to Content: The relative strength of a magnet is dependent upon the orbital and spin motions of the electrons of the material and how these electrons interact with each other. All matter is affected by magnets in some way. However, some are more affected than others. In the most magnetic materials there are a large number of interactive moments between the electrons.

There are four categories of magnetic materials. These include paramagnetic materials, ferromagnetic materials, ferrimagnetic materials and diamagnetic materials. Substances like gold and copper are very weakly attracted to magnets because they are paramagnetic - a property that allows them to become very weak magnets. Ferromagnetic materials like iron and steel are strongly attracted to magnets and are greatly affected by magnetic fields. This allows them to actually become strong magnets. Magnetite is a crystal that is ferrimagnetic. Everything else is considered diamagnetic, which means they do not appear to respond to magnetic fields. However, all matter is made of atoms or molecules which do have a slight response to magnetic fields. Diamagnetic materials include plants, animals, paper and even you.

Possible Procedure(s): Some possible ways of determining a magnet's strength include:
- Counting the number of paper clips picked up.
- Counting the number of sheets of paper that separate the magnet from a paperclip that is held in place by the magnet force.
- Measuring the distance between a magnetic compass and the point at which a magnet, approaching the needle from the east or the west, causes the needle to move.
- Measuring the distance between a paper clip (hanging by a thread) and the point at which a magnet causes the paper clip to move.
- Weighing the amount of iron filings a magnet will pick up (put test magnets in a plastic bag to keep them clean).

Precautions: A directional compass is actually a small magnet balanced and spinning on a pivot. It is possible to reverse the polarity of these devices by touching them with a magnet. Should this happen to your compasses they will still point in the north/south direction only the north seeking end of the needle (usually the colored end) will be pointing south. These reversed compasses can be changed back to their original condition once again getting them close to a regular magnet. It may take some practice because the trick is to get the like poles of the compass and the magnet to touch…something they do not want to do. But take heart, the compass needle is a very weak magnet and will be re-polarized as soon as the regular magnet is brought close by. Hint: Bring the regular magnet down toward the center of the compass needle and then move it out to the end. This will usually do the trick.

While the problem solving techniques used by each team may be different, the diversity of thinking is beneficial for enhancing the problem solving repertoire of each student. Sharing is not only encouraged it is a strategy used throughout the program.

THE CIVIL WAR

- Design a solution to a problem. *NSES*
- Think critically and logically to make the relationships between evidence and explanations. *NSES*
- Apply and adapt a variety of appropriate strategies to solve problems. *NCTM*
- Students employ a wide range of strategies as they write and use different writing process elements appropriately to communicate with different audiences for a variety of purposes. *NCTE*

The Context: Solving a puzzle often depends on how the pieces appear or how they interact.

The Scenario: The Cheapo Magnet Company experienced a power failure last week at the end of its production line. As a result, the poles of the magnets produced were never labeled North (N) and
South (S).

The Challenge: Your team has been given the task of finding a way to identify and correctly label the poles of the magnets produced. You know that unlike poles attract one another and like poles repel one another.

The Limitations:
- Each team will receive a similar set of unmarked magnets.
- Each team must create and record a procedure for solving the problem.
- Each team must also provide a rationale for why it believes its procedure will result in the accurate labeling of the unmarked magnets.
- Each team will have one day to gather any additional materials it believes will be helpful in solving the problem.
- All work, including labeling, must be done within one class period.

The Rules:
- Each team will have two periods to complete this challenge - one day for writing the procedure, rationale and magnet labeling, and one day for presenting the findings.
- Each team must create and record a procedure for solving the problem.
- A materials list must be created.
- Each team must present its findings, but in a form other than a written report.

TEACHER NOTES

Suggested Materials: Each design team should receive the same number of unlabeled magnets. The quantity is not as important as the variety. Ball magnets and flat refrigerator magnets can often pose an further challenge. In addition to the supply of magnets a few magnetic compasses, plastic caps that will float or cork slices, steel pins, nails, steel and copper wire, shallow dishes and water might also be left out for students to consider. Some of these materials could be red herrings.

Suggested Use: After the students have investigated magnets, this challenge could be used as a performance assessment. The challenge requires students to apply the concept that the opposite poles of magnets attract one another and the like poles of magnets repel one another. Understanding how a magnetic compass functions is also pertinent. Alternately, this challenge could be used as an introduction to the properties of magnets. In such a case, the students would learn through discovery.

Ties to Content: Finding the poles of unmarked magnets is not an easy task for some students because of the confusion between the labels that are usually found on the magnets and the actual polarity of the magnets. In sum, they are opposite and thus the mental confusion. For example, the end of a magnet that is labeled with an "N" for north, is actually the "north seeking" end of the magnet. Applying the rule that the opposite poles of two magnets attract then the "north seeking" end is actually the south pole of that magnet. To demonstrate this, suspend the magnet by a string tied in the center. The magnet will come to rest with the "north seeking" pole pointing to the magnetic north pole of the earth. This demonstration can easily be observed when using a magnetic compass which is nothing more than a magnet balanced on a needle with the "north seeking" end, or south pole, indicated by a bright color.

Possible Procedure(s): Students will probably have little difficulty in finding the like and unlike poles of the magnets supplied. However, the question of accurately labeling the poles remains. Using a magnet with labeled poles as a reference may provide some help. Using a magnetic compass is yet another way of solving the puzzle since it is a magnet as well.

Precautions: Be sure that your students keep all magnets away from any computer equipment or other electronic devices including televisions.

While the problem solving techniques used by each team may be different, the diversity of thinking is beneficial for enhancing the problem solving repertoire of each student. Sharing is not only encouraged it is a strategy used throughout the program.

MAGNETIC METAL MADNESS

- Design a solution to a problem. *NSES*
- Think critically and logically to make the relationships between evidence and explanations. *NSES*
- Apply and adapt a variety of appropriate strategies to solve problems. *NCTM*
- Students adjust their use of spoken, written, and visual language (e.g., conventions, style, vocabulary) to communicate effectively with a variety of audiences and for different purposes. *NCTE*

The Context: Change is often a chain reaction, in that the changes that occur in one place usually cause changes somewhere else.

The Scenario: You family manages a small scrap yard on the outskirts of town. As various metals are delivered to your yard, they are sorted in different ways. The aluminum, brass and copper are separated by hand, while cast iron and steel are handled by a strong electromagnet attached to a movable crane. Until recently the equipment was able to easily handle the weight of the materials. But your family has started accepting junk cars which are too heavy for your present electromagnet to lift.

The Challenge: The cost of a new electromagnet is too expensive for your family business. You begin to wonder if the lifting capacity of your current electromagnet could somehow be doubled. You decide to proceed by constructing and testing a model electromagnet to determine how many paper clips it can pick up. Once you find the magnet's capacity then you need to find out if it can be modified to double the strength. If your idea works with the model you'll use the same procedure to change the real electromagnet in the scrap yard.

The Limitations:
- Each team will receive a supply of basic materials.
- Each team may supply one additional material or item of its choice.
- Two class periods will be devoted to this investigation at the discretion of the teacher.
- Each electromagnet must have an on/off switch.
- Small paper clips will be used as the standard unit of measurement.

The Rules:
- Each team must display the lifting capacity of its original electromagnet.
- Each team must create a data chart showing the parts of the electromagnet.
- Each team will get two chances to demonstrate its improved electromagnet.
- Electromagnets may not be altered between demonstrations.
- Students should refer to the *Project Assessment Rubric* for guidance when designing, constructing, testing and presenting their project.

TEACHER NOTES

Suggested Materials: The suggested basic materials for each design team include: four fresh 1.5 volt batteries, three meters of insulated copper wire (22-24 gauge), several two meter lengths of insulated copper wire, a variety of steel nails (12, 16, & 20 common), a switch, 30 cm of masking tape and a copy of the *Project Assessment Rubric*. Different gauges of insulated copper wire may also be added if available.

Suggested Use: This application challenge was designed for students who have had at least an introduction to electromagnets. Once students have constructed an electromagnet it is a natural transition to inquire about how to make the magnet stronger.

Ties to Content: In an electromagnet, the coils of wire that are wrapped around the iron core create a magnetic field around that core. As more and more coils are overlapped, the magnetic field becomes stronger. Other ways to increase the strength of the magnet include adding batteries in series to the power source, decreasing the gauge of the wire or increasing the size of the iron core. The electromagnet is considered a temporary magnet because it is dependent upon the current flowing through the wire. When the current is interrupted the magnetism stops.

Possible Procedure(s): The challenge, to double the lifting capacity of the electromagnet, could be different for each design team since the outcome is dependent upon the original lifting capacity of each electromagnet. A series circuit with an in-line switch is generally used with an electromagnet. The strength of an electromagnet is generally increased by adding batteries to the power source, adding additional windings of insulated copper wire around the iron core, using a smaller gauge wire or increasing the size of the iron core of the electromagnet. The inclusion of an in-line switch is necessary since the electromagnet is a direct short and as such will quickly drain the batteries. The switch allows the circuit to remain open unless in use, thus preventing a drain of the batteries. Recall that teams were required to identify the parts of their electromagnets (type of nail, # of windings of wire, # or batteries used, and paper clips picked up).

Precautions: Using 1.5 volt dry cells for teaching simple circuitry in schools has been a standard for a number of years and has not presented a major safety issue. There are, however, a few precautions that should be followed. First, inspect student circuits for short circuits (a direct connection between the positive and the negative poles of the power source that can cause the connecting wire to become hot enough to cause a burn). Second, never take a dry cell apart. Batteries are filled with a corrosive paste and should never be opened or cut apart. Third, always dispose of batteries in an environmentally safe manner. Batteries are comprised of heavy metals and other elements and should never be sent to the landfill.

While the problem solving techniques used by each team may be different, the diversity of thinking is beneficial for enhancing the problem solving repertoire of each student. Sharing is not only encouraged it is a strategy used throughout the program.

I WONDER ???

- Design a solution to a problem. *NSES*
- As a result of activities in grades 5-8, all students should develop an understanding of transfer of energy. *NSES*
- Apply and adapt a variety of appropriate strategies to solve problems. *NCTM*
- Students employ a wide range of strategies as they write and use different writing process elements appropriately to communicate with different audiences for a variety of purposes. *NCTE*

The Context: Permanent and temporary magnets possess similar characteristics. Electromagnets appear to behave exactly like permanent magnets... but do electromagnets have poles like permanent magnets and can these poles be reversed?

The Scenario: Following a break-in, the security at your building has been increased. Outside video cameras have been installed and the front entrance has been converted to a security door that can only be opened after someone on the inside deactivates the electromagnetic lock. But there is a problem... the lock is working backwards. The security door will not lock unless someone inside the building throws the switch. The lock is working backwards and must be corrected so that throwing the switch will unlock the door.

The Challenge: You and your engineering team have been called in to fix the problem. After discussing a number of suggestions, you wonder if the problem has something to do with magnetic poles. You know that permanent magnets have poles; but is this true of electromagnets? Since the lock is working backwards, you wonder if the problem could be solved by finding out if electromagnets have north and south poles and, if so, can these poles be reversed?

The Limitations:
- Each team must create and submit an action plan before gathering materials.
- Two class periods will be set aside for the completion of this entire investigation including pre-planning and documentation.
- Each team is responsible for its own time management.
- All materials must be obtained from the general supply of magnetic and electrical items.

The Rules:
- Each team member must write a report documenting what was done to solve the problem.
- All conclusions made about the poles of the electromagnets must be supported by data.
- Each team member must use investigative data to write a set of directions that could be used to correct the problem with the lock

TEACHER NOTES

Suggested Materials: For each design team supply the following materials. Three 1.5 volt dry cells, a supply of 22 gauge insulated copper wire (40 cm long pieces for making connections and a 2 meter piece for making the electromagnets, one #16 or #20 common nail, a magnet, a directional compass, and a switch. In addition, all other equipment used in the study of magnetism and electricity should be made available for student use.

Suggested Use: Students who have had some experience with magnets, electrical circuits and electromagnets should be ready to apply that knowledge in completing this challenge. The students will have to understand the attraction and repulsion of magnetic poles, how to construct a series circuit, how to wire an in-line switch, and how to construct an electromagnet.

Ties to Content: A Danish physics teacher, Hans Christian Oersted, hypothesized that an electric current moving through a wire produced a magnetic field around the wire. He also observed that the direction of the magnetic field changed with a change in the direction of the current. In an electromagnet, the coils of wire that are wrapped around the iron core induce a magnetic field in that core. As more and more coils are overlapped the stronger the magnetic field becomes. As with every other magnet, the core of the electromagnet has a north and a south pole.

Possible Procedure(s): The polarity of an electromagnet can be reversed by either switching the positive and the negative wires on the power source or by reversing the coils that are wrapped around iron core.

A series circuit is generally used with an electromagnet with an in line switch. The strength of an electromagnet is generally altered by changing the number of batteries serving as the power source or adding additional windings of insulated copper wire around the iron core. An in-line switch is necessary because electromagnets are a direct short and as such will quickly drain the batteries. The switch allows the current to remain open unless the magnet is in use.

In an electromagnet, the coils of wire that are wrapped around the iron core create a magnetic field around that core. As more and more coils are overlapped, the magnetic field becomes stronger. Other ways to increase the strength of the magnet include adding batteries in series to the power source, decreasing the gauge of the wire or increasing the size of the iron core. The electromagnet is considered a temporary magnet because it is dependent upon the current flowing through the wire. When the current is interrupted, the magnetism stops.

Precautions: Using 1.5 volt dry cells for teaching simple circuitry in schools has been a standard for a number of years and has not presented a major safety issue. There are, however, a few precautions that should be followed. First, inspect student circuits for short circuits (a direct connection between the positive and the negative poles of the power source that can cause the connecting wire to become hot enough to cause a burn). Second, never take a dry cell apart. Batteries are filled with a corrosive paste and should never be opened or cut apart. Third, always dispose of batteries in an environmentally safe manner. Batteries are comprised of heavy metals and other elements and should never be sent to the landfill.

While the problem solving techniques used by each team may be different, the diversity of thinking is beneficial for enhancing the problem solving repertoire of each student. Sharing is not only encouraged it is a strategy used throughout the program.

TELEGRAPH TROUBLE (PART 1)

> - Design a solution to a problem. *NSES*
> - As a result of activities in grades 5-8, all students should develop an understanding of transfer of energy. *NSES*
> - Apply and adapt a variety of appropriate strategies to solve problems. *NCTM*
> - Students adjust their use of spoken, written, and visual language (e.g., conventions, style, vocabulary) to communicate effectively with a variety of audiences and for different purposes. *NCTE*

The Context: Improvements in technology can often increase the usefulness of a device.

The Scenario: In 1854 Samuel Morse was granted a patent for his invention of the telegraph and his device was hailed as a technological breakthrough. Your model telegraph is similar to the one Samuel Morse created in that it uses a switch, an electromagnet and a flexible metal arm that makes an audible "click" when it makes contact with the electromagnet. Your telegraph is dependent upon an external switch. Wonderful...but that's not exactly how a real telegraph works. The telegraph that Samuel Morse invented did not use an external switch and functioned as a sending device as well as an instrument that responded to incoming messages.

The Challenge: Your design team has been called together to solve the telegraph. Presently, your device will only send signals from an external switch. You need to redesign two telegraph systems so that they will both send and receive signals to one another without using additional switches.

The Limitations:
- Each team will have two class periods to complete this challenge
- A labeled drawing of the electric circuitry must be submitted before design teams can begin the construction phase.
- Each team will need to use two telegraphs.
- Each telegraph must function as a sender as well as a receiver.
- Each team will have access to the general electrical supplies for this challenge.

The Rules:
- Each team must provide a labeled sketch showing the circuitry in the final version of its system and be able to explain that system to others via an oral presentation.
- Telegraphs may not be changed or adjusted after the demonstrations begin.
- Students should refer to the *Project Assessment Rubric* for guidance when designing, constructing, testing and presenting their projects.

TEACHER NOTES

Suggested Materials: This challenge is an obvious extension of the commonly used telegraph investigation. In addition to the items the students used to construct their original telegraphs (see the following Telegraph Picture), the only material the students should need is additional lengths of 22-24 gauge wire and a copy of the *Project Assessment Rubric*. Other electrical supplies might also be made available to allow for creativity.

Suggested Use: Students who have successfully constructed a working telegraph should be ready for this challenge. In it also assumed that students have also had a number of experiences constructing simple circuits with in-line switches.

Ties to Content: The electromagnet is considered a temporary magnet because it is dependent upon current flowing through a wire that is wrapped around the iron core. In a standard classroom telegraph when the external switch is closed the electromagnet is powered and attracts the metal bar causing it to come in contact with the iron core thus producing the familiar "click".

Possible Procedure(s): The key to this challenge is for the students to think about rewiring each telegraph to function as a switch, or control, for the other telegraph. In fine tuning the telegraph, students may have to adjust the height of the iron core in the base, bend the steel banding, increase the strength of the electromagnet by adding batteries in series, adding coils of wire around the core, or a combination of all three. Each telegraph will then function as a sending instrument when forwarding a message and as a responding instrument when receiving a message.

Precautions: Using 1.5 volt dry cells for teaching simple circuitry in schools has been a standard for a number of years and has not presented a major safety issue. There are, however, a few precautions that should be followed. First, inspect student circuits for short circuits (a direct connection between the positive and the negative poles of the power source that can cause the connecting wire to become hot enough to cause a burn).Second, never take a dry cell apart. Batteries are filled with a corrosive paste and should never be opened or cut apart. Third, always dispose of batteries in an environmentally safe manner. Batteries are comprised of heavy metals and other elements and should never be sent to the landfill.

While the problem solving techniques used by each team may be different, the diversity of thinking is beneficial for enhancing the problem solving repertoire of each student. Sharing is not only encouraged it is a strategy used throughout the program.

HOMEMADE TELEGRAPH

Begin with two blocks of ¾ inch pine approximately 3 inches by 4 inches. Join them at one end with glue and finishing nails. Drill a small hole in the opposite end of the base block large enough to accommodate the nail of the electromagnet. Cut a piece of banding steel long enough to extend from the narrow cut in the vertical support to beyond the head of the nail. Banding steel is usually discarded as trash in lumber yards and home improvement stores. It is used to hold bundles of lumber together during shipping.

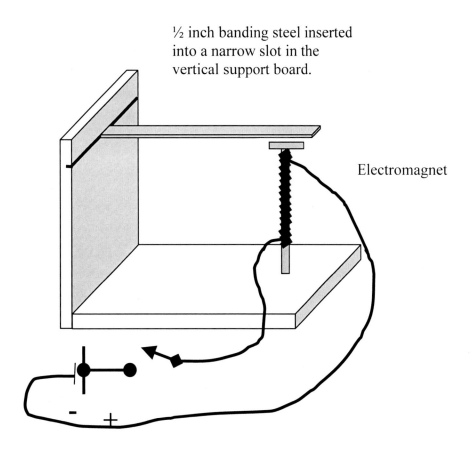

½ inch banding steel inserted into a narrow slot in the vertical support board.

Electromagnet

Battery and Switch

TELEGRAPH TROUBLE (PART 2)

- Design a solution to a problem. *NSES*
- As a result of activities in grades 5-8, all students should develop an understanding of transfer of energy. *NSES*
- Apply and adapt a variety of appropriate strategies to solve problems. *NCTM*
- Students employ a wide range of strategies as they write and use different writing process elements appropriately to communicate with different audiences for a variety of purposes. *NCTE*

The Context: In the event of an emergency, quick and creative thinking often solves a problem.

The Scenario: You are the "wireless" operator aboard the Titanic and are responsible for sending and receiving telegraph messages to and from other ships as well as the shore. At approximately 11:00 PM on the third night of your voyage, the Titanic hits an iceberg. The main lights are out and to make matters worse the incredible noise of the impact has caused you to be temporarily deaf. You are the only one on board that knows how to use the telegraph but now you are not able to hear the familiar "clicking" of the key.

The Challenge: Using any equipment available you are to re-design your telegraph so that it will be able to send messages that can be seen as well as heard…remember, you are unable to hear the telegraph key.

The Limitations:
- The ship is sinking and each team only has two periods to complete the challenge.
- The telegraph key must still work, in addition to any visual adaptations created.
- Each team must provide a procedure and a rationale for its telegraph alterations before gathering any materials.
- Each team may use any materials available to complete the task.

The Rules:
- The new telegraph design must work every time without adjustments.
- Each team must create a color sketch, with metric measurements and labels, so that someone else could use to change an existing telegraph so that it would function like your "advanced" model.
- Each team member must individually write a paragraph describing the invention, what equipment was used, how the equipment was set up, what problems were encountered, and how these problems were solved.
- Students must obtain a copy of the Morse Code.
- Each team must also create and transcribe a message to the other teams using Morse Code. It is expected that the other teams will translate sent messages.
- Students should refer to the *Project Assessment Rubric* for guidance when designing, constructing, testing and presenting their projects.

TEACHER NOTES

Suggested Materials: This challenge is an obvious extension of the commonly used telegraph investigation. In addition to the items the students used to construct their original telegraphs (see the following Telegraph Picture), the only material the students should need is additional lengths of 22-24 gauge wire and a copy of the *Project Assessment Rubric*. Other electrical supplies might also be made available to allow for creativity.

Suggested Use: Students who have successfully constructed a working telegraph should be ready for this challenge. In it also assumed that students have also had a number of experiences constructing simple circuits with in-line switches.

Suggested Use: Students who have successfully constructed a working telegraph should be ready for this challenge. In it also assumed that students have also had a number of experiences constructing simple circuits with in-line switches.

Ties to Content: The electromagnet is considered a temporary magnet because it is dependent upon a current flowing through a wire that is wrapped around the iron core. In a standard classroom telegraph, when the external switch is closed, the electromagnet is powered and attracts the metal bar causing it to come in contact with the iron core thus producing the familiar "click".

Possible Procedure(s): For this specific challenge students could wire a bulb, in series, with the switch that controls the telegraph. The key to this challenge is for the students to think about rewiring each telegraph to function as a switch, or control, for the other telegraph. In fine tuning the telegraph, students may have to adjust the height of the iron core in the base, bend the steel banding, increase the strength of the electromagnet by adding batteries in series, adding coils of wire around the core, or a combination of all three. Each telegraph will then function as a sending instrument when forwarding a message and as a responding instrument when receiving a message.

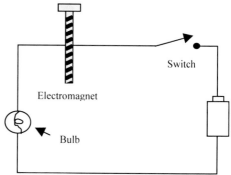

Precautions: Using 1.5 volt dry cells for teaching simple circuitry in schools has been a standard for a number of years and has not presented a major safety issue. There are, however, a few precautions that should be followed. First, inspect student circuits for short circuits (a direct connection between the positive and the negative poles of the power source that can cause the connecting wire to become hot enough to cause a burn). Second, never take a dry cell apart. Batteries are filled with a corrosive paste and should never be opened or cut apart. Third, always dispose of batteries in an environmentally safe manner. Batteries are comprised of heavy metals and other elements and should never be sent to the landfill.

While the problem solving techniques used by each team may be different, the diversity of thinking is beneficial for enhancing the problem solving repertoire of each student. Sharing is not only encouraged it is a strategy used throughout the program.

LIGHTS OUT!

- Design a solution to a problem. *NSES*
- As a result of activities in grades 5-8, all students should develop an understanding of transfer of energy. *NSES*
- Apply and adapt a variety of appropriate strategies to solve problems. *NCTM*
- Students employ a wide range of strategies as they write and use different writing process elements appropriately to communicate with different audiences for a variety of purposes. *NCTE*

The Context: All electrical systems are wired to perform in a specific way.

The Scenario: The Baker family just moved into a new house and they were very excited about their fresh surroundings. However, their joy quickly changed to concern when they discovered that in order for the light in any downstairs room to work the lights in the other three rooms also had to be on. They decided to call The Edison Group, the best electrical contractor in town.

The Challenge: As a member of the Edison Group, you are curious about the Baker's electrical problem and begin making plans to fix it. You decide to build a model of the Baker's first floor to duplicate their problem on a smaller, more manageable scale. Once that has been accomplished you'll need to rewire the model house so that the lights in each room work independently. Once your model is functioning properly, you will transfer the modifications to the actual house.

The Limitations:
- Each team will have two class periods to complete this challenge at the discretion of the teacher.
- The materials supplied to each team will be the same.
- Each team must present wiring diagrams of the circuits it plans to create in the model house before gathering any materials.
- Each team must wire at least three bulbs in the Baker house.
- In the revised wiring system each bulb must work independently of the others.
- Bulbs need not be attached to the walls of the model.

The Rules:
- Two schematics must be drawn, one labeled BEFORE and one labeled AFTER.
- Upon successfully rewiring the model house, each team member must independently write a report that compares the two different circuits including why they work differently.

TEACHER NOTES

Suggested Materials: Each team should receive the same materials which include (2) 1.5 volt dry cell batteries, three bulbs, (12) 25 cm lengths of copper wire (22-24 gauge), three switches, and if available two battery holders and three bulb holders. Purchasing strings of Christmas lights and cutting them between each bulb, allowing for wire leads, is an inexpensive way of obtaining large numbers of lights for classroom use. In order to easily simulate the first floor of the Baker's house have the design teams use cardboard boxes. Many of these boxes contain dividers that can represent interior walls.

Suggested Use: This challenge was developed as an application of series and parallel circuits. Students need to be conversant with wiring in-line switches and these two basic wiring systems before being given this challenge.

Ties to Content: The two kinds of circuits that students will be expected to use in most of their projects are series circuits and parallel circuits. In a series circuit the current, moving from the battery, has a single pathway to follow. Any interruption in this pathway will result in an incomplete circuit (fig. 1).

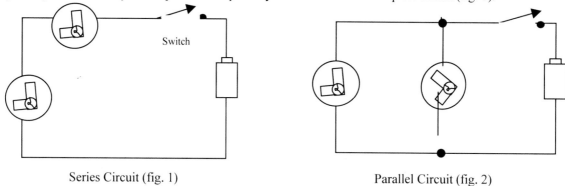

Series Circuit (fig. 1)   Parallel Circuit (fig. 2)

In a parallel circuit the current has separate branches to move through. The advantage to using parallel circuits in most settings is that if one appliance or light is removed, or becomes nonfunctional, the current to the other appliances or lights will not be interrupted (fig. 2).

The purpose of a switch in a circuit is to provide a way to interrupt the electrical circuit. In a battery and bulb system the switch can be placed on the negative or the positive side of the power source. When the switch is closed the current from the power source is given a completed pathway and the bulbs will light up. When the switch is opened the circuit is incomplete and no bulbs will light.

Possible Procedure(s): There are two basic ways to rewire the Baker's house so that when one light goes out the others will stay on. The most common procedure would be to rewire the entire first floor using a parallel wiring system. An alternative would be to wire each light as a completely separate system.

Precautions: Using 1.5 volt dry cells for teaching simple circuitry in schools has been a standard for many of years and has not presented a major safety issue. There are, however, a few precautions that should be followed. First, inspect student circuits for short circuits (a direct connection between the positive and the negative poles of the power source that can cause the connecting wire to become hot enough to cause a burn). Second, never take a dry cell apart. Batteries are filled with a corrosive paste and should never be opened or cut apart. Third, always dispose of batteries in an environmentally safe manner. Batteries are comprised of heavy metals and other elements and should never be sent to the landfill.

While the problem solving techniques used by each team may be different, the diversity of thinking is beneficial for enhancing the problem solving repertoire of each student. Sharing is not only encouraged it is a strategy used throughout the program.

ENLIGHTENING

- Design a solution to a problem. *NSES*
- As a result of activities in grades 5-8, all students should develop an understanding of transfer of energy. *NSES*
- Apply and adapt a variety of appropriate strategies to solve problems. *NCTM*
- Students adjust their use of spoken, written, and visual language (e.g., conventions, style, vocabulary) to communicate effectively with a variety of audiences and for different purposes. *NCTE*

The Context: Products we use are often changed and re-introduced into the marketplace.

The Scenario: The "Everbright" Flashlight Company has fallen on hard times. Sales are slumping and rumors of employee lay-offs are sure to become a reality.

The Challenge: Your design team has been called in to save the company from going bankrupt. Your job is to boost sales by re-inventing the "Everbright" flashlight making it more appealing to consumers.

The Limitations:
- Each team will have the same materials
- Each product must contain a working switch.
- Each team will be given one class period to design and construct the device.
- One additional period will be allotted for creating detailed sketches and presentations.
- Only authorized materials may be used.

The Rules:
- Each team must create an advertisement that publicizes its product, highlighting product advantages.
- Each team must draw a detailed sketch of its product, including a schematic of the circuit, identifying the type of circuit used, and noting its advantages over other circuits.
- Each team must present its invention to the "Everbright Board of Trustees" at the annual stockholders meeting.
- Presentations should include details about the positive product features, manufacturing costs, user friendliness, and suggested sales slogans.
- Students should refer to the *Project Assessment Rubric* and the *Team Presentation Rubric* for guidance when designing, constructing, testing and presenting their projects.

TEACHER NOTES

Suggested Materials: Each design team will need two 1.5 volt dry cell batteries, 30 cm insulated copper wire (22-24 gauge), a switch, a flashlight bulb, masking tape, a square of aluminum foil (15 centimeter square), a few rubber bands, a square of oak tag (15 centimeter square) and a copy for the *Project Assessment Rubric* and the *Team Presentation Rubric*.

Suggested Use: Prior to introducing this challenge students should have investigated series and parallel circuits. In addition, students should also have a working knowledge of how switches function and how they can be wired within circuits.

Ties to Content: The two kinds of circuits that students will be expected to use in most of their projects are series circuits and parallel circuits. In a series circuit the current, moving from the battery, has a single pathway to follow. Any interruption in this pathway will result in an incomplete circuit (fig. 1).

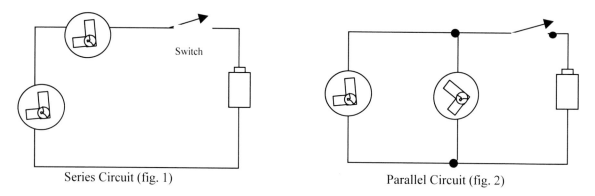

Series Circuit (fig. 1)   Parallel Circuit (fig. 2)

In a parallel circuit the current has separate branches to move through. The advantage to using parallel circuits in most settings is that if one appliance or light is removed, or becomes nonfunctional, the current to the other appliances or lights will not be interrupted (fig. 2).

The purpose of a switch in a circuit is to provide a way to interrupt the electrical circuit. In a battery and bulb system the switch can be placed on the negative or the positive side of the power source. When the switch is closed the current from the power source is given a completed pathway and the bulbs will light up. When the switch is opened the circuit is incomplete and no bulbs will light.

Possible Procedure(s): Flashlights are usually wired as a series circuit. In this type of circuit the more dry cells used the brighter the bulb will light. This is so because the voltages of the batteries in series are added together because the batteries are stacked positive to negative one on top of the other. Students will find that this is the optimum wiring procedure for this challenge, providing that they want to create a regular flashlight including a switch. More elaborate designs may require more elaborate circuitry.

Precautions: Using 1.5 volt dry cells for teaching simple circuitry in schools has been a standard for a number of years and has not presented a major safety issue. There are, however, a few precautions that should be followed. First, inspect student circuits for short circuits (a direct connection between the positive and the negative poles of the power source that can cause the connecting wire to become hot enough to cause a burn). Second, never take a dry cell apart. Batteries are filled with a corrosive paste and should never be opened or cut apart. Third, always dispose of batteries in an environmentally safe manner. Batteries are comprised of heavy metals and other elements and should never be sent to the landfill.

While the problem solving techniques used by each team may be different, the diversity of thinking is beneficial for enhancing the problem solving repertoire of each student. Sharing is not only encouraged it is a strategy used throughout the program.

THE MONSTER LIGHT

- Design a solution to a problem. *NSES*
- As a result of activities in grades 5-8, all students should develop an understanding of transfer of energy. *NSES*
- Apply and adapt a variety of appropriate strategies to solve problems. *NCTM*
- Students adjust their use of spoken, written, and visual language (e.g., conventions, style, vocabulary) to communicate effectively with a variety of audiences and for different purposes. *NCTE*

The Context: All electrical systems are wired to perform in a specific way.

The Scenario: The Monster-Lite Flashlight Company just discovered that they had a communication problem in their engineering department. It seems that the Power Division created an awesome four battery, 6 volt camping lantern. However, the Illumination Division created bulbs designed to work with no more than one battery. If these bulbs are used with the 6 volt system they will blow out immediately and with them the company's profits.

The Challenge: You are a member of the Wiring Division for the Monster-Lite Flashlight Company and have been asked to help solve the problem. Your team has been given the task of designing a wiring system that will use all four batteries but will only produce the light of a single battery system. If you are successful the Power Division and the Illumination Division will not have to suffer the embarrassment created by their lack of communication.

The Limitations:
- The new lighting system must consist of on bulb and 4 batteries.
- Each team must submit a wiring diagram must before starting construction.
- Each team will receive the same materials.
- The design and construction of the light will be limited to one class period.
- At the time of testing each team must compare the brightness of its four battery lighting system to a standard one battery lighting system that uses a similar bulb.

The Rules:
- As a result of testing, any changes in circuit design must be accompanied revised wiring diagram.
- Each team must demonstrate that each battery in the system is connected, and that removing any battery will not affect the brightness of the bulb.

TEACHER NOTES

Suggested Materials: The materials needed for each team include four 1.5 volt dry cell batteries, approximately 10 pieces of copper wire (22-24 gauge), a flashlight bulb, and a bulb holder. Prior to testing, set up a single battery and bulb system as a standard for comparison purposes using the same type of bulb that the students will have.

Suggested Use: After the students have had experience using bulbs to create series and parallel circuits they will be better prepared to try this challenge.

Ties to Content: This investigation is an application of connecting batteries in parallel. Usually batteries are connected in series as in a flashlight. In series, the voltage from each battery is cumulative. Thus, the more batteries used, the brighter the bulb will become. When wired in parallel, as in this investigation, the voltage is not cumulative but the storage capacity of the system is increased four times longer than in a single battery system. The bulb, however, will not be any brighter than with a single battery. Both systems will be rated as 1.5 volts.

Possible Procedure(s): The easiest way to accomplish this task is to use a non-insulated wire to connect the bottoms of all the batteries, one after the other. Use a second non-insulated wire to connect all the tops of the batteries, one after the other. The free ends of the wires should be

attached to the flashlight bulb in an appropriate fashion. The batteries will then be wired in series and the bulb will be receiving only as much power as it would from a single battery but will be able to receive that energy four times longer.

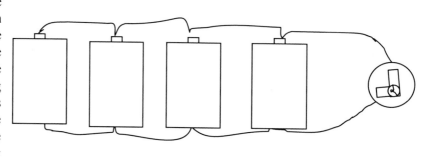

Precautions: Using 1.5 volt dry cells for teaching simple circuitry in schools has been a standard for a number of years and has not presented a major safety issue. There are, however, a few precautions that should be followed. First, inspect student circuits for short circuits (a direct connection between the positive and the negative poles of the power source that can cause the connecting wire to become hot enough to cause a burn). Second, never take a dry cell apart. Batteries are filled with a corrosive paste and should never be opened or cut apart. Third, always dispose of batteries in an environmentally safe manner. Batteries are comprised of heavy metals and other elements and should never be sent to the landfill.

While the problem solving techniques used by each team may be different, the diversity of thinking is beneficial for enhancing the problem solving repertoire of each student. Sharing is not only encouraged it is a strategy used throughout the program.

RECEPTIVE RECEPTACLE

- Design a solution to a problem. *NSES*
- As a result of activities in grades 5-8, all students should develop an understanding of transfer of energy. *NSES*
- Apply and adapt a variety of appropriate strategies to solve problems. *NCTM*
- Students adjust their use of spoken, written, and visual language (e.g., conventions, style, vocabulary) to communicate effectively with a variety of audiences and for different purposes. *NCTE*

The Context: All electrical systems are wired to perform in a specific way.

The Scenario: The holiday decorations are in place, a candle in each window, the electric train surrounds the base of the tree and as usual you have to crawl under, around and through the branches every time you want to plug or unplug the lights.

The Challenge: Your group has been contacted to solve this homeowner's problem by designing an electrical circuit wherein the receptacle can be controlled by a switch. This would allow the homeowner to control the lights on the tree and in the windows simply by closing the wall switch.

The Limitations:
- Each team will have one class period to solve this problem.
- An additional class period will be set aside for documentation purposes.
- Each team will be given a standard household receptacle, wall switch, and lamp plug. All other materials will be determined by the design team.

The Rules:
- A detailed sketch and written description of the electrical circuit must be completed by each team member after successfully completing the circuit.
- Each circuit must be demonstrated to prove it actually works.
- No adjustments in the circuitry may be made once the demonstrations begin.
- Students should refer to the *Project Assessment Rubric* for guidance when designing, constructing, testing and presenting their projects.

TEACHER NOTES

Suggested Materials: Each design team should receive a standard household receptacle, a household wall switch, and an inexpensive, replacement type lamp plug. These items are available at home improvement stores and are not too expensive. General supply items include a flashlight bulb and bulb holder, a 1.5 volt dry cell battery, a battery holder, simple switches, eight 20 cm lengths of copper wire (22-24 gauge), a screw driver to loosen and tighten the screws on the receptacle, a switch and a copy of the *Project Assessment Rubric*.

Suggested Use: This challenge was written to bridge the gap between classroom activities and real world household wiring, which is a mystery for most people. Students will be expected to apply and extend their knowledge of simple circuits as they manipulate and wire standard household electrical devices.

Ties to Content: The simple circuits that students have been creating are pretty much the same as those used in household wiring projects. The difference between the simple circuits being used in the classroom and household wiring is the size of the wire, the voltage and the electrical devices being used. For the most part homes are wired using parallel circuits, which allows each device to be relatively independent in relation to other devices in the same circuit.

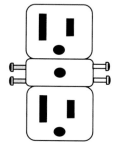

There may be some confusion as to how household electrical devices function. It is suggested that the students be given some time to compare the household devices to the simplified items with which they have been working. For example, regardless of the structure or type, single pole switches function the same way as the simplified versions found in most school science programs. They both open and close the circuit.   Side-wired receptacles, the most common type used in homes, have two terminal screws on each side. One pair is black or brass colored the other side, silver colored. The black or "hot" wire in a home electrical system always connects to the brass terminal. The white wire connects to the silver terminal.

Possible Procedure(s): Prior to distributing the household devices it is suggested that you allow the students to create a sample circuit using the same materials they have used for their other assignments.

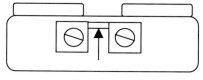

Once the circuit is completed the students can tackle the problem of wiring the unfamiliar devices. Should you want to extend and enhance the original challenge, ask your students to design an electrical circuit that would permit one half the receptacle to be controlled by a switch and the other half to maintain power at all times. In order for this to be possible the "break-off" tab along the side with the brass colored terminals must be broken off. Simply grab the break-off with a pair of pliers and bend it back and forth until it snaps off. Now the two halves of the receptacle are independent.

Precautions: Using 1.5 volt dry cells for teaching simple circuitry in schools has been a standard for a number of years and has not presented a major safety issue. There are, however, a few precautions that should be followed. Inspect student circuits for short circuits (a direct connection between the positive and the negative poles of the power source that can cause the connecting wire to become hot enough to cause a burn). Never take a dry cell apart. Batteries are filled with a corrosive paste and should never be opened or cut apart. Third, always dispose of batteries in an environmentally safe manner. Batteries are comprised of heavy metals and other elements and should never be sent to the landfill.

While the problem solving techniques used by each team may be different, the diversity of thinking is beneficial for enhancing the problem solving repertoire of each student. Sharing is not only encouraged it is a strategy used throughout the program.

THREE'S COMPANY

> - Design a solution to a problem. *NSES*
> - As a result of activities in grades 5-8, all students should develop an understanding of transfer of energy. *NSES*
> - Apply and adapt a variety of appropriate strategies to solve problems. *NCTM*
> - Students use a variety of technological and information resources (e.g., libraries, databases, computer networks, video) to gather and synthesize information and to create and communicate knowledge. *NCTE*
> - Students adjust their use of spoken, written, and visual language (e.g., conventions, style, vocabulary) to communicate effectively with a variety of audiences and for different purposes. *NCTE*

The Context: All electrical systems are wired to perform in a specific way.

The Scenario: Your school has started an after school program and you and your friends have decided to join the photography club. Since your house has a large, unused basement, the group suggests that locating the developing lab there would be ideal.

After the lab is set up you discover a major problem. The basement light is only controlled by a switch at the top of the stairs. You need the light to go down the stairs safely but the film developing process must be done in the dark. There must be a way to control the light from the top and the bottom of the stairs.

The Challenge: The challenge for your design team is rather clear. Using the equipment provided, you must design an electrical circuit that will allow the basement light to be controlled from two different locations, the top and the bottom of the stairs.

The Limitations:
- Each team will have the same materials
- All designs, construction, and documentation must be completed in two class periods.

The Rules:
- Each team member must individually submit a final wiring diagram and written explanation after the successful completion of the project.
- Each team must compile a bibliography of resources used in completing this project.
- Completed projects will be demonstrated at the end of the second class period.
- No adjustments may be made to projects once the demonstrations begin.
- Students should refer to the *Project Assessment Rubric* for guidance when designing, constructing, testing and presenting their projects.

TEACHER NOTES

Suggested Materials: This investigation uses 3-way switches which can be purchased, in bulk, at the local home improvement store for under two dollars each. In addition to the 3-way switches (2 per group), each design team will need two 1.5 volt dry cell batteries, about ten 20 cm lengths of copper wire (22-24 gauge), a flashlight bulb and a copy of the *Project Assessment Rubric*. If available, battery and bulb holders could also be added. The 3-way switches have a number of connection screws located along the sides of the devices. It is suggested that these screws be "backed out" far enough for the students to make their wire connections. While straight slot screw drivers are actually not needed they could come in handy for this investigation.

Suggested Use: This design brief should not be addressed until after the students have had the opportunity to work with the household electrical devices in the Receptive Receptacle Challenge. The Three's Company design brief is intended to stretch the circuit designing capabilities of the students and provide a necessary opportunity for them to research this type of circuit.

Ties to Content: The three way switch is a different from most wall mounted switches. These switches are installed in pairs. Three-way switches control the current to a light or other device, from two separate locations. The most common use can be found at stairways where a switch at the bottom and one at the top control a single light. Three-way switches require a four-wire system which includes a power wire, two interconnecting wires and a ground wire.

Each of the switches has four terminal screws, two on one side, and one on the other side (and a green colored ground screw). As with most household electrical devices, the terminals are color coded. The dark terminal on the three –way switch is reserved for the power wire. The other two terminals are for the two interconnecting wires.

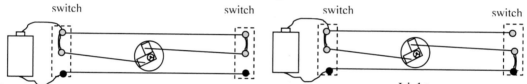

Possible Procedure(s Light   a three way switch can be a most cha   Light   ısk. Some students will persist in creating this circuit by applying their knowledge of simple parallel and series circuits. However, this particular circuit is unique and as such may require more than just a trial and error approach. It is suggested that students seek reliable references in gathering pertinent information to complete this challenge.

Precautions: Using 1.5 volt dry cells for teaching simple circuitry in schools has been a standard for a number of years and has not presented a major safety issue. There are, however, a few precautions that should be followed. First, inspect student circuits for short circuits (a direct connection between the positive and the negative poles of the power source that can cause the connecting wire to become hot enough to cause a burn). Second, never take a dry cell apart. Batteries are filled with a corrosive paste and should never be opened or cut apart. Third, always dispose of batteries in an environmentally safe manner. Batteries are comprised of heavy metals and other elements and should never be sent to the landfill.

While the problem solving techniques used by each team may be different, the diversity of thinking is beneficial for enhancing the problem solving repertoire of each student. Sharing is not only encouraged it is a strategy used throughout the program.

PATENT OFFICE

CONSTRUCTION CONUNDRUM

- Design a solution to a problem. *NSES*
- Implement a proposed design and evaluate completed technological designs or products. *NSES*
- Apply and adapt a variety of appropriate strategies to solve problems. *NCTM*
- Students employ a wide range of strategies as they write and use different writing process elements appropriately to communicate with different audiences for a variety of purposes. *NCTE*

The Context: Direct communication is more effective than indirect communication.

The Scenario: The small architectural firm of Munchkin, Inc. has designed a new cultural center for your community. They have built a model of the structure, and plan to hold an open bid for all construction companies. Your organization would like to participate but obviously needs to see the model prior to bidding.

The Challenge: Your construction company is required to make an exact copy of the model, but you will only have limited access to the model (located in the very tiny office complex of Munchkin, Inc.). Considering this constraint you decide to send the company Foreman to view the model. The Foreman will report back to the contractors to describe the model so that the remainder of team can duplicate the model from his/her instructions.

The Limitations:
- Teams have one class period to complete this challenge.
- Each team will have an identical container of materials.
- Each team is responsible for selecting its own Foreman, the only team member permitted to view the original model.
- The Foreman may make as many visits as needed to view the model.
- The Foreman may only use verbal skills to communicate to the contractors and may not make any notes or record any sketches.
- The Foreman must keep his/her hands behind him/her at all times.
- The Contractors (remainder of team) are in charge of constructing the model based upon the Foreman's verbal directions.
- Only the Contractors may touch the building materials.

The Rules:
- Team work locations must be separated as much as possible throughout the room.
- At the conclusion of this challenge, all team members must individually write a report to Munchkin, Inc. describing:
  - their role in the communication process.
  - how they felt during the challenge and why they felt this way.
  - what they would change if they had to repeat this process at another time.
  - what they would do differently if they were to change roles.
  - what suggestions they could offer to make the communication process easier between others.
- The team that constructs the most accurate model in the shortest time will be awarded the community contract.

TEACHER NOTES

Suggested Materials: Prior to this challenge, you will need to construct a model of some kind using everyday materials from the classroom. Name brand plastic or wooden construction pieces like K'NEX®, Tinker Toys®, or Legos® may also be used. However, general classroom or office supplies will also suffice. Prepare identical containers of materials for each team. Extra materials may also be included as a distraction.

Ties to Content: The ability to accurately communicate is often more of an assumption than a reality. We can "tell" someone how to do something, or write out the directions for others to follow, or create a data display to convey the results of an investigation but will our efforts be successful? If not, then who or what is to blame? The purpose of this challenge is for the students to develop a better understanding of the importance of precise and accurate verbal communication.

Possible Procedure(s): The procedure for this challenge should be followed as scripted. It should be noted that the most important segment is the last paragraph of the rules section. Since the purpose of this challenge is for the students to gain a deeper appreciation of accurate verbal communication they should be given the opportunity to reflect on their experience and process how they might do things differently. In sum, this challenge is an object lesson for students to help expand, enhance and more fully appreciate the need for precise communication.

Precautions: Student groups will be located in different parts of the room and the hidden model should be positioned so that all the Foremen will have to walk approximately the same distance to view the model. Caution the Foremen that running is not permitted, especially since they must keep their hands behind them at all times.

While the problem solving techniques used by each team may be different, the diversity of thinking is beneficial for enhancing the problem solving repertoire of each student. Sharing is not only encouraged it is a strategy used throughout the program.

ACCOMMODATIONS

- Design a solution to a problem. *NSES*
- Implement a proposed design and evaluate completed technological designs or products. *NSES*
- Apply and adapt a variety of appropriate strategies to solve problems. *NCTM*
- Students use a variety of technological and information resources (e.g., libraries, databases, computer networks, video) to gather and synthesize information and to create and communicate knowledge. *NCTE*

The Context: Designing accommodations for the physically impaired has become the purview of technology and engineering.

The Scenario: Mr. Mathews will be coming home from the hospital following a double knee replacement. He lives alone and will need a full time nurse as he will be wheelchair bound for at least two months. In addition, he has no way of entering and exiting his house because it is 4 meters higher than the street level. The Mathews' building lot is 20 meters long and 35 meters wide. His house is 13 meters long, 8 meters wide. It sits 8 meters from the street in the center of the lot. There is a very rocky stream that runs from the back of the property to the front on the right side of the lot.

The Challenge: Your challenge is to design a system that will allow Mr. Mathews to enter and exit his home in his wheel chair.

The Limitations:
- Each team must present an action plan and rationale before construction begins.
- Each team must construct a demonstration model of their wheelchair accommodation system.
- If the accommodation system contains moving parts these parts must also function in the demonstration model.
- Each team will be given four class periods to complete this challenge. Class periods will be at the discretion of the teacher.
- All materials will be the responsibility of the design team.

The Rules:
- Any references/research used must appear in a bibliography.
- Each team must prepare a scale drawing (top view) of the Mathews property. Scale drawings must be in color, contain a key with the scale and symbolic references.
- Each team must present their models, explain how and why they decided on this design and demonstrate its effectiveness. Construction changes and other problems must be recorded and solutions explained.
- Students should refer to the *Team Presentation Rubric* and the *Project Assessment Rubric* as they progress through this challenge.

TEACHER NOTES

Suggested Materials: All materials for this design brief are the responsibility of the design teams. Teams have the option of working on this project at home, but while in school, it is suggested that they have access to general school supplies like paper, tape, glue, as well as general science equipment. Students will also need copies of the *Team Presentation Rubric*, Design loop and *Project Assessment Rubric* for reference.

Suggested Use: The focus of this design brief is project oriented and relies heavily on the appropriate use the Design Loop and the collaborative abilities of each team member. As with many design problems, it will be necessary for student teams to be acutely aware of the time constraints and the variety of design components for which they are responsible. Students will be expected to use the Design Loop and the *Project Assessment Rubric* as guides in their planning, construction, testing and presentation phases. Having your students meet with a physically disabled person may also provide an increased sense of purpose, awareness, and guidance for this challenge.

Ties to Content: There are a number of potential content ties associated with this challenge and each is determined by the method which the student teams select to solve the problem. Teams could potentially use electricity, mechanical leverage, ramps, gears, pulleys or pneumatics to name a few possible directions.

Possible Procedures(s): While there will probably be differences in the approach that each team takes to solve this problem the time frame for each group will remain the same. Time management may become an issue with some groups. It is therefore suggested that a production schedule be established as a way to keep design teams focused and on task. This is especially important since the four class periods are at the discretion of the teacher and could possibly stretch over several weeks.

Precautions: Whenever students are involved in a construction project there is the possibility of a mishap, especially if tools, hot glue guns and other sharp objects are available. Students should be shown proper tool use and be expected to sign a safety contract. Students should wear safety glasses whenever working with sharp objects in close quarters. Appropriate safety contracts can be obtained from Flinn Scientific at www.flinnsci.com

While the problem solving techniques used by each team may be different, the diversity of thinking is beneficial for enhancing the problem solving repertoire of each student. Sharing is not only encouraged it is a strategy used throughout the program.

GOING UP?

- Design a solution to a problem. *NSES*
- Implement a proposed design and evaluate completed technological designs or products. *NSES*
- Apply and adapt a variety of appropriate strategies to solve problems. *NCTM*
- Students adjust their use of spoken, written, and visual language (e.g., conventions, style, vocabulary) to communicate effectively with a variety of audiences and for different purposes. *NCTE*
- Students apply knowledge of language structure, language conventions (e.g., spelling and punctuation), media techniques, figurative language, and genre to create, critique, and discuss print and non-print texts. *NCTE*

The Context: Advances in design and technology have enabled the physically disabled to function more normally.

The Scenario: The American's With Disabilities Act of 1992 created much needed improvements for the physically handicapped individual. Public buildings and other public access facilities had to be retro-fitted to accommodate the handicapped. But finding a retro-fitted house, or reconstructing a house to make it more handicap accessible, is more of a challenge. The engineers of your design company had a different idea. Rather than completely changing the house, why not change the wheel chair?

The Challenge: Your engineering team has been asked to help with this project. Your challenge is to design and construct a working model of a wheel chair that would help a handicapped person reach objects far above his or her head. Kitchen countertops and cabinets are but two examples of the obstacles that most handicapped persons face in a standard kitchen.

The Limitations:
- Each team will have four class periods to complete this challenge at the discretion of the teacher. These times may be spread out over a period of two weeks.
- All materials will be the responsibility of the design teams.
- Each team is encouraged to work outside of class.
- Each team must budget their time and personnel wisely.
- Each team must craft an advertising campaign highlighting their wheel chair design.
- There is no size or material restriction on the model wheel chair.
- Each team must keep a journal of plans, from the original to the final model. The journal must include all sketches and explanations for modifications. Each entry must be dated.

The Rules:
- Model chairs will be demonstrated during the fourth class meeting.
- Each team member must turn in journals prior to their presentations.
- Students should refer to the *Project Assessment Rubric* for guidance when designing, constructing, testing and presenting their project.
- Each team must also present their advertising campaign at the time their wheel chair is demonstrated.
- Each team member must write a letter to a local newspaper explaining their class project and the reasons they felt it was worthwhile.

TEACHER NOTES

Suggested Materials: All materials for this project are the responsibility of the design teams. Teams have the option of working on this project at home but while in school it is suggested that they have access to general school supplies like paper, tape, glue, as well as general science equipment. Students will also need copies of the *Project Assessment Rubric, Team Presentation Rubric,* and the Advertising Guidelines

Suggested Use: The focus of this design brief is project oriented and relies heavily on the appropriate use the Design Loop and the collaborative abilities of each team member. As with many design problems, it will be necessary for student teams to be acutely aware of the time constraints and the variety of design components for which they are responsible. Students will be expected to use the Design Loop and the *Project Assessment Rubric* as guides in their planning, construction, testing and presentation phases. In addition to the foregoing, this challenge could be used as an opportunity for students to research other handicap accommodations that society has implemented. Having your students meet with a physically disabled person may also provide an increased sense of purpose, awareness, and guidance for this challenge.

Ties to Content: There are a number of potential content ties associated with this challenge and each is determined by the method which the student teams select to solve the problem. Teams could potentially use electricity, mechanical leverage, gears, pulleys or pneumatics to name a few possible directions.

Possible Procedures(s): While there will probably be differences in the approach that each team takes to solve this problem the time frame for each group will remain the same. Time management may become an issue with some groups. It is therefore suggested that a production schedule be established as a way to keep design teams on task and focused. This is especially important since the four class periods will be divided over a two week period at the discretion of the teacher.

Precautions: Whenever students are involved in a construction project there is the possibility of a mishap, especially if tools, hot glue guns and other sharp objects are available. Students should be shown proper tool use and be expected to sign a safety contract. Students should wear safety glasses whenever working with sharp objects in close quarters. Appropriate safety contracts can be obtained from Flinn Scientific at www.flinnsci.com

While the problem solving techniques used by each team may be different, the diversity of thinking is beneficial for enhancing the problem solving repertoire of each student. Sharing is not only encouraged it is a strategy used throughout the program.

BIG FOOT

> - Design a solution to a problem. *NSES*
> - Implement a proposed design and evaluate completed technological designs or products. *NSES*
> - Apply and adapt a variety of appropriate strategies to solve problems. *NCTM*
> - Students use a variety of technological and information resources (e.g., libraries, databases, computer networks, video) to gather and synthesize information and to create and communicate knowledge. *NCTE*
> - Students adjust their use of spoken, written, and visual language (e.g., conventions, style, vocabulary) to communicate effectively with a variety of audiences and for different purposes. *NCTE*

The Context: Sometimes, the old ways of doing things are better. Sometimes they are a necessity.

The Scenario: Your community just received six times its average snowfall and the drifts are dangerously deep. The roads are completely closed and will be for some time. The best way to travel is the old fashioned way…by foot, but only if you have snowshoes.

The Challenge: You must design, build, and test a snowshoe capable of supporting the weight of one team member in a heavy snow drift.

The Limitations:
- Each team may make as many rough copies of their design as they deem necessary. A final copy, in color, with measurements labeled, must be presented at the time of testing.
- The snowshoe must be constructed from only natural materials.
- Each team is responsible for all materials except general classroom supplies.
- Each team has one class period to research this project and two additional periods to construct, test and present.

The Rules:
- Along with the color design, all team members must write a set of directions to the Gooding Snowshoe Company so they will be able to accurately reproduce the snowshoes.
- All research and resources must be appropriately noted.
- There are no weight requirements for testers.
- All snowshoes will be tested for effectiveness by measuring how far the test person sinks into the snow when compared to their foot without the snowshoe. A difference of 75%, or more, between the plain shoe and the one with the snowshoe will be deemed acceptable.

TEACHER NOTES

Suggested Materials: Students are responsible for all materials except general classroom supplies.

Suggested Use: This design challenge was written to serve as a seasonal problem solving/construction project.

Ties to Content: This brief addresses the physics of weight distribution, the process skills and the use of the Design Loop as a problem solving technique. The success of a device, like a snow shoe, is directly related to how the weight of its wearer is distributed. Much like the wide, soft tires of a dune buggy, the weight of a person wearing snowshoes is distributed over a larger area and as such allows the person not to penetrate the snow as much. The larger the snowshoe the greater the weight distribution.

Students are responsible for collaborating on the design of a device to accomplish a specific job. It is suggested that students conduct research about snow shoes including the history and use of available materials.

Possible Procedures(s): It is suggested that a work schedule be established to keep student teams on task. Students should also be encouraged to assign responsibilities within their group since multiple tasks need to be accomplished at the same time.

In the event that there is no snow to test the completed snowshoes, Styrofoam egg cartons will suffice. The effectiveness of the snowshoe can be measured by how much the egg cartons are depressed when compared to a regular shoe. Standards could be established for comparing snowshoes.

Precautions: No safety precautions are associated with this design brief.

While the problem solving techniques used by each team may be different, the diversity of thinking is beneficial for enhancing the problem solving repertoire of each student. Sharing is not only encouraged it is a strategy used throughout the program.

TOWER POWER

- Design a solution to a problem. *NSES*
- Implement a proposed design and evaluate completed technological designs or products *NSES*
- Apply and adapt a variety of appropriate strategies to solve problems. *NCTM*
- Students adjust their use of spoken, written, and visual language (e.g., conventions, style, vocabulary) to communicate effectively with a variety of audiences and for different purposes. *NCTE*

The Context: Thomas Edison successfully used bamboo poles as reinforcing rods in the construction of a concrete swimming pool. Plastic soda bottles are melted and spun into micro fiber fill for insulating winter clothing. And now...

The Scenario: Each year the city holds its annual "Creative Engineering Competition (**CEC**)". The director of your engineering firm has selected you and your team to be this year's company representative at the **CEC**.

The Challenge: The challenge is to construct a model tower with a cantilevered, spherical shaped restaurant at its pinnacle. The rules committee has determined that the only materials that can be used are newspaper and masking tape. A golf ball will serve as the restaurant.

The Limitations:
- The tower may only be constructed of newspaper and masking tape.
- The tower may not be taped to anything for support.
- The tower must be at least 150 cm tall.
- The golf ball must be at the top of the tower and lean out from the main tower a minimum of 12 cm (as measured from the center of the tower to the center of the golf ball).
- Each team has 45 minutes to complete the tower.

The Rules:
- Each team member must be actively involved.
- There are costs associated with this challenge and your team must keep an accurate account of how much money it spends.
    > Newspaper = $2.00 per full, double sided sheet (only full sheets may be purchased)
    > Masking Tape = $.25 per centimeter
- When finished, each team must divide the total cost of its tower by its height in centimeters. The lowest cost per centimeter tower will be declared the winner, providing that the other construction parameters have been met.
- No materials may be returned.
- Any team that finishes early will receive $1.00 off their construction costs for each full minute.
- Extra time may be purchased by any team at $2.00 per minute up to a total of five minutes.

TEACHER NOTES

Suggested Materials: The materials provided for this challenge are inexpensive and easily obtained. Each team will need newspaper, a golf ball, metric tapes, masking tape, and possibly a calculator. The only preparation required is to unfold the newspaper so that only double sheets are available. If golf balls are not available then tennis balls would do. The issue here is to have some object that has enough weight to present problems in a cantilever design.

Ties to Content: There are three general principles that many construction projects seem to follow. The first is in reference to the base of a structure. The wider the base the taller the structure can be. This is especially true of structures like the newspaper tower that is not attached to any permanent structure or anchored in the ground. The second principle is that the triangle is the strongest building shape. Gustave Eiffel understood this when he designed his now famous tower. Modern examples of this principle can also be found in the design of bridges containing a myriad of triangles. The third engineering principle relates to changing the shape of a material. It can be demonstrated that altering the shape of a material can often affect its structural properties. For example, newspaper is usually very flimsy. But, if the sheets are folded or rolled up tightly the strength of the material can change dramatically.

Possible Procedure(s): Students will probably pursue a variety of approaches in meeting this challenge. Regardless of their methods and prior to gathering materials, all groups should spend a few minutes designing, sketching, sharing and discussing their ideas in some form of group decision making process (refer to the Design Loop).

It has been our experience that materials distribution for this challenge is best done by the bulk storage method where every group is responsible for gathering and keeping track of that which they need and use. This materials strategy is also in keeping with the open ended philosophy of this design brief.

Timing is everything and managing the clock may be the determining factor in the success of some of the student teams. Time is also a great motivator and it would be prudent to provide frequent time checks to your individual teams. Should you find that 45 minutes is not sufficient then extend this to an hour. If extending is not an option, then splitting this lesson into a planning session and a building/testing session would be a viable option.

Should you want to add an additional constraint to the construction project, issue each team an equal amount of play money for its material purchases. This limits the amount of material they can procure and adds another layer of reality to the entire project.

Precautions: The only precaution associated with this challenge involves the enthusiastic students building a tower too tall. While 150 cm is the minimum height there is no limit to how high the students might try to build their tower. Should this become the situation in your room it is suggested that you establish a maximum height as well.

While the problem solving techniques used by each team may be different, the diversity of thinking is beneficial for enhancing the problem solving repertoire of each student. Sharing is not only encouraged it is a strategy used throughout the program.

A TITANIC CHALLENGE

- Design a solution to a problem. *NSES*
- Implement a proposed design and evaluate completed technological designs or products. *NSES*
- Apply and adapt a variety of appropriate strategies to solve problems. *NCTM*
- Students employ a wide range of strategies as they write and use different writing process elements appropriately to communicate with different audiences for a variety of purposes. *NCTE*

The Context: Safety devices must perform up to their advertised level of effectiveness.

The Scenario: The Potomac Princess Cruise Line is preparing to refurbish its ships and purchase new lifeboats for the remainder of its fleet. Your design team is interested in submitting a bid to build the lifeboats for the cruise line. Along with your bid you must also submit a prototype (model) for testing.

The Challenge: You must design, build, and test a lifeboat model that will not exceed a certain volume and still be able to carry a large number of people.

The Limitations:

- Each team will have two class periods to complete this challenge
- The volume of your lifeboat must not exceed 350 cubic centimeters.
- The only material that is approved for lifeboat construction is heavy duty aluminum foil.
- Aluminum foil squares must not exceed 225 square centimeters.
- The lifeboat must carry a minimum of 30 passengers.
- Extra materials <u>may not be added</u> to the lifeboat.
- Pennies or washers will simulate passengers.

The Rules:

- Each team will be allowed only one piece of aluminum foil for each member of the team.
- All lifeboats must be tested two different times to make sure they would work during an emergency.
- Each team member must write a letter to the president of the Potomac Princess Cruise Line suggesting the how the cruise line should construct their life boats. In addition, the letter must provide detailed instructions describing how the passengers should enter and sit to assure maximum capacity.
- In the event that more than one boat meets the required specifications additional passengers will be added until the most efficient boat is determined.
- Teams should refer to the *Project Assessment Rubric* as they craft their projects.

TEACHER NOTES

Suggested Materials: In addition to a water container and sponge, each team will require a supply of pennies or washers. Students will need copies of the *Project Assessment Rubric*.

Suggested Use: This design challenge was written to serve as a problem solving/construction project addressing the concept of buoyancy. Please note that pennies minted prior to 1982 weigh approximately 3.1 grams. In 1982 the Federal Government changed the composition of the coin and they now weigh approximately 2.5 grams. Of course, if you did not pre-sort the pennies and also did not tell the students about it, this discrepancy could serve as a real life problem for the students to pursue.

Ties to Content: Buoyancy is the ability of an object to float in a liquid, such as water and understanding this principle helps to explain why some things float while other objects sink. More than 2,000 years ago Archimedes discovered that an object is buoyed up by a force equal to the weight of the water the object displaces. If an object that would normally sink, like a block of steel, were reshaped into a boat, the steel would float because it now displaces more water than it did before.

Students will find that the shape of their boat does have an affect on the number of passengers that it will hold (the barge shaped vessels generally carry more). In addition, the placement of the passengers also affects the carrying capacity.

Possible Procedures(s): It is suggested that a work schedule be established to keep student teams on task as only two class periods are allotted to complete this challenge. The first period could be devoted to designing crafting and testing the aluminum boats. The second period could be devoted to boat modifications, final testing and individual data processing.

Precautions: No safety precautions are associated with this design brief.

Titanic Extensions and Assessments:

- Create a data table and graph that compares the capacity of a lifeboat to the number of passengers it can hold.
  Use class data to create a rule that would help explain this comparison.
- Write a letter to a classmate who was absent today telling him/her about the lifeboat investigation. Be sure to describe the steps you took to create your lifeboats, what things you did to make your lifeboat carry more passengers.
- If your lifeboat had to carry twice as many passengers what would be the easiest way to solve this problem?
- What could you do so your lifeboat would only hold half the number of passengers?
- Imagine that you and your sweetheart, Penny, are passengers aboard the luxury cruise ship "The Widowmaker". In the center of the ocean the ship develops trouble and begins to sink. There are 700 passengers and 50 lifeboats designed to safely hold 10 people. Describe what happened and how everyone managed to survive.
- There may be a better design for a lifeboat than the "cup" shape. What other shape/shapes do you "think" would be better and what kind of a "fair test" could you perform to prove your new design was better?

While the problem solving techniques used by each team may be different, the diversity of thinking is beneficial for enhancing the problem solving repertoire of each student. Sharing is not only encouraged it is a strategy used throughout the program.

SOLE SEARCHING

- Design a solution to a problem. *NSES*
- Implement a proposed design and evaluate completed technological designs or products. *NSES*
- Apply and adapt a variety of appropriate strategies to solve problems. *NCTM*
- Students adjust their use of spoken, written, and visual language (e.g., conventions, style, vocabulary) to communicate effectively with a variety of audiences and for different purposes. *NCTE*

The Context: To stay competitive, manufacturers modify products for better performance.

The Scenario: The Bullwinkle Shoe Company is looking for of a new, improved, and inexpensive sole for its most popular running shoe.

The Challenge: Your team must design a resilient, comfortable sole for the company's most popular running shoe. To simulate the shock absorbing qualities of the sole, a raw egg will be dropped from a height of six feet, on the prototype sole material that your team designs.

The Limitations:
- Each design team has two class periods to complete this challenge at the discretion of the teacher.
- Out of school research and development is strongly encouraged.
- Your sole design may be no larger than 30 square centimeters in area and no thicker than one centimeter.
- The sole must be made from at least two different materials.
- Each team is responsible for supplying all of their materials.
- The egg must not be treated in anyway such as being hard-boiled, have attached wings, parachutes, etc.
- Raw eggs will be dropped from a height of six feet.
- Each team must supply two raw eggs for testing.

The Rules:
- All eggs will be dropped in the same manner.
- If the egg breaks when dropped the sole material will be considered unacceptable.
- If a dropped egg bounces off the sole, the trial may be repeated but not more that twice.
- In the case of a tie, the thinnest designed sole will be declared the most efficient. If a tie exists between two or more designed shoe soles the drop height of the egg will be increased.
- Teams should refer to the *Project Assessment Rubric* as they pursue this challenge to fruition.
- Each team member must prepare a written description of how the sole was constructed and why shoe manufacturers should be interested in this innovative design. This report must be supported by data.

TEACHER NOTES

Suggested Materials: Students are responsible for all materials except general classroom supplies. Students should have copies of the *Project Assessment Rubric* as a reference.

Suggested Use: This design challenge was written to serve as a general problem solving/construction project. It is also a real-life application of the shock absorbing characteristics of particular materials.

Ties to Content: This brief addresses the physics of weight distribution and also addresses the process skills and the use of the Design Loop as a problem solving technique. Shock absorbing materials have a variety of applications from orthotics to protective packaging materials. While the process of closed foam technology is a common characteristic in shock absorbing materials there also exists a number of natural materials that exhibit similar properties. Living things are made up of cells, generally have a high water content and can act like mini shock absorbers when pressure is applied. Humans have used this idea…consider the water filled barriers that are often installed at the end of highway guide rails. Currently, research is being conducted on cone shaped granules as an energy absorbing material.

Possible Procedures(s): It is suggested that a work schedule be established to keep student teams on task. Students should also be encouraged to conduct trial test at home since only two class periods are set aside for this challenge. The first class period could be devoted to the introduction of the challenge and to the teams discussing their action plan. The research related to shock absorbing materials will be the responsibility of the student teams. It should be noted that the written report is the responsibility of each student and should be done outside of class.

Once the teams have designed and constructed their shock absorbing materials at home set a class period aside for testing. In the interest of fairness, dropping the eggs in the same manner is critical for this challenge and using six foot step ladder, while helpful, is not the only way that this can be accomplished. You might find that dropping eggs down paper tube or shaft might be helpful as well. It might be interesting to present this "egg dropping issue" as an additional challenge to the class in conjunction with the Sole Searching Challenge.

Precautions: No safety precautions are associated with this design brief.

While the problem solving techniques used by each team may be different, the diversity of thinking is beneficial for enhancing the problem solving repertoire of each student. Sharing is not only encouraged it is a strategy used throughout the program.

SNOW ALERT

- Design a solution to a problem. *NSES*
- Implement a proposed design and evaluate completed technological designs or products. *NSES*
- Apply and adapt a variety of appropriate strategies to solve problems. *NCTM*
- Students use a variety of technological and information resources (e.g., libraries, databases, computer networks, video) to gather and synthesize information and to create and communicate knowledge. *NCTE*
- Students adjust their use of spoken, written, and visual language (e.g., conventions, style, vocabulary) to communicate effectively with a variety of audiences and for different purposes. *NCTE*
- Students apply knowledge of language structure, language conventions (e.g., spelling and punctuation), media techniques, figurative language, and genre to create, critique, and discuss print and non-print texts. *NCTE*

The Context: Specialized equipment must often be created to meet specialized needs.

The Scenario: The task of removing snow from a suburban neighborhood is very different than removing snow from narrow city streets. In the suburbs, and in rural communities, trucks usually push the snow to the sides of the streets with plows. This cannot be done in many of the locations in the city because of the narrow streets, the parked cars, and the lack of any "catchment" area along the sides. Because police, fire and other city services cannot get through these narrow streets this is a matter of public safety as well as a personal burden on those who live there.

The Challenge: Your engineering team has been contacted to design a new snow removal system specifically for the narrow city streets, many of which match the description in the scenario. A model must also be constructed for demonstrative purposes.

The Limitations:
- Each team has five class periods to complete this project.
- Each team is required to research and document their findings in bibliographical form.
- Rough drawings must be approved before the team can begin work on the final copy.
- Each team must create a scale drawing of its snow removal invention.
- Drawings must be labeled and contain metric measurements.
- The final drawing must be in color to highlight the different systems of the invention.
- The narrow city streets are approximately 8 meters wide.
- The snow removal system should fit through a city street with cars parked on both sides.
- Each team is responsible for project material except for paper.

The Rules:
- Each team must construct a model of their snow removal system.
- The models do not have to function but they should represent the designed system.
- Each team must craft a letter to the governing body of a major city explaining the invention, its different systems, how it works, and a rationale as to why the city should consider funding its construction.
- Each team must present its project, explaining how its invention works, while referencing drawings and models.
- Students should refer to the as they craft their presentations.

TEACHER NOTES

Suggested Materials: Students should have access to general classroom supplies. Students are responsible for all other materials.

Suggested Use: This design challenge was written to serve as a problem solving/construction project.

Ties to Content: This brief has no direct ties to any specific science content but addresses the process skills and the use of the Design Loop. Students are responsible for collaborating on the design of a device to accomplish a specific job. It is suggested that students conduct research about existing snow removal systems in order to gather information that would enable them to adapt engineered systems to solving their problem.

Possible Procedures(s): It is suggested that a work schedule be established to keep student teams on task. Students should also be encouraged to assign responsibilities within their group since multiple tasks need to be accomplished at the same time. At the discretion of the teacher, five class periods are allotted to complete this challenge. The first period could be devoted to researching snow removal systems and procedures. The second and third class periods could be devoted designing and constructing. The fourth period could be reserved to project presentations while individual letter writing could be done during the last period. Should the time allotment for this challenge be too extensive, then assign some of the work to be done at home.

Precautions: No safety precautions are associated with this design brief.

While the problem solving techniques used by each team may be different, the diversity of thinking is beneficial for enhancing the problem solving repertoire of each student. Sharing is not only encouraged it is a strategy used throughout the program.

SE-PA-RA-TION

- Design a solution to a problem. *NSES*
- Implement a proposed design and evaluate completed technological designs or products. *NSES*
- Apply and adapt a variety of appropriate strategies to solve problems. *NCTM*
- Students adjust their use of spoken, written, and visual language (e.g., conventions, style, vocabulary) to communicate effectively with a variety of audiences and for different purposes. *NCTE*

The Context: Efficiency is an important factor in reducing the cost of process.

The Scenario: For many years the BOZO Recycling Company, located on the northern edge of the city, was a small operation and generally recycled iron, steel, and aluminum. However, times have changed and BOZO needs to upgrade its material separation process to handle an increasing variety of different items like plastic, paper and glass.

The Challenge: Your engineering team has been contacted by BOZO Recycling to design a new materials separation process. The revised system must account for different metals like steel, aluminum and copper, common plastics like soda bottles, glass bottles, and newspaper.

The Limitations:
- Each team will have four class periods to complete this challenge.
- There will be a set of common recycling materials available for the class use for reference.
- Each team must spend at least the first day researching the recycling process.
- It is expected that all teams will create a detailed, colored drawing of the different systems in their separation process.
- A model of the complete process is not required however, teams must demonstrate how each subsystem in the recycling process will work.
- The separation process must be environmentally friendly.
- General classroom materials will be provided, but teams may supply additional materials.

The Rules:
- Each team must create a name for their process.
- Each individual team member must write a detailed report about how the recycling system works.
- Each team must present its separation system to the BOZO Board of Directors at the annual stockholder's meeting. This presentation should include details about the process in general as well as how each subsystem works, how possible environmental issues have been addressed, and what the company might consider doing with the different piles of separated materials.

TEACHER NOTES

Suggested Materials: The reference materials supplied to the teams are totally up to the discretion of the teacher. Plastics, aluminum foil, paper clips, small pieces of copper wire, pieces of plastic, small pieces of paper and so on. The larger the variety the more involved the recycling process will be. Students will also need general school supplies including large pieces of drawing paper. For presentation purposes students should refer to the *Team Presentation Rubric*.

Suggested Use: This design brief can be classified as a general design challenge that would help to increase the students' understanding of the recycling process. In addition, this challenge provides an opportunity for teachers to observe the problem solving and research application abilities of students.

Ties to Content: This design brief is obviously connected to a unit on recycling. Schools and communities have recycling programs but rarely do the students understand what happens to those materials after they leave the curb. How are these different items separated? Mechanically, manually, gravitationally? The focus of this specific design brief is project oriented and relies heavily on the appropriate use the Design Loop, the use of appropriate process skills and the collaborative abilities of each team member. Although this challenge does not require students to construct any models or actual systems, it does expect design teams to research the recycling industry and ferret out how each recyclable material is handled. Students also need to be aware of the *Team Presentation Rubric* in planning, construction, testing and presenting.

Possible Procedures(s): While there are a variety of ways students can approach this design challenge. As students research the recycling industry they will discover that the different materials that enter such a facility are handled by different means. For example, ferrous materials like iron and steel are usually removed with the use of an electromagnet. Aluminum and copper are generally removed manually however, aluminum cans and plastic bottles because of their light weight, can also be separated by a strong blast of air as the materials move along a conveyor belt.

Precautions: No safety precautions are associated with this design brief.

While the problem solving techniques used by each team may be different, the diversity of thinking is beneficial for enhancing the problem solving repertoire of each student. Sharing is not only encouraged it is a strategy used throughout the program.

SKY CAM

- Design a solution to a problem. *NSES*
- Develop an understanding of abilities of technological design and understandings about science and technology. *NSES*
- Apply and adapt a variety of appropriate strategies to solve problems. *NCTM*
- Students adjust their use of spoken, written, and visual language (e.g., conventions, style, vocabulary) to communicate effectively with a variety of audiences and for different purposes. *NCTE*

The Context: Today's technology has enabled fans to view sporting events from locations previously considered impossible.

The Scenario: Several domed football stadiums have installed a movable camera in the ceiling of the structure. This camera can be automatically moved over any spot of the playing field giving the audience a unique view of team formations and plays. How else can this technology be used?

The Challenge: Your special effects film crew has been contacted to produce a documentary about the very secretive lowland gorillas of equatorial Africa. In order to accomplish this task your crew decides that a sky cam, similar to that used in sports stadiums, would be ideal for this assignment.

Your initial challenge is to design and construct a working model of a mechanical system that would function like a sky cam. Once this model is working properly a large scale sky cam can be constructed.

The Limitations:
- Each crew will have four class periods to complete this challenge at the discretion of the teacher.
- Each special effects crew must submit detailed, labeled sketch before construction may begin.
- Materials will be the responsibility of the special effects crew except for general laboratory equipment.
- Each crew member must keep a journal documenting each phase of this project.
- Journals must contain a description of work done in written or illustrative form (or both), problems incurred, solutions tried, results and questions or issues that need to be addressed the next time the group meets.
- Each crew member is encouraged to work outside of class as long as this is documented in the journal.

The Rules:
- All sky cam systems must be demonstrated and presented during the final class period.
- Each crew must create a movie poster that would interest passersby to want to see the documentary.
- At the conclusion of this project each crew must submit at least two sky cam questions that they would like to investigate.
- Crews should refer to the Team Presentation Assessment for direction in crafting their oral presentation.

TEACHER NOTES

Suggested Materials: Teams are responsible for supplying all materials for this design challenge except for general classroom supplies and regular laboratory equipment. If you want to supply some helpful materials for the students then pulleys, string, binder clips, scraps of wood, K'NEX® or Tinker Toys®. Students will need a copy of the *Team Presentation Rubric* and the Team Project Assessment as reference guides.

Suggested Use: This design brief was developed as an application challenge for students following a unit on simple machines.

Ties to Content: Machines are found throughout our daily lives…from opening a door to cutting a string with a pair of scissors. Some machines are considered simple machines, devices that perform a task most with only one moving part. Other machines are more complex such as compound machines, two or more simple machines working together. Simple and complex machines make work easier by reducing the effort needed to perform a task. Actually, the same amount of work is done it just seems easier because of the distance trade off. For example, it is easier to move a rock by using a pry bar but our hands have to move the top of the pry bar further than the responding distance of the rock. The amount of effort force reduced by using simple or complex machines is called mechanical advantage (MA). The mechanical advantage of a machine is the ratio of the output force, that which the machine exerts, to the input force, that which is applied to the machine. The mechanical advantage of a simple machine not only tells how much the effort force is multiplied but how much the effort needs to be moved in relation to the resistance distance.

Possible Procedures(s): An actual sky cam relies on cables, pulleys, motors and computerized motor controls. Students can design and construct a less sophisticated model by using pulleys, pulley supports and string. It will not be necessary for students to use movable pulleys since creating a machine with a large mechanical advantage is not the issue. The mechanics behind the sky cam is rather simplistic. There is a pulley and cable retrieving system at each of four corners. In the center of this system is the sky cam, attached to each of the four cables. The sky cam can be moved to any place in the field by reeling in and letting out the four cables in combination.

Precautions: Whenever students are involved in a construction project there is the possibility of a mishap, especially if tools, hot glue guns and other sharp objects are available. Students should be shown proper tool use and be expected to sign a safety contract. Students should wear safety glasses whenever working with sharp objects in close quarters. Appropriate safety contracts can be obtained from Flinn Scientific at www.flinnsci.com

While the problem solving techniques used by each team may be different, the diversity of thinking is beneficial for enhancing the problem solving repertoire of each student. Sharing is not only encouraged it is a strategy used throughout the program.

THE BUSYBODY

- Design a solution to a problem. *NSES*
- Implement a proposed design and evaluate completed technological designs or products. *NSES*
- Apply and adapt a variety of appropriate strategies to solve problems. *NCTM*
- Students use a variety of technological and information resources (e.g., libraries, databases, computer networks, video) to gather and synthesize information and to create and communicate knowledge. *NCTE*
- Students adjust their use of spoken, written, and visual language (e.g., conventions, style, vocabulary) to communicate effectively with a variety of audiences and for different purposes. *NCTE*
- Students apply knowledge of language structure, language conventions (e.g., spelling and punctuation), media techniques, figurative language, and genre to create, critique, and discuss print and non-print texts. *NCTE*

The Context: The ideas behind old inventions are sometimes applied to modern situations.

The Scenario: Residents of Colonial Philadelphia often used a sighting device from to see who was standing at their door. This "Busybody", as it was called, contained mirrors and could be adjusted to be used from any floor of the house. The Authentic Reproduction Company is interested in reproducing and improving upon this device but without a research and engineering department the possibility of this actually happening is simply wishful thinking.

The Challenge: Your design team has been contacted by Authentic Reproduction Company to help them make their dream a reality. Before you can improve upon this invention, you must research and reproduce a working device that functions as described. Your ultimate challenge, however, will be to modify the original design of this old idea to create a new device.

The Limitations:
- Each team will have four class periods to complete this challenge. The class periods will be spaced over a period of time at the discretion of the teacher.
- Some materials will be made available while others will be the responsibility of the team.
- Each team will work outside of class. Budgeting time wisely is essential.

The Rules:
- Each team must submit their initial research and illustrations before they can begin construction of their Busybody.
- Once completed, teams must demonstrate the effectiveness of their Busybody.
- Each team must submit a detailed plan and sketch of how they intend to redesign their Busybody.
- Each team must create a name for its invention and a descriptive advertising slogan, song or poem.
- Each team must also craft a set of illustrated instructions that would describe how the device works and how it is most commonly used. Other uses of the device could also be included.

TEACHER NOTES

Suggested Materials: The "Busybody" is a device invented by Benjamin Franklin and is still manufactured today by a few reproduction companies. General classroom supplies will be needed for this challenge as well as a supply of stiff wire (like coat hangers), strips of wood, cardboard, duct tape and ring stands and test tube clamps which are perfect for this project. Inexpensive plastic mirrors are available in bulk at science supply houses as well as dollar store outlets. This challenge may require additional time. It is suggested that a completion schedule be created for each segment as this will help to keep the students on task.

Suggested Use: This design brief was developed as an application activity for students to demonstrate their understanding of the Law of Reflection.

Ties to Content: The reflective behavior of light is addressed in this challenge. Reflection occurs when a beam of light is strikes an object, like a mirror and bounces off. The incoming light beam

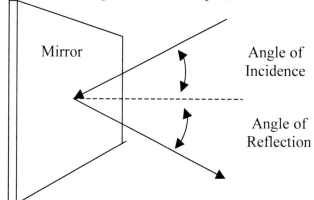

is called the incident beam, the beam that bounces off is the reflected beam. When using a mirror the angle of incidence is equal to the angle of reflection. This is called the Law of Reflection and applies to both smooth and uneven surfaces. The difference however is that on smooth surfaces the light bounces off in one direction and is scattered when bouncing off uneven surfaces like crumpled aluminum foil.

Possible Procedures(s): Students must begin this challenge by researching the busybody device. Once the students have acquired pictures, illustrations and/or descriptions they should have sufficient information to construct a prototype. As mentioned in the materials section, ring stands and test tube clamps are ideal for this challenge as mirrors can be held in place by the clamps and rotated in a variety of directions.

Precautions: Whenever students are involved in a construction project there is the possibility of a mishap, especially if tools, hot glue guns and other sharp objects are available. Students should be shown proper tool use and be expected to sign a safety contract. Students should wear safety glasses whenever working with sharp objects in close quarters. Appropriate safety contracts can be obtained from Flinn Scientific at www.flinnsci.com

While the problem solving techniques used by each team may be different, the diversity of thinking is beneficial for enhancing the problem solving repertoire of each student. Sharing is not only encouraged it is a strategy used throughout the program.

A CHILLY CHALLENGE

- Design a solution to a problem. *NSES*
- Implement a proposed design and evaluate completed technological designs or products. *NSES*
- Apply and adapt a variety of appropriate strategies to solve problems. *NCTM*
- Students adjust their use of spoken, written, and visual language (e.g., conventions, style, vocabulary) to communicate effectively with a variety of audiences and for different purposes. *NCTE*

The Context: The inspiration for new ideas favors the good observer.

The Scenario: Your employer has sent you to represent the company at the Annual Engineer's Banquet for another cold, overpriced meal and a series of long winded speeches. Out of sheer boredom you begin playing with the ice cubes in your glass and notice that they are perfectly clear. The ice cubes you make at home are always cloudy. How do they make them clear? And why not make them in colors? These colored cubes might be able to change the appearance of a person's drink as they melted. What a novel idea. All of a sudden attending this banquet was not such a bad thing.

The Challenge: The next morning you tell the rest of your engineering team your idea for multicolored ice cubes. They are skeptical at first but you convince them that with a good marketing campaign, your company could make a lot of money.

The Limitations:
- Each team must complete an action plan of how they intend to proceed.
- Each team member is expected to work independently at home on this project.
- All materials are the responsibility of the engineering team.
- Three class periods may be needed for this project. One for initial planning, and the remainder of the time divided over several days in ten-fifteen minute segments for teams to meet, plan and present.
- Each team member must keep a journal detailing the initial experiment and subsequent changes in the procedure, the rationale, the results and related questions.

The Rules:
- Multicolored ice cubes must be made using only two of the three primary colors.
- The color layers in the ice cube must be stacked vertically, one color atop the other.
- Each team must demonstrate proof of their success.
- Each team must create a marketing campaign for this new product in the form of a poster, newspaper or magazine article or a radio/television commercial.
- Upon completion, each member of the engineering team must write out a set of directions for their making multicolored ice cubes.
- As an extension, teams could be asked to prepare a brief report about it might be possible to create a three color ice cube with the colors layered from the inside out.
- Another option would be to suggest or research methods of creating clear ice cubes.

TEACHER NOTES

Suggested Materials: No materials need be supplied for this challenge since it is the responsibility of the students.

Suggested Use: This design challenge an opportunity for students to explore ice, a common, everyday material. Teachers may decide to take this opportunity to introduce or reinforce the Design Loop, its structure and use. This format, predominantly used in technology education, is an alternative to the linear structure of the traditional scientific method and also more aligned with problem solving strategies.

Ties to Content: Water freezes when cooled below 0^0 Celsius at standard atmospheric pressure. This transition from liquid water to a solid is known as a phase change. Water also demonstrates another phase change when it is heated above $100\,^{\circ}$ Celsius and steam is formed. For the purposes of this challenge knowing exactly how water changes into ice might provide important information. When ice forms on ponds it does so from the outside edges towards the center. Another unique feature of water is that it actually expands when it cools to 0^0 Celsius. This occurs because of the hydrogen bonds that are formed between the water molecules. The hydrogen molecules line up, and in doing so, create a structure that takes up more volume that liquid water. Ice also floats because it is approximately 8 % lighter than the surrounding liquid water.

So…what happens in your freezer? Do ice cubes freeze from the outside in or the inside out? Does the top freeze before the bottom? The sides before the middle? And so on.

When ice cubes are formed in a freezer they generally form from the outside in on all sides, the center being the last section to solidify. Proof of this can be found when cubes are extracted from the tray before they are completely frozen.

Possible Procedures(s): This design challenge can be approached from several angles. Creating a two colored, layered ice cube is the easiest process and is usually accomplished by freezing colored water in stages. The trick here is to cool the colored water for the top layer to almost freezing so that it will not melt, or fuse with, the bottom layer.

Another way to accomplish this task would be to layer the two colors of water before freezing. Add a little salt or sugar to the bottom layer making a more dense solution. Carefully add the second layer (plain water and food coloring) by slowly pouring it down the side of the container before freezing.

Creating an ice cube that is colored from the inside out is another problem all together. However, knowing that ice cubes form from the outside, creating hollow ice boxes should provide a clue to how this challenge could be accomplished.

Precautions: There are no precautions associated with this challenge.

While the problem solving techniques used by each team may be different, the diversity of thinking is beneficial for enhancing the problem solving repertoire of each student. Sharing is not only encouraged it is a strategy used throughout the program.

CA'-CHING

> - Design a solution to a problem. *NSES*
> - Implement a proposed design and evaluate completed technological designs or products. *NSES*
> - Apply and adapt a variety of appropriate strategies to solve problems. *NCTM*
> - Students use a variety of technological and information resources (e.g., libraries, databases, computer networks, video) to gather and synthesize information and to create and communicate knowledge. *NCTE*

The Context: Mechanical devices often save time and increase accuracy.

The Scenario: The students at the Money Penny Middle School have been collecting money for a local charity. Most of the donations have been in the form of change and, after a month, the five gallon jug sitting in the school office is almost full. Moving this very heavy container is going to be a problem but counting it may take forever.

The Challenge: Your student design team has been made aware of the problem and decides that they can help. Their challenge is to design and construct a way to separate the coins by denomination and to count them as well.

The Limitations:
- Each team will have four class periods to work on this challenge at the discretion of the teacher over a two week period.
- Students are strongly urged to work on this project outside of class.
- Each team may use two separate processes or devices to complete this challenge.
- Each team member must make a rough sketch of its coin separating and counting system/systems.
- Each team will be responsible for completing a final sketch of its coin system/systems before they begin construction.
- Standard science equipment will be available for team use. However, all teams are responsible for all other materials used except for the coins.

The Rules:
- Each team will receive the same number and types of coins to separate and count.
- For testing purposes, each team must separate and count a different supply of coins. The number of coins will be the same for each group but their denomination and the total amount of money will be different. Results must be kept secret during the testing.
- All coin devices will be tested on the same day.
- The efficiency of the devices will be determined by the speed and the accuracy of the coin counting process.
- Each team must report the total number of coins counted, the total number for each denomination, the value for each denomination and the total value for the coins counted.
- Students should refer to the *Project Assessment Rubric* for guidance when designing, constructing, testing and presenting their project.
- Students should refer to the *Team Presentation Rubric* for guidance as they craft their presentation.

TEACHER NOTES

Suggested Materials: In addition to standard laboratory equipment each team will require a supply of coins. The number of coins will be the same for each group but their denomination and the total amount of money will be different. Students will need copies of the *Team Presentation Rubric* as well as the *Project Assessment Rubric*.

Suggested Use: This design challenge was written to serve as a problem solving/construction project.

Ties to Content: This brief has no direct ties to any specific science content but addresses the process skills and the use of the Design Loop. Students are responsible for designing and constructing a device that works repeatedly without adjustments. Students should also be encouraged to follow the Design Loop paying particular attention to the process of testing, modifying, and retesting.

Possible Procedures(s): It is suggested that a work schedule be established to keep student teams on task. At the discretion of the teacher, four class periods are allotted to complete this challenge. The first period could be devoted to crafting a plan and assigning responsibilities within each student group. The second and third class periods could be devoted constructing, modifying and retesting. Student team presentations would take up the fourth class period. Students should be made aware that they may have to spend time outside of school collecting the required data.

Students might solve this problem by using a sieve arrangement that would separate the different denominations of coins. Determining the number of coins in each denomination could be done by weighing or by a graduated stacking system. There is a hitch with using the weight of the coins as a separating procedure. You will also need a supply of pre-sorted pennies. Please note that pennies minted prior to 1982 weigh approximately 3.1 grams. In 1982 the Federal Government changed the composition of the coin and they now weigh approximately 2.5 grams. Of course, if you did not pre-sort the pennies and also did not tell the students about it, this discrepancy could serve as a real life problem for the students to pursue.

Precautions: No safety precautions are associated with this design brief.

While the problem solving techniques used by each team may be different, the diversity of thinking is beneficial for enhancing the problem solving repertoire of each student. Sharing is not only encouraged it is a strategy used throughout the program.

"THE INCREDIBLE BULK"?

> - Design a solution to a problem. *NSES*
> - Implement a proposed design and evaluate completed technological designs or products. *NSES*
> - Apply and adapt a variety of appropriate strategies to solve problems. *NCTM*
> - Students adjust their use of spoken, written, and visual language (e.g., conventions, style, vocabulary) to communicate effectively with a variety of audiences and for different purposes. *NCTE*
> - Students apply knowledge of language structure, language conventions (e.g., spelling and punctuation), media techniques, figurative language, and genre to create, critique, and discuss print and non-print texts. *NCTE*

The Context: The consistent packaging of materials is essential for the consumer and the manufacturer as well.

The Scenario: Under certain circumstances large manufacturing companies may produce products in bulk for smaller businesses under another name. The smaller businesses then have the option of selling the product to the consumer in bulk, saving the cost of packaging, or if they have the capability, repackaging the product in smaller amounts before selling. The Bulky Bits Outlet has been selling bulk products for a number of years and has decided to offer a line of pre-packaged goodies as a convenience for their customers. (Actually, the marketing department figured out that Bulky Bits could make more money selling products this way).

The Challenge: Your engineering team has been contracted by Bulky Bits to design and construct a system that will consistently measure out the same amount of product for their re-packaging program.

The Limitations:
- Each team will have three class periods to complete this challenge at the teacher's discretion.
- Students must research outside of class.
- Each team may choose one of three different products to repackage.
- Each team must submit a labeled design sketch and written explanation before construction may begin.
- Each team member must keep a journal for this challenge. Journal entries must be in ink, contain entry dates, and include procedures, problems, problem solving measures, design modifications and test results.
- All materials, except the products to be packaged, will be the responsibility of the design teams.
- Each team must design an advertising campaign for their "new" product.

The Rules:
- Each team must design an attractive package, with appropriate labeling, for their product.
- The repackaging system must consistently measure out the same amount of product.
- Each team will have three minutes to present their completed repackaging system and advertising campaigns to the Bulky Bits Board of Directors during the third class period.
- Students should refer to the *Team Presentation Rubric*, The Advertising Guidelines and the *Project Assessment Rubric* for guidance as they pursue this challenge.

TEACHER NOTES

Suggested Materials: Three different products should be supplied for students to use. These products should be as diverse as possible. Items like hard candy, gummy worms, and small crackers would suffice. Students should also have access to regular science equipment and standard school supplies. In addition, student teams should have copies of the *Team Presentation Rubric*, The Advertising Guidelines and the *Project Assessment Rubric* for reference as they work through this design challenge.

Suggested Use: This design brief can be classified as a general consumer protection challenge and can provide an opportunity for teachers to observe the problem solving and data processing abilities of students.

Ties to Content: The focus of this design brief relies heavily on the appropriate use the design loop as students design, construct, test and modify their product repackaging system. Students also need to keep an accurate, on-going journal that chronicles the challenge from beginning to end. In addition, teachers should also take notice of students' appropriate use of the process skills.

Possible Procedures(s): While there are a variety of ways students could approach this design challenge. The object is to repackage bulk material into smaller amounts in a consistent manner. Students might decide to use product weight or volume to accomplish this task. If the product is large enough simple hand counting might prove to be the most efficient technique.

  As with many design problems, it will be necessary for student teams to be acutely aware of the time constraints. It is suggested that a completion schedule be provided to keep students on task. Three class periods have been allotted for this challenge. These periods are at the discretion of the teacher and could be spread over a longer period of time if necessary. Students are encouraged to work on this project outside of class.

Precautions: Whenever students are involved in a construction project there is the possibility of a mishap, especially if tools, hot glue guns and other sharp objects are available. Students should be shown proper tool use and be expected to sign a safety contract. Students should wear safety glasses whenever working with sharp objects in close quarters. Appropriate safety contracts can be obtained from Flinn Scientific at www.flinnsci.com .

While the problem solving techniques used by each team may be different, the diversity of thinking is beneficial for enhancing the problem solving repertoire of each student. Sharing is not only encouraged it is a strategy used throughout the program.

SCIENTIFIC REASONING

CHARIOTS OF THE GODS

- Design a solution to a problem. *NSES*
- Use visualization, spatial reasoning, and geometric modeling to solve problems. *NCTM*
- Apply and adapt a variety of appropriate strategies to solve problems. *NCTM*
- Students adjust their use of spoken, written, and visual language (e.g., conventions, style, vocabulary) to communicate effectively with a variety of audiences and for different purposes. *NCTE*

The Context: There is a difference between scientific fact and a belief system. In other words, a colloquial theory is often very different from a scientific theory.

The Scenario: In *Chariots of the Gods* (1974), Erich von Daniken claimed that the large scale drawings on the Plains of Nazca could only have been made with help from aliens. The rationale for this belief was that the symmetry and proportions of the immense pre Inca drawings that were etched into the earth's surface. How else could an ancient culture produce these sketches if they didn't receive directions from hundreds of feet above?

The Challenge: Your research team has been asked to investigate the claim that the large scale sketches found on the Plains of Nazca were the result of extraterrestrial intervention. Your goal is to propose and test an alternative method of creating large scale drawings in the hopes of debunking the alien intervention theory.

The Limitations:
- Each research team will have two weeks to complete this investigation <u>outside of school</u>.
- Each team must prepare a detailed plan of how it intends to produce the large scale drawing.
- Each team will be responsible for supplying all materials except for school/scientific equipment that would normally be available.
- Large scale drawings must be a minimum of 25 square meters.
- Once drawings begin they must be completed in one class period.
- All drawings must be <u>temporary</u> and may not destroy school property.
- One class period will be devoted to creating the large scale drawing and another presenting the procedure.

The Rules:
- Each member of the research team must complete a written report detailing the team's procedure, rationale, and results.
- Following the completion of the large scale drawings, each team must present its procedure and rationale with the class.
- Students should refer to the *Team Presentation Rubric* as they craft their presentations.

TEACHER NOTES

Suggested Materials: Student teams may require general school and science supplies to complete this task. For presentation purposes, students will need a copy of the *Team Presentation Rubric*.

Suggested Use: This challenge has been used in conjunction with the study of scale. According to the *NCTM Standards*, middle school students should have experience in drawing, measuring, visualizing, comparing, transforming, and classifying geometric objects.

Ties to Content: As noted, this design brief is directly associated with the study of scale. The scale of a drawing can be easily increased or decreased by transferring it through a variety of different sized grids. Large scale drawings can also be made by creating a sketch on a small grid, orienting the grid to magnetic north and then, using a directional compass and a pacing system, transfer the drawing from the grid to the ground.

Possible Procedures(s): In typical *Myth Busters* tradition, have students create sketches on grid paper and identify a starting point somewhere on the grid. After they establish a scale (like one grid square = one pace) have the students go outside and orient their sketches to the magnetic north by using the directional compass. Now, it's a matter of transferring the grid sketch to the school grounds by using the compass and pacing. Usually, one team member stays with the sketch and the others pace, help with orienting and marking the trail. Students can use flour to mark their trail or playground chalk to actually sketch it on the paved areas.

Precautions: No safety precautions are associated with this design brief.

While the problem solving techniques used by each team may be different, the diversity of thinking is beneficial for enhancing the problem solving repertoire of each student. Sharing is not only encouraged it is a strategy used throughout the program.

A PECK OF PROBLEMS

- Design a solution to a problem. *NSES*
- Apply and adapt a variety of appropriate strategies to solve problems. *NCTM*
- Understand measurable attributes of objects and the units, systems, and processes of measurement. *NCTM*
- Apply appropriate techniques, tools, and formulas to determine measurements. *NCTM*
- Students apply knowledge of language structure, language conventions (e.g., spelling and punctuation), media techniques, figurative language, and genre to create, critique, and discuss print and non-print texts. *NCTE*

The Context: Measurement is something that is done every day, almost without thought. But what happens when you don't have the necessary tools?

The Scenario: The Biodome, a once self-sustaining living environment and research facility has been abandoned due to lack of funding. Because most of the facilities and equipment are still in good condition, Second Hand Science, Inc., an independent research firm, has decided to purchase the Biodome. The only major problem they found is that the emergency cooling system overheats and needs to be repaired. This task can easily be completed if the large rectangular-shaped coolant tank is filled to capacity. Because coolant is potentially unsafe for the environment and is very expensive, the coolant company will only let you transport the exact amount you need and no more. With no standard measuring equipment available, Second Hand Science, Inc. is in a quandary.

The Challenge: Your "Think Tank" research team has decided to take up the challenge to develop a new system of measurement. Like the metric system, your scheme of measurement must allow the user to convert between volume and length.

The Limitations:
- Each team will have three class periods to complete this challenge.
- Each team must devise a measurement system structured around a "basic unit".
- Each team must create a name for their "basic unit" and any other units created.
- Each team is encouraged to work outside of class.
- Standard laboratory equipment will be available for this challenge.

The Rules:
- Each team member will be responsible for maintaining a journal that includes, measurement ideas, changes, rationales, illustrations and data.
- Each team will prepare and present a poster describing its system of measurement, including length and volume increments.
- Posters must include formulae for converting between the units of length and volume.
- Each team member will individually prepare a written description of how to determine the volume of the coolant tank using the new system.
- Students should refer to the *Team Presentation Rubric* for guidance as they craft their presentation.

TEACHER NOTES

Suggested Materials: Suggestions include but are not limited to large paper clips, small paper clips, any type of dried bean, metal washers, pennies, popsicle sticks, M&M's, or hex nuts. Students will also need a copy of the *Team Presentation Rubric* as a reference.

Suggested Use: In 1790 Thomas Jefferson proposed a decimal-based measuring system similar in structure to the Metric System. His believed that "to obtain uniformity in measures, weights, and coins, it is necessary to find some measure of invariable length, with which, as a standard, they may be compared." Well, it's been more than 200 years and the United States is still without such a system.

Ties to Content: A team may use a "paperclip" (2 clips = 1 diclip, 3 clips = 1 triclip, etc.). Having students develop, defend and justify their measurement system is the fundamental goal.

Possible Procedures(s): Prepare sandwich bags containing 12-15 "basic units" such as paperclips, pennies, coffee stirrers, craft sticks, metal washers, seeds, marbles, sticks of chalk, pencils, ping pong balls or anything that is uniform in size. You will need a different "basic unit" to randomly distribute to each research team or have them blindly select their own. Also provide each team with an empty "coolant tank" for measuring. Cereal boxes work nicely.

Extensions:
- Each team will devise a formula or procedure that will enable them to convert a measurement unit (linear or volumetric) in their system to a similar unit from another team's measurement system.
- Each team will use its measurement system to determine the volume of an irregularly shaped "coolant tank."

Precautions: No safety precautions are associated with this design brief.

While the problem solving techniques used by each team may be different, the diversity of thinking is beneficial for enhancing the problem solving repertoire of each student. Sharing is not only encouraged it is a strategy used throughout the program.

"WHAT GOES UP..."

- Design a solution to a problem. *NSES*
- Implement a proposed design and evaluate completed technological designs or products. *NSES*
- Apply and adapt a variety of appropriate strategies to solve problems. *NCTM*
- Students adjust their use of spoken, written, and visual language (e.g., conventions, style, vocabulary) to communicate effectively with a variety of audiences and for different purposes. *NCTE*

The Context: Everyday problems can sometimes be solved in simple ways.

The Scenario: Floyd's Party Service was having a problem with its party and specialty balloons; they would not stay inflated for more than 24 hours. Floyd could not afford to buy the Mylar balloons, which are the shiny, foil coated variety, and was looking for a less expensive substitute.

The Challenge: Your research team decides that they could help Floyd out of his dilemma. Your challenge is to find a way to alter/treat the cheaper balloons that Floyd uses so that they will stay inflated longer.

The Limitations:
- Each team will have two class periods to complete this challenge. The class periods will be spaced out over time at the discretion of the teacher.
- Each team must design and submit a "Fair Test" action plan before it may begin investigating.
- The action plan must identify the conditions that will be held constant and how that will be accomplished.
- Each team must design both a data collection format and a data display format.
- Each team will be responsible for all materials.
- Each team must create a name for the process or materials they use to increase the inflation time of the balloon.

The Rules:
- Each team member must craft a written report of the investigation including the procedure, the results, the data supported conclusions, and recommendations for further study.
- Air will be the only gas permitted for inflating balloons.
- A balloon pump will be used to assure equity in the amount of air between balloons.
- The entire class must determine how they will measure the amount of deflation in test balloons.
- Each team must demonstrate its "decreasing deflation" process in class.
- Balloons will be supplied for this test. The balloon that loses the least amount of air in 48 hours will be declared the winner.

TEACHER NOTES

Suggested Materials: You will need to supply identical balloons for testing purposes. These balloons must be the same in every respect including color. Party supply stores are good places for bulk purchases like this. A balloon hand pump will also be required so as to control the amount of air that each balloon receives. In addition, students should also have access to general laboratory equipment and standard school supplies.

Suggested Use: This design brief can be classified as a general consumer protection challenge and can provide an opportunity for teachers to observe the problem solving, implementation and data processing abilities of students. However, it could also be used in conjunction with a study on permeability, semi-permeable membranes, polymers, and molecular arrangement, etc. During this challenge students will need to describe how they intend to identify and control the variables in the investigation. Teachers should take notice of this and if students use appropriate process skills throughout. As with many design problems, it will also be necessary for student teams to be acutely aware of the time constraints. Students should refer to the *Team Presentation Rubric* in planning, construction, testing and presenting.

Ties to Content: The focus of this design brief relies heavily on the appropriate use the Design Loop as students craft a fair test to determine the most effective way to prevent a balloon from deflating. Latex balloons are semi-permeable membranes, and as such, allow air to escape over time. On the other hand, Mylar balloons are <u>aluminized</u> through the application of a thin metal coating. The result is a material that is much less permeable to gasses. Another content application may be one relating to the study of polymers and/or molecular arrangement. For example, why does the balloon stretch when inflated, and not burst? Or, why is the balloon permeable to air in the first place, and why does the coating alter that?

Possible Procedures(s): There are a variety of ways students can approach this design challenge and making a semi-permeable membrane less permeable would be a logical course of action. Coating the inside of the balloon with something like mineral oil might just do the trick.

Precautions: Whenever students are involved in a construction project there is the possibility of a mishap, especially if tools, hot glue guns and other sharp objects are available. Students should be shown proper tool use and be expected to sign a safety contract. Students should wear safety glasses whenever working with sharp objects in close quarters. Appropriate safety contracts can be obtained from Flinn Scientific at www.flinnsci.com.

While the problem solving techniques used by each team may be different, the diversity of thinking is beneficial for enhancing the problem solving repertoire of each student. Sharing is not only encouraged it is a strategy used throughout the program.

URBAN LEGENDS

- Think critically and logically to make the relationships between evidence and explanations. *NSES*
- Design a solution to a problem. *NSES*
- Implement a proposed design and evaluate completed technological designs or products. *NSES*
- Apply and adapt a variety of appropriate strategies to solve problems. *NCTM*
- Students adjust their use of spoken, written, and visual language (e.g., conventions, style, vocabulary) to communicate effectively with a variety of audiences and for different purposes. *NCTE*

The Context: Urban legends are the folklore of the modern world.

The Scenario: Urban legends travel throughout society. Although in every legend there is a relatively unchanging core, adjustments are often added to match the local surroundings thus lending a layer of truthfulness and believability. Urban legends can be found throughout the media, in history and in stories associated with famous people, events and discoveries.

The Challenge: Your research team has been issued the challenge of "debunking" a commonly accepted urban legend. Some possibilities include:
- A raw egg will balance on its end only during the vernal equinox.
- Tapping the top of a soda can will prevent it from foaming out when opened.
- The Coriolis effect causes toilets to flush clockwise in the northern hemisphere.
- A tooth will dissolve in coke overnight.
- Hot water will make ice cubes faster than cold water.
- There are more crimes when the moon is full.
- Ants will not cross a chalk line.
- The liquid squeezed from outer layer of citric peels can be used as a pesticide.
- Bay leaves will repel crawling insects.
- Coffee grounds and egg shells are good for house plants.

The Limitations:
- Each team will have three weeks, at the teacher's discretion, to complete this challenge.
- Each team must note research references in bibliographical form.
- Although the application of science to these legends is generally flawed, teams must note the rationale associated with the legend.
- Each team must write out an action plan prior to testing.
- The materials needed for this investigation are the responsibility of the team.
- Each team member must prepare a written report describing the procedures, the variables that were controlled and how, the results of the testing supported by data charts and graphs, the conclusions supported by data and suggestions or questions for further study.

The Rules:
- If someone on the team is aware of a legend not listed, you have the option of pursuing this instead providing that the legend lends itself to testing.
- Each team must present its research to the remainder of the class.
- Students should refer to the *Team Presentation Rubric* for guidance as they craft their presentations.

TEACHER NOTES

Suggested Materials: All the materials for this design brief are the responsibility of the research teams. However, teachers should be prepared to supply general laboratory equipment and standard school supplies.

Suggested Use: This design brief was crafted to serve as a general research and experimental design challenge. Students should understand the basic requirements of crafting a "fair test" investigation prior to attempting this design brief. Critical issues such as controlling variables, designing data tables, data displays and processing and interpreting data are considered essential for success. In addition, understanding how to research a topic and ferret out primary sources would also be of value.

Ties to Content: It is our belief that people who engage in scientific research should possess a healthy sense of skepticism and getting to the bottom of an urban legend is a real life, somewhat enjoyable way, to encourage this.

Possible Procedures(s): Since this is an open ended investigation there are no possible procedures offered as the direction taken by each research team is not scripted in any way. It is suggested that since the time frame for this challenge is at the discretion of the teacher that a schedule be established to help keep the research teams on track.

Precautions: Students will be expected to wear appropriate eye protection during any investigation. Care should be taken when using any chemical. Check the MSDS sheet for each chemical prior to use. Should these sheets not be available check the Flinn Scientific Catalog or the Flinn Scientific website at www.flinnsci.com. Click on the chemistry link and then the MSDS link.

While the problem solving techniques used by each team may be different, the diversity of thinking is beneficial for enhancing the problem solving repertoire of each student. Sharing is not only encouraged it is a strategy used throughout the program.

TEACHER SUPPORT

How to Create Design Briefs

The use of design briefs can extend or enhance an investigation by challenging students to think, to apply and to evaluate science concepts and processes. However, crafting design briefs can be a challenge in itself. Therefore, it is helpful to keep in mind the following salient points, which were used throughout the development of this book. The design brief format:

- places added responsibility onto the shoulders of the learner.
- requires more time than traditional activities.
- requires the students to apply knowledge.
- provides concise guidelines for initially channeling students.
- describes what is required but not how to get there.
- provides assessment and project evaluation criteria to the students before an investigation starts.

A teacher might go through the following thought process when attempting to develop a design brief while her sixth grade class is investigating the states of matter. Let's say that the students have been compiling descriptive attributes to help classify each state, when they notice that liquids differ in thickness. Some liquids are thicker than others, but by how much? Does this difference in thickness affect other properties? These questions could easily be turned over to the students in the form of a design brief.

Before beginning the actual details of the brief, the teacher must present a factual rationale for the investigation in the form of a **context** statement. This sentence or two establishes the focus for the investigation. In the example above this might be, *"Liquids differ in their resistance to flow. The thicker the liquid the slower it moves. This characteristic is known as viscosity."*

The second segment of the design brief is a short story that is not only plausible but contains a real life connection or application. This is referred to as the **scenario**. A possible scenario for her design brief might be, *"The Gonzo Oil Company uses descriptive terms like thick, very thick, super thick and super-duper thick. As new products are developed this system is becoming more confusing and inadequate. The company has decided that its classification system would work better if a number was associated with each viscosity."*

When creating the **challenge**, the third component of the design brief, the teacher sets forth a task for the students to pursue. In this case the teacher might state, *"Your research team has been contacted by the Gonzo Oil Company to help them solve their problem. The company wants you to develop a viscosity rating system for their product line, one that would assign a number to each product based on its relative viscosity."*

Real-world limitations often make problem solving more difficult because of little things like the laws of physics, the cost or availability of materials, and time. These are but a few of the issues that make problem solving a predicament. The **limitations** and **rules** sections of the design brief set forth the conditions and guidelines under which the students must work and the criteria for assessing the quality of their projects. In addition, they provide supplementary challenges for the students in the form of constraints.

When crafting limitations and rules for a design brief the teacher should consider some of the following, which will vary based on the nature of the design brief.

Time

- How much time will the students be allowed to complete this project?
- Will the time be broken into segments? If so, how many segments?
- Will the students be permitted or encouraged to work on this project outside of class?
- Are there penalties associated with exceeding the time limit or benefits for staying under?

Materials

- Will all research teams be supplied with the same materials?
- Will they be allowed to supply some of their own materials?
- Will the research teams be responsible for acquiring the materials?
- If materials are supplied, are there limits associated with the amount that may be used?
- Will there be fictitious material costs which the students have to consider in the design and construction of a product or prototype?
- If materials are supplied, do teams need to use everything?

Data

- Will students be held responsible for creating their own tables, graphs and charts?
- Will the form of the data presentation be up to the students or will this be prescribed?
- How do you expect students to use the collected data?
- Will students be expected to present the data along with any conclusions?

Presentation of Results

- What form will the student presentation take?
- Will the entire team be involved in the presentation?
- What will be the extent of team member involvement?
- Will the students self assess? If so, how?
- Will the students evaluate each others' projects? If so, how?
- Will students be required to document their findings?

Procedural Issues

- Will students be permitted to make procedural changes?
- Will students have to make note of any procedural changes they make?
- Will students be expected to develop their own testing procedures?
- Are there a minimum number of trials required for a procedure to be considered valid?
- Will it be necessary for students to submit their procedures, or action plans, prior to construction?
- Will detailed sketches or illustrations be required as part of the procedure or presentation?
- What types of resources will students be permitted to use?
- Upon completion will students have to craft additional investigable questions about their project?
- Will the students be expected to research and include a real life example/application of the challenge?

Static and Working Models

- If a working model is associated with the project how well does it have to work?
- Will modifications be permitted to working models at all times?
- Will student models or systems be expected to function equally well in the light of added constraints?

- Will there be size or weight limitations associated with the model?
- Will there be minimum/maximum performance criteria established for designed models and systems?

Assessment Concerns

- Will a rubric be provided for student and/or project assessment?
- How will individual student assessments be conducted and will the collaborative attitude of team members be assessed?
- Will there be a variety of ways that students can demonstrate that they have successfully completed the project, or their parts of the project?
- Will students be required to critically evaluate their own projects and suggest alterations should they have the opportunity to repeat the challenge?

Six Easy Pieces
(Responding to Student Answers)

According to the National Science Education Standards (NSES) changes in the delivery of instruction must be implemented in order for inquiry to occur. Among these changes are:

- Increasing the emphasis on understanding and responding to individual student interests, strengths, experiences and needs.
- Guiding students in active and extended inquiry.
- Encouraging debate among students.
- Providing opportunities for students to apply scientific knowledge, ideas and inquiry processes.

Specific teacher behaviors that are paramount to implementing inquiry-based instruction include the following.

1. Calling for Clarification*: *Could you rephrase that? What do you mean by that? I'm not sure I understand, could you please explain that again? Is there anything that you could add that could make that more understandable?*

2. Calling for Evidence*: *How do you know that? What is your proof? What did you find that would help explain your conclusion? What does your data show?*

3. Calling for Evaluation*: *What did find to support that answer? What else do you think could have caused that? If you did this again what would you do differently? Why do you consider your answer reasonable?*

4. Using Wait Time I**: *The time between the teacher's question and the student's response or the repetition/rephrasing of the question.*

5. Using Wait Time II**: *The time between a student's response and the introduction of another question or direction by the teacher.*

6. Not Looking for the "Right" Answer: *When teachers seek a pre-determined response to a question that may be answered in a variety of ways they close down further student thought and discussion. In the same light, if students are seeking a single response they too shut down further thought and discussion.*

*Adapted from:
Reynolds, W. A., Abraham, E. C. & Nelson, M.A. (1971, February). The classroom observational record. Paper presented at the annual convention of the American Research Association.

**Adapted from:
Rowe, M. B. (1974). Wait-time and rewards as instructional variables, their influence on language, logic, and fate control: part one - wait-time. *Journal of Research in Science Teaching*, *11*(2), pp. 81-94.

PROJECT ASSESSMENT RUBRIC
All project limitations and rules must be met before using this rubric

	4	3	2	1
Understanding the Problem	Thorough understanding of problem. Effective use of problem solving strategies.	Problem is generally understood. Evidence of problem solving strategies.	Partial understanding of problem. Attempted use of problem solving strategies.	Unable to demonstrate understanding of problem. Some attempt to respond was made.
Modifications to Original Design	Modifications made to initial design were important improvements and backed by a logical rationale. Documentation present	Modifications made to initial design were improvements. Rationale for changes somewhat sketchy. Documentation present.	Modifications to initial design made no difference in model performance. Rationale for change not present. Documentation present but limited.	Modifications to initial design reduced model performance but were continued. Documentation and rationale not present.
Operation of Model	The model works smoothly and no adjustments are required.	The model works but is somewhat awkward.	The model works but requires constant adjustments.	The model does not work.
Repeated Operation of Model	Model works repeatedly without lengthy re-set period.	Model works repeatedly but re-setting model is difficult.	Model will work more than once but requires a lengthy re-set period.	Model works only once.
Collection of Data	Data collected, well organized, and appropriately displayed	Data collected, organized, and displayed.	Some data is collected. Ineffectively organized or displayed.	Little, if any data collected. No organization is present.

Advertising Guidelines

Advertising approaches usually include one or more of the following:
1.   Humor = Cartoons, funny situations, humorous visual/sound effects
2.   Sorrow = Used mainly by charities
3.   Fear = Used in selling personal or property protection equipment
4.   Need = Used in an effort to convince people they "can't live without it".
5.   Personal Appeal = Used to convince people they will look better, feel better, live longer, be stronger, have whiter teeth, etc.

Magazine/Brochure Advertisement
Your magazine advertisement must include:
1.   Unique and colorful lettering
2.   Bright colors
3.   Descriptive statements
4.   Picture/pictures
5.   Data display (charts, tables, graphs)
6.   Evidence that advertisement is supported by testing results.
7.   Cost of product and payment plan if necessary (number of payments, acceptance of credit cards)
8.   Ordering information (phone, mail, Internet)
9.   Internet address may be included
10.   Special offers or discounts may be included

Radio Commercial
Your radio commercial must include:
1.   Story-board and script must be pre-approved by teacher before proceeding
2.   Sound props
3.   30 second time limit
4.   Data
5.   Evidence that advertisement is supported by testing results.
6.   Cost of product and payment plan if necessary (number of payments, acceptance of credit cards)
7.   Ordering information (phone, mail, Internet)
8.   Internet address may be included
9.   Background music (optional)

Television Commercial
Your television commercial must include:
1.   Story-board and script which must be pre-approved by teacher before proceeding
2.   Participants must be in costume
3.   45 second time limit
4.   Data displayed and presented
5.   Evidence that advertisement is supported by testing results.
6.   Background music
7.   Cost of product and payment plan if necessary (number of payments, acceptance of credit cards)
8.   Ordering information (phone, mail, Internet)
9.   Internet address (optional)
10.   Special visual effects (optional)

TEAM PRESENTATION RUBRIC

	4	3	2	1
Group Participation	Each member contributed to the presentation, knew what to do, and when to do it. Each member showed confidence.	Each member contributed to the presentation	Majority of the members contributed to the presentation.	Only a few members contributed to the presentation.
Organization	Organized, sequential, concrete, on topic	Organized, sequential, and on topic	Somewhat disorganized and off topic at times.	Disorganized, jumped from one idea to another.
Transitions	Transitions from one presenter to the next were successful and clear.	Transitions from one presenter to the next were evident.	Transitions not always apparent.	No transitions.
Closing	Concise, effective, and summarizes the main idea.	Clear, effectively brought to an end.	Somewhat abrupt, short.	No closing.
Volume	Everyone could be heard and was confident.	Everyone could be heard.	Majority of the group could be heard.	Only a few could be heard.
Assessment	Focused on most important points. Accommodations made for different learning styles of classmates.	Focused on most important points. Some accommodations made for different learning styles of classmates.	Focused on some important points. No accommodations made for different learning styles of classmates.	Not focused. No accommodations made for different learning styles of classmates.

Different Ways Students Can Demonstrate They Have Learned

Through Construction:

Design and build a model
Construct a mobile
Design and construct a working model
Develop a new product
Do a technical drawing
Create an invention
Design a new way to make music
Draw or paint a picture
Construct a map
Create a sculpture
Make a scale drawing
Create a flowchart
Design a poster

Through Writing:

Write a poem or song
Write a story
Write and direct a video
Write a newspaper or magazine article
Write out steps for doing a project
Write a play
Craft an editorial
Write the specifications for a model
Keep an accurate journal

Through Integrated Processes:

Create a slide show with audio
Create an animated video
Create a board game
Plan, perform and discuss a demonstration
Develop a learning center
Teach someone something
Apply knowledge in a novel manner
Modify an existing activity to make it new
Create a comic book
Make up a scoring rubric
Put together an advertising campaign
Create a radio or television piece
Solve a problem in a unique way
Create a new recipe
Create a computer program for data
Design an investigation
Create an informational brochure
Design and write a guidebook
Create a sales campaign for a product
Collect and accurately display data
Make up a rule to explain experimental results
Compare the opinions of others
Make reasonable predictions based on data
Formulate a working hypothesis
Revise an activity
Summarize an investigation
Propose possible solutions to a problem
Create a way to verify a suggested solution
Analyze collected data
Prepare and deliver a persuasive speech
Critique a position
Create a computer program for data

A Few Notes About Notebooks:

Science notebooks have been successfully used for many years and their importance continues to grow as a viable assessment tool. As students engage in the pursuing the challenges presented by design briefs, it is anticipated that they will record and interpret their observations, thoughts, data and illustrations. Furthermore, they will also need to reprocess this information in order to draw conclusions, to summarize and to formulate investigable questions, thus setting the stage for additional inquiries.

So what is a science notebook? It is a place where students can record what they do, what they observe and what they think during all the phases of an investigation. The notebook is a timeline of sorts that chronicles student progress and may include daily observations, reflective thoughts, investigative procedures, data displays, illustrations, shared information, rationales and summaries. The notebook is a living document, one that evolves, one that records change, both procedural and cerebral, and one that serves as an informational source for both the teacher and the student.

Teachers have found that science notebooks not only provide evidence of how students are thinking, but also indicate their grasp of the process skills. These notebooks are permanent places to provide continuous feedback and afford teachers with opportunities to formatively assess student learning and to discover student misdirection. Since most of the work done in the notebook is descriptive and narrative, its qualitative nature also provides the teacher with information about how the students are interpreting and processing collected data.

Students benefit from maintaining a science notebook in that they have a continuous record of prior learning that can be used for self assessment and reflection. Maintaining a notebook also provides opportunities for students to engage in authentic writing and a chance to organize information in a way that makes sense to them because they are investigating their own questions. Moreover, science notebooks have a positive impact on writing achievement because of the increased practice in reflective writing which requires students to revisit and reprocess investigative data.

Assessment of science notebooks is used to provide insight to students about how they learn and to inform the teacher of what the student needs next. Notebooks also serve as an excellent resource to demonstrate growth to parents-growth not only in science, but in multiple areas of the curriculum. The notebook is centered on authentic tasks such as collaborative, researching, analyzing and evaluating. There is seldom one right answer or conclusion. In fact, it is not uncommon for the teacher to "discover" alternative explanations within the context of students writing.

Process Skill Matrix – An Overview of Expectations Kindergarten – Grade 12

The following pages contain information adapted from the 1976 publication, *Science: A Process Approach,* by the American Association for the Advancement of Science. The content has since become public domain, but it bears noting its source here as these process skills are as valid today as in 1976.

The Basic Process Skills
(Target Population Kindergarten-Grade 6)

Observing: This process is considered to be the basic process from which all others emerge and dependent upon the five senses. It is through these senses that students learn to make observations and gather data. As students gain understanding in this process they will be increasingly able to articulate a wider range of attributes when describing objects and phenomena. With technologies such as a hand lens, and other scientific equipment students can further expand their observations to include more complicated and detailed descriptions of systems and constructs.

Classifying: Classifying begins as children observe and compare two or more objects…a process that enriches the observations of each item involved. As students progress through the grades they should be able to serial order objects, which is tantamount to making multiple, simultaneous comparisons. Eventually, the children should become conversant with crafting and interpreting multi-stage classification systems such as those found in taxonomies.

Communicating: This is the process of crafting or transferring accurate information either by oral, written, tabular, or other illustrative means. Students often begin this process by creating pictographs, which evolve into bar and line graphs by grade four or five. As students progress through the grades it is expected that they also master, and appropriately apply, of a variety of communication tools such as computers, calculators and video technologies.

Measuring and Using Numbers: The measuring process often begins with students determining the length of objects using non-standard units. This process develops into using standard units and applying these units in multidimensional ways when computing area, perimeter and volume. Liquid volume, mass, weight, temperature, force and speed are just some of the other parameters measured by students as they advance through the science curriculum.
Using Numbers begins with the identification of numbers and sets. The process then transitions through ordering, counting and the basic arithmetical operations including finding and correctly applying averages, decimals and exponents.

Inferring: Inferences are general ideas constructed from observations or judgments derived from past experience. As students progress through the grades they are expected to draw inferences from hypotheses as well. Inferences should not be considered right or wrong but judged on their appropriateness to the task or their reasonableness when compared to the observations from which they emerged.

Predicting: It is the presence of data that distinguished predicting from the process of inferring. Once students have data to consider the door to additional investigations stands ready to be opened. Students should be encouraged to compare and analyze a number of observations for similarities, use a graph to interpolate and extrapolate untested outcomes, identify generalizations or trends that might forecast the results of a similar but untested experiment and so on.

Using Space-Time Relationships: Students at the primary level use this process as they describe shapes, the movement of objects from one place to another and the direction in which these objects move. As students proceed through the grades their egocentrism diminishes and they become more capable of understanding scale, perspective and changes in the relative position and motion of objects such as the movement of the planets in our solar system, the phases of the moon and the reason for earth's seasons.

The Integrated Process Skills
(Target Population Grade 5 and Above)

Defining Operationally: The purpose of this process is to clarify procedures and terms. As students conduct investigations it becomes increasingly important for them to accurately define what it is they are doing. Students often need to share data. It is therefore necessary that they reach consensus regarding procedures, tests, and definitions. Everyone needs to be on the same page and defining operationally is an essential first step.

Controlling Variables: The first step in controlling variables is to identify if these factors might affect the outcome of an investigation. Some variables are not readily controllable, like the air flow in a room, or gravity for example. As students gain experience in recognizing these "non-controllable factors" they are better able to focus on the variables that can be controlled and how they can be used to craft reasonable, investigable questions. Students conversant with identifying variables should then expected to design ways to manage these factors in constructing "fair test" investigations.

Formulating Hypotheses: In simple terms, a hypothesis is a theory that serves as the basis for an investigation. A hypothesis must be <u>testable</u> and generally will be based upon previous <u>observations</u> or the results of other investigations.

Interpreting Data: When interpreting data students are expected to accurately compare observations, translate tables, graphs, sketches, and technical illustrations such as schematic diagrams. It is also anticipated that students will also be able to explain the information presented, in their own words, and recognize general patterns and trends for the purposes of predicting future outcomes.

Experimenting: This process is the compilation of all the other process skills and often begins when an investigable question is raised. However, the foundation for an experiment can really come from something as basic as a simple observation. During this process students are expected to construct hypotheses, identify and control variables, craft procedures to guide their progress, design appropriate data displays, collect data, predict outcomes, interpret findings, communicate results, raise additional queries and summarize results in a reflective manner.

Process Skill Matrix – An Overview of Expectations Kindergarten – Grade 12

Skill	K	1	2	3	4	5
OBSERVING	- Explores the function and the use of the five senses. - Identifies the body part with which each sense is associated. - Uses properties of color, shape, size & texture to describe & differentiate between objects. - Observes & describes weather & seasonal changes. **I**	- Uses more than one sense to describe object characteristics. - Identifies the taste of objects as sweet, sour, or salty. **I**	- Describes objects using three or more properties - Uses observations to gather data about how objects change and interact. **I**	- Observes and communicates using complete, accurate, detailed, and objective descriptions. **I**	- Observes and communicates using complete, accurate, detailed, and objective descriptions. **E** - Distinguishes between two sounds in terms of volume, duration and pitch. **I**	- Observes and communicates using complete, accurate, detailed, and objective descriptions. **M**

Skill	K	1	2	3	4	5
CLASSIFYING	-Differentiates likenesses and differences of objects. **I**	- Groups objects according to two characteristics. - Accurately orders objects according to a variety of observable properties. **I** - Distinguishes among solids and liquids. - Separates solid materials. **I**	- Groups objects according to three characteristics. **E** - Devises and explains self generated ordering system. **I**	- Groups objects according to three characteristics. **E** - Devises and explains self generated ordering system. **E**	- Groups a collection of objects using a multi-stage system that is capable of including additional items. **E**	- Uses multi-stage classification system to sort items and is able to incorporate new items into system. Identifies and explains the ordering system of others. **M**

Skill	K	1	2	3	4	5
DEFINING OPERATIONALLY				-Describes the need for using operational definitions **I**	-Describes the need for using operational definitions **E**	-Describes the need for using operational definitions **M**

244

I = Introduction, E = Extension, M = Mastery, R = Reinforcement

6	7	8	9	10	11	12
- Observes & communicates using complete, accurate, detailed, and objective descriptions. **R**	- Observes & communicates using complete, accurate, detailed, and objective descriptions. **R**	- Observes & communicates using complete, accurate, detailed, and objective descriptions. **R**	- Observes & communicates using complete, accurate, detailed, and objective descriptions. **R**	- Observes & communicates using complete, accurate, detailed, and objective descriptions. **R**	- Observes & communicates using complete, accurate, detailed, and objective descriptions. **R**	- Observes & communicates using complete, accurate, detailed, and objective descriptions. **R**

6	7	8	9	10	11	12
- Develops multi-stage classification system to separate items and revises classification system as new items are introduced. - Uses taxonomy chart as a research tool. **I**	- Uses taxonomy chart as a research tool. **E**	- Uses taxonomy chart as a research tool. **E** -Creates taxonomy chart as a data display. **E**	- Uses taxonomy chart as a research tool. **M** -Creates taxonomy chart as a data display. **M**	- Uses taxonomy chart as a research tool. **R** -Creates taxonomy chart as a data display. **R**	- Uses taxonomy chart as a research tool. **R** -Creates taxonomy chart as a data display. **R**	- Uses taxonomy chart as a research tool. **R** -Creates taxonomy chart as a data display. **R**

6	7	8	9	10	11	12
- Constructs and uses appropriate operational definitions. **I**	- Constructs and uses appropriate operational definitions. **E**	- Constructs and uses appropriate operational definitions. **E**	- Constructs and uses appropriate operational definitions. **M**	- Constructs and uses appropriate operational definitions. **R**	- Constructs and uses appropriate operational definitions. **R**	- Constructs and uses appropriate operational definitions. **R**

Process Skill Matrix – An Overview of Expectations Kindergarten – Grade 12

Skill	K	1	2	3	4	5
COMMUNICATING	- Writes short descriptions about pictures. **I** - Uses pictures to construct representational graphs. **I** - Describes an object in detail - Identifies and names the number of items represented by a graph. **I**	Constructs pictographs from data and explains data from pictograph. **I** - Describes changes in living and non-living materials through illustrations, oral and written communication. **I**	- Uses illustrations and a written paragraph to explain the results of an investigation. **I** - Describes the sequence of events of a class investigation. **I** - Completes and interprets simple bar graphs. **I**	- Uses illustrations and sentences to explain the results of an investigation. **E** - Describes the sequence of events in a class investigation. **E** - Constructs a bar graph from data. **E** - Interprets the data from a bar graph. **E** - Participates in self and peer evaluation. **I**	- Writes a report on a student selected topic. **I** Orally presents and adds additional information as appropriate. **E** -Answers oral questions. E -Independently completes bar and line graphs given formatted grid. **E** - Chooses appropriate labels and title for graphs. **I**	- Writes a report on a science topic. **E** -Gives a three minute oral report with appropriate visual aids. **E** -Answers oral questions about report. **E** - Creates appropriate bar and line graphs as well as storage tables for collected data. **I**

Skill	K	1	2	3	4	5
MEASURING	- Compares objects by using an equal arm balance - Recognizes situations where measurement is appropriate. - Finds the volume of different containers using agreed upon units. **I**	- Measures to the nearest centimeter or inch. Uses non-standard units to measure other attributes - Estimates the length of objects by comparing them to a standard scale. **I**	- Measures an object to the nearest gram or other standard unit - Measures the volume of a container using standard units (milliliters, ounces) - Estimates the weight of objects by comparing them to some standard unit. **I**	- Measures an object to the nearest gram or other standard unit - Measures the volume of a container using standard units (milliliters, ounces) - Estimates the weight of objects by comparing them to some standard unit. **I**	- Chooses appropriate tool and uses it to the smallest unit marked. -Records measurement using appropriate unit - Uses the tools of measurement to determine a quantity as well as to create a specific quantity - Estimates the volume of containers in standard units. - Makes close estimates of anticipated purchases. **I**	- Measures to the smallest unit marked and converts among the units within a system. - Selects most appropriate unit for measurement process during investigations and records using respective unit. **E**

Skill	K	1	2	3	4	5
CONTROLLING VARIABLES					- Identifies and names some of the variables in an investigation. **I**	- Identifies and names the major variables in an investigation. - Accurately describes a "fair test" investigation. **I**

I = Introduction, E = Extension, M = Mastery, R = Reinforcement

6	7	8	9	10	11	12
- Writes a report on a student selected topic. -Gives a three minute oral report with appropriate diagrams, illustrations, graphs and charts. Answers oral questions about report. **I**	- Writes a report on a student selected topic. -Gives a three minute oral report with appropriate diagrams, illustrations, graphs and charts. Answers oral questions about report. **E**	- Writes a report on a student selected topic. -Gives a three minute oral report with appropriate diagrams, illustrations, graphs and charts. Answers oral questions about report. **E**	- Writes a report on a student selected topic. -Gives a three minute oral report with appropriate diagrams, illustrations, graphs and charts. Answers oral questions about report. **E**	- Writes a report on a student selected topic. -Gives a three minute oral report with appropriate diagrams, illustrations, graphs and charts. Answers oral questions about report. **M**	- Writes a report on a student selected topic. -Gives a three minute oral report with appropriate diagrams, illustrations, graphs and charts. Answers oral questions about report. **R**	-Writes a report on a student selected topic. -Gives a three minute oral report with appropriate diagrams, illustrations, graphs and charts. Answers oral questions about report. **R**

6	7	8	9	10	11	12
- Measures to the smallest unit marked and converts among the units within a system. - Selects most appropriate unit for measurement process during investigations and records using respective unit. **I**	- Selects most appropriate unit for measurement process during investigations and records data using respective unit. **E**	- Selects most appropriate unit for measurement process during investigations and records data using respective unit. **E**	- Selects most appropriate unit for measurement process during investigations and records data using respective unit. **M**	- Selects most appropriate unit for measurement process during investigations and records data using respective unit. **R**	- Selects most appropriate unit for measurement process during investigations and records data using respective unit. **R**	- Selects most appropriate unit for measurement process during investigations and records data using respective unit. **R**

6	7	8	9	10	11	12
Uses variables and constants within an investigation. **I** Constructs "fair test" investigations. **I**	Uses variables and constants within an investigation. **E** Constructs "fair test" investigations. **E**	Uses variables and constants within an investigation. **E** Constructs "fair test" investigations. **E**	Uses variables and constants within an investigation. **M** Constructs "fair test" investigations. **M**	Uses variables and constants within an investigation. **R** Constructs "fair test" investigations. **R**	Uses variables and constants within an investigation. **R** Constructs "fair test" investigations. **R**	Uses variables and constants within an investigation. **R** Constructs "fair test" investigations. **R**

Process Skill Matrix – An Overview of Expectations Kindergarten – Grade 12

Skill	K	1	2	3	4	5
INFERRING	- Draws inferences based upon observations. **I**	- Draws inferences based upon observations. **I**	- Distinguishes between statements that are inferences and statements that are observations. Identifies observations that support inferences. **I**	- Constructs one or more inferences from a set of observations - Constructs situations to test inferences. **I**	- Describes expected outcomes based on inferences. **E**	- Develops ideas and theories about what may be happening when presented with new and unfamiliar situations. **I**

Skill	K	1	2	3	4	5
PRESICTING	- Constructs a prediction based upon collected or observed data. - Predicts secondary color resulting from the mixing of different primary colors. **I**	- Constructs a prediction based upon data presented on a graph. **E**	- Constructs a prediction based on data collected from an investigation. **E**	- Constructs a prediction based on data collected from an investigation. **E**	- Recognizes the relationship between two variables used to make predictions. - Revises predictions based on additional data. - Uses graph to predict uncollected data (interpolation &extrapolation). **E**	- Constructs tests for predictions of student collected data. **I**

Skill	K	1	2	3	4	5
SPACE-TIME RELATIONSHIPS	- Identifies objects that possess bilateral symmetry. **I**	- Tells time to the nearest half hour. - Locates objects in environment based upon a series of reference points. - Describes the location of objects by using a series of reference points. **I**	- Tells time to the nearest five minutes. - Constructs pictures of common objects as viewed from another perspective. - Identifies the relative speed of two objects. **I**	- Tells time to the nearest minute. - Constructs pictures of common objects as viewed from another perspective. - Identifies the speed of an object as the distance moved per unit of time. - Describes changes in the position of objects relative to one's own position. **I**	- Constructs pictures of common objects as viewed from another perspective. - Describes changes in the position of objects relative to one's own position. **I**	-Describes the position of objects relative to perspectives other than self. -Describes the motion of objects relative to a variety of perspectives **E** -Transfers data from a two dimensional model to a three dimensional model and visa versa. **I** - Identifies and describes the changes in motion as evidence of energy transfer. **I**

I = Introduction, E = Extension, M = Mastery, R = Reinforcement

6	7	8	9	10	11	12
- Develops theories to explain observed phenomena and proposes ways to test theories. **I**	- Develops theories to explain observed phenomena and proposes ways to test theories. **E**	- Develops theories to explain observed phenomena and proposes ways to test theories. **E**	- Develops theories to explain observed phenomena and proposes ways to test theories. **E**	- Develops theories to explain observed phenomena and proposes ways to test theories. **M**	- Develops theories to explain observed phenomena and proposes ways to test theories. **R**	- Develops theories to explain observed phenomena and proposes ways to test theories. **R**

6	7	8	9	10	11	12
Constructs tests for predictions of student collected data. **E**	- Constructs tests for predictions of student collected data. **E**	- Constructs tests for predictions of student collected data. **E**	- Constructs tests for predictions of student collected data. **E**	- Constructs tests for predictions of student collected data. **M**	- Constructs tests for predictions of student collected data. **R**	Constructs tests for predictions of student collected data. **R**

6	7	8	9	10	11	12
-Describes the position and motion of objects relative to a variety of perspectives. **E** -Transfers data from 2-D models to 3-D models and visa versa. **E** - Creates reasonable mental constructs to help explain observations. **I**	- Constructs tests for predictions of student collected data. **E**	- Constructs tests for predictions of student collected data. **E**	- Constructs tests for predictions of student collected data. **E**	- Constructs tests for predictions of student collected data. **M**	- Constructs tests for predictions of student collected data. **R**	Constructs tests for predictions of student collected data. **R**

249

Process Skill Matrix – An Overview of Expectations Kindergarten – Grade 12

Skill	K	1	2	3	4	5
FORMULATING HYPOTHESES						- Constructs hypotheses for simplified investigations. - Generates questions about an investigation and constructs a "fair test" for the hypothesis. - Separates data that support an hypothesis from data that do not support an hypothesis. **I**

Skill	K	1	2	3	4	5
INTERPRETING DATA						- Constructs one or more inferences to account for the results of an investigation - Constructs and demonstrate a procedure for conducting an investigation. **I**

Skill	K	1	2	3	4	5
EXPERIMENTING	- Helps plan simplified large group investigations. **I**	- Helps plan simplified large group investigations. **E**	- Helps plan simplified large group investigations. **E**	- Follows the steps in small group investigations - Plans and conducts simple small group investigations - Draws reasonable conclusions. **I**	- Follows the steps in small group investigations - Plans and conducts simple small group investigations - Draws reasonable conclusions. **E**	- Follows steps in small group investigations - Plans and conducts simple small group investigations -Communicates findings using graphs, charts and tables. - Draws reasonable conclusions. **M**

I = Introduction, E = Extension, M = Mastery, R = Reinforcement

6	7	8	9	10	11	12
- Constructs hypotheses for simplified investigations. - Generates questions about investigations and constructs "fair tests" for hypotheses. - Separates data that support a hypothesis from data that do not. **E**	- Constructs hypotheses for simplified investigations. - Generates questions about investigations and constructs "fair tests" for hypotheses. - Separates data that support a hypothesis from data that do not. **E**	- Constructs hypotheses for simplified investigations. - Generates questions about investigations and constructs "fair tests" for hypotheses. - Separates data that support a hypothesis from data that do not. **E**	- Constructs hypotheses for simplified investigations. - Generates questions about investigations and constructs "fair tests" for hypotheses. - Separates data that support a hypothesis from data that do not. **M**	- Constructs hypotheses for simplified investigations. - Generates questions about investigations and constructs "fair tests" for hypotheses. - Separates data that support a hypothesis from data that do not. **R**	- Constructs hypotheses for simplified investigations. - Generates questions about investigations and constructs "fair tests" for hypotheses. - Separates data that support a hypothesis from data that do not. **R**	- Constructs hypotheses for simplified investigations. - Generates questions about investigations and constructs "fair tests" for hypotheses. - Separates data that support a hypothesis from data that do not. **R**

6	7	8	9	10	11	12
- Describes changes between observations, given a set of at least two observations. - Interprets data tables. -Interprets graphs and charts, correctly explaining the relationship between two variables. **I**	- Describes between observations, given a set of at least two observations. - Constructs a data table for collecting appropriate information. - Constructs a graph, including labels and scales to show relationships between two variables. **E**	- Describes between observations, given a set of at least two observations. - Constructs a data table for collecting appropriate information. - Constructs a graph, including labels and scales to show relationships between two variables. **E**	- Describes between observations, given a set of at least two observations. - Constructs a data table for collecting appropriate information. - Constructs a graph, including labels and scales to show relationships between two variables. **E**	- Describes between observations, given a set of at least two observations. - Constructs a data table for collecting appropriate information. - Constructs a graph, including labels and scales to show relationships between two variables. **M**	- Describes between observations, given a set of at least two observations. - Constructs a data table for collecting appropriate information. - Constructs a graph, including labels and scales to show relationships between two variables. **R**	- Describes between observations, given a set of at least two observations. - Constructs a data table for collecting appropriate information. - Constructs a graph, including labels and scales to show relationships between two variables. **R**

6	7	8	9	10	11	12
- Identifies a problem to be answered. Designs and conducts a scientific investigation to answer the stated problem. **I**	- Identifies a problem to be answered. Designs and conducts a scientific investigation to answer the stated problem. **E**	- Identifies a problem to be answered. Designs and conducts a scientific investigation to answer the stated problem. **E**	- Identifies a problem to be answered. Designs and conducts a scientific investigation to answer the stated problem. **E**	- Identifies a problem to be answered. Designs and conducts a scientific investigation to answer the stated problem. **E**	- Identifies a problem to be answered. Designs and conducts a scientific investigation to answer the stated problem. **M**	Identifies a problem to be answered. Designs and conducts a scientific investigation to answer the stated problem. **R**

BIBLIOGRAPHY

Donovan, S.M. & Bransford, J. D. (Eds.). (2005). *How Students Learn Science in the Classroom.* Washington, DC: National Academies Press.

Klein, K. & Boals, A. (2001). Expressive writing can increase working memory capacity. *Journal of Experimental Psychology: General*, 130, pp. 520-533.

National Research Council. (1996). *National Science Education Standards.* Washington, DC: National Academy Press.

National Research Council. (2000). *Inquiry and the National Science Education Standards: A Guide for Teaching and Learning.* Washington, DC: National Academy Press.

Pearson, Greg A. & Young, T. (2002). *Technically Speaking: Why all Americans Need to Know More About Technology.* Washington, DC: National Academy Press.

Reynolds, W. A., Abraham, E. C. & Nelson, M.A. (1971, February). *The classroom Observational record.* Paper presented at the annual convention of the American Research Association, New York, NY.

Rowe, M. B. (1974). Wait-time and rewards as instructional variables, their influence on language, logic, and fate control: part one - wait-time. *Journal of Research in Science Teaching, 11*(2), pp. 81-94.

Sousa, D. R. (1995). *How the Brain Learns.* Reston, VA: National Association of Secondary School Principals.

von Daniken, E. (1999). *Chariots of the Gods.* New York: Berkley Publishing Group.

Zubrowski, Bernard. (2002). Integrating science into design technology projects: Using a standard model in the design process. *Journal of Technology Education. 13*(2). http://scholar.lib.vt.edu/ejournals/JTE/v13n2/zubrowski.html